SEWING
VICTORIAN
Doll
CLOTHES

SEWING

VICTORIAN *Doll* CLOTHES

Authentic Costumes from Museum Collections

MICHELLE HAMILTON

Lark Books

Asheville, North Carolina

EDITOR: **Kate Mathews**
ART DIRECTOR: **Chris Bryant**
PHOTOGRAPHER: **Tony Salamone**
ILLUSTRATOR: **Michelle Hamilton**

Library of Congress Cataloging-in-Publication Data

Hamilton, Michelle, 1952–
    Sewing Victorian doll clothes : authentic costumes from museum
collections / Michelle Hamilton.
      p.   cm.
    Includes bibliographical references and index.
    ISBN 1-887374-06-X
    1. Doll clothes—Patterns.   2. Doll clothes—History—19th century.   3. Dolls—History—19th century.
    4. Costume—History—19th century.   I. Title.
    TT175.7.H36   1996
    745.592'21—dc20   96-15430
                      CIP

10 9 8 7 6 5 4 3

Published in 1996 by Lark Books
50 College Street
Asheville, NC 28801

© 1996 by Michelle Hamilton

Distributed in the U.S. by Sterling Publishing
   387 Park Avenue South, New York, NY 10016; 1-800-367-9692

Distributed in Canada by Sterling Publishing,
   c/o Canadian Manda Group, One Atlantic Avenue, Suite 105, Toronto, Ontario, Canada M6K 3E7

Distributed in Great Britain and Europe by Cassell PLC,
   Wellington House, 125 Strand, London, England WC2R OBB

Distributed in Australia by Capricorn Link (Australia) Pty Ltd.,
   P.O. Box 6651, Baulkham Hills Business Centre, NSW, Australia 2153

Printed in Hong Kong.

ISBN 1-887374-06-X

Contents

PAGE

ACKNOWLEDGMENTS … … … … … … … … … … … … vi

FOREWORD … … … … … … … … … … … … … vii

GALLERY … … … … … … … … … … … … … … 8

PART ONE: DOLLS WITH SHOULDERPLATES (1835–1860)

CHAPTER

    I. Day dress, c.1837–1845 … … … … … … … … 74

        Chemisette … … … … … … … … … … 86

    II. Pagoda sleeve day dress, c.1850–1855 … … … 89

        Undersleeves… … … … … … … … … 101

    III. Yoke bodice day dress, c.1855 … … … … … 102

    IV. Wrapper, c.1860 … … … … … … … … … 111

PART TWO: FRENCH FASHION DOLLS (1865–1885)

CHAPTER

    V. Walking costume, c.1865 … … … … … … … 119

    VI. Promenade dress, c.1873 … … … … … … … 130

    VII. Princess polonaise, c.1877 … … … … … … 142

PART THREE: GERMAN COMPOSITION LADIES (1900–1915)

CHAPTER

    VIII. Edwardian five-gore skirt and waist, c.1905 … 156

    IX. Bridge dress, c.1910 … … … … … … … … 168

THE PATTERNS … … … … … … … … … … … … 177

APPENDICES

    A. Sewing by hand … … … … … … … … … 195

    B. Making things fit … … … … … … … … … 208

GLOSSARY … … … … … … … … … … … … … 213

BIBLIOGRAPHY … … … … … … … … … … … … 216

SUPPLY SOURCES … … … … … … … … … … … 221

INDEX … … … … … … … … … … … … … … 224

Acknowledgments

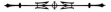

Fɪʀsᴛ of all, many thanks to the curators and administrators of the Wenham Museum and Yesteryears Historical Association. Needless to say, without the generous extension of access to these wonderful collections, there would have been no book. Lorna Lieberman, at the Wenham Museum, gave me the opportunity to work for the first time with authentic items, and from that experience came the idea for this book. Also at Wenham, Diane Buck, for moral support extraordinaire; and Anne Foley, who spent several weeks packing and unpacking practically everything in the costume collection for use as photographic props. At Sandwich, Eileen Fair and Janet Shaw spent several freezing days dismantling their exhibits for photography. And thanks are due to Diane Costa for thinking this was a good idea. All have been very generous with their time and counsel.

Then there are the people who allowed me to talk them into reading drafts of portions of the book. Diane Buck, Anne Foley, Diane Costa, Eileen Fair, and Janet Shaw have all read portions of the manuscript, in addition to my brother and sister-in-law, Josh and Melissa Hamilton, and my friends Susan Kenfield, Joan Walther, Carolyn McDade, and Sandy Gamble. I am also indebted to Margaret Ordoñez of the University of Rhode Island for review of the text beyond the call of duty. Nancy Rexford has also rendered much sound and kindly advice.

The project would have been impossible without the generous forbearance of my long-suffering employer, Goodwin, Procter & Hoar, especially Fran DiChiappari and Donna Manion in the personnel department; and Tony Downs, a partner in the litigation department; also Bryan Batson of The Greater China Business Network. In addition, Larry Campbell, George Wilkinson, and the staff of Pitney Bowes Services handled volumes of copies of pencil drawings and text for years with efficiency and good humor.

I am also obliged to Tony Salamone, not only for his expertise, but also (fortunately for all involved) the patience of Job over several days of photography.

Many thanks, one and all.

Foreword

THIS book was written to illustrate the history of 19th century clothing through a selection of dolls' clothes of the period. It is intended for doll collectors and dressers who are interested in finding out how the authentic dolls' clothing was made. The emphasis is on cut and sewing technique.

The original garments pictured in this book are in the collections of the Wenham Museum, in Wenham, Massachusetts, and Yesteryears, at Sandwich. Although these two collections are not all-inclusive, they do contain a large enough sample to provide a representative overview of the period, and, moreover, a pretty fair illustration of the interests that drive collectors.

The collection at Wenham was established in the late 1890s by Elizabeth Horton, who created it as a traveling attraction to raise money for children's charities. The collection was donated to the town of Wenham and ultimately found a permanent home in a wing of the renovated Wenham Museum in the 1950s. Like many Victorian collectors, Mrs. Horton was a dedicated amateur who enthusiastically took in any interesting object that appealed to her, irrespective of its value, and her legacy is of large-minded eclecticism.

Yesteryears, in Sandwich, was conceived as a retirement project of Eloise and Ron Thomas. Mrs. Thomas had been a hobbyist collector when her husband was posted to Japan after the Second World War. While there, and during a subsequent tour in Germany, she developed a keen appreciation for dolls as cultural artifacts. It was her husband who perceived their potential as investment objects. Opened to the public in 1961, the collection is still housed in its original quarters in the Old First Parish Meeting House, built in 1833.

All of the dolls photographed in color for the Gallery are old. The selection includes some dolls wearing their own original clothing, and some wearing clothing that is authentic and contemporary with them. I felt this was an acceptable deviation from the usual doll-history ideal, since my emphasis is on the clothing itself. There are also several dolls wearing reproduction dresses; the collections include several dressed with great skill, and it seemed useful to illustrate how difficult it can be to identify a reproduction when it is made well. (The reproductions are identified clearly enough, I hope, so that there is no confusion in the text.)

Following the Gallery are patterns of costumes chosen from each period. The models wearing them were selected as "typical" dolls of the period when the fashions were current. They are all approximately 18" tall; their measurements are provided in an appendix at the back of the book along with some suggestions for altering the patterns to fit dolls of other sizes.

It is prudent to read a pattern through before beginning. The patterns illustrate general principles rather than provide a fixed set of steps from which no deviation is allowable. In attempting to explain how the Victorian dressmaker worked, I have taken some liberties with operations that seemed difficult, but for the most part, the patterns follow the original garments closely. The instructions, therefore, may seem somewhat "foreign."

The patterns indicate how many buttons, how many yards of tape or cording, are needed to complete a pattern. Estimates are generous. However, I have not attempted to specify the fabric requirements, as many people would be working from old garments, scraps, and oddments, making a yardage requirement pointless. No pattern in the book requires more than a yard, and most considerably less. Planning is necessary, since you have to decide how you will be cutting bindings, tapes, plackets, and other interior constructions. Some are cut from the dress self-fabric, others from contrast, and so forth. Both the original garments and the fabrications chosen for the copies are described closely, and I think for most people this should be adequate.

It is very important to measure everything as you work, and to keep trying the garment on the doll. Relatively small errors or variations can have a disproportionately unfortunate effect on dolls' clothes scale.

The patterns have to be enlarged to full size before they can be used. This can be done at any good copy shop; the patterns are labeled as to the amount of enlargement necessary.

Appendix A at the back of the book is a short chapter on hand-sewing and related techniques that many modern dressmakers may find useful. The clothing explained in Part I, designed for china shoulderplate dolls, was originally made entirely by hand. The sewing machine came into general use in the 1860s, and after that machine work is found commonly. Most of the long seams of the garments can be done by machine if you cannot face the prospect of sewing an entire garment by hand. Dolls' clothes, however, because of their small scale, are often easier to do by hand than by machine. This appendix also deals with topics like cleaning old fabrics and various other techniques that arise in clothing construction.

My personal inspiration has always been the wonderful Pingree collection at the Wenham Museum. The ladies who made it worked on it for nearly ten years. Sometime I hope to find an explanation for why stitching dolls' clothes is so fascinating for so many grown women. In the meantime, I share their pleasure in it and hope that this book improves your own.

Gallery

THE period we call "Victorian" was the beginning of modernity as we know it. Although we often associate the 19th century with a particular style of deep social conservatism, to those who lived it, it was a period of enormous stress and rapid change, a culture whose advances in knowledge and material prosperity seemed to be purchased with a worrisome degree of social turmoil.

The second quarter of the 19th century, when this book begins, saw the rise of a middle class of a size, prosperity, and power never known before, but even its beneficiaries worried about the cost. It was at about this time that the middle-class family practices we have come to regard as quintessentially "Victorian" emerged, among them the "angel of the house" theory of marital life. Although its philosophical roots reach back to the 18th century, the modern family, with its focus on the nurturance of children perceived to be innocent and intrinsically valuable, is an early 19th century invention. Most people of the Victorian era believed deeply that men's and women's very natures were different and complementary. While men dealt with the public world, women were responsible for family life.

In general, it was expected that women would marry, might in fact be obligated to marry, and that they would spend their lives, essentially, "at home." In a time of great economic and social upheaval, the ability of women to provide a safe haven from the world and to raise their children to be responsible, productive adults, was considered to be crucially important to the survival of civilized life. In the self-consciously egalitarian United States, the concept of "republican motherhood" invested women with unprece-dented moral stature. In innumerable 19th century illustrations, idealized, genteel, middle-class families are depicted seated around the parlor table: father is reading aloud, and while the younger children quietly busy themselves with improving projects, mother and the older girls sew.

Most of the dresses on these pages were made at home. The quality of the workmanship varies widely, from exquisitely detailed miniature representations of fashionable dress to mere suggestions of popular styles. Nevertheless, the history of the 19th century is clearly represented in the costumes of these small women.

The dolls on these pages were manufactured as playthings. They were intended not as art, but as toys, some expensive and now relatively rare, but most produced in quantity and priced well within the reach of middle class parents wishing to provide a pleasant and materially comfortable environment for their children. To the collector of old dolls, one of their most fascinating attributes is their tendency to acquire personality. Carefully packed away when outgrown and sentimentally passed down to others, dolls are not only artifacts of the world in which they were made but emblems of the girls for whom they were made.

Over the course of the century, conventional notions of family life would be subject to increasingly severe revision by social critics unhappy with the place occupied by women. While it is unlikely that the Victorian family ever actually existed as pictured, the safe and orderly world the Victorians tried to make in its image remains an elusive but compelling ideal.

Plate 1. *Lady doll, 20½" (52 cm) tall, with papier-mâché head and ungusseted kid body; human hair wig styled à la giraffe." Left, wearing a green silk ensemble with velvet bonnet sewn in 1828. Center, printed cotton dress c.1837. Right, pink satin cottage bonnet and cotton day cap, both c.1835. Background, maroon and ivory silk satin parasol, worn with a wedding ensemble c.1835.*

COURTESY OF THE WENHAM MUSEUM.

Plate 2. *Corset of jean, c.1828, showing the back lacing. The straps are secured with hooks and eyes to the upper edge of the corset front. The corset pulls the shoulders back; the breasts are flattened and pushed up and out.* COURTESY OF THE WENHAM MUSEUM.

Plate 3. *Bonnet of the late 1840s of mustard-colored silk damask, bound with striped ribbon and lined with yellow silk.* COURTESY OF THE WENHAM MUSEUM.

Plate 4. *Left, lady doll with papier-mâché head c.1835, 20" (51 cm) tall, body of ungusseted kid; finely detailed human hair wig. Center, child doll with head and arms of papier-mâché c.1845, 16" (40.5 cm) tall; cloth body; human hair wig. Right, lady doll with head of papier-mâché and painted features, 18½" (47 cm); body of ungusseted cloth and leather hands; hair à la giraffe," c.1830.* COURTESY OF YESTERYEARS.

Centerpiece, child's dress c.1835, of mustard-colored silk jacquard; skirt is fully lined with boldly printed cotton. COURTESY OF THE WENHAM MUSEUM.

Plate 5. *Annabelle, c.1845, wearing her white cap.*
COURTESY OF YESTERYEARS.

Plate 6. *Bride and groom with papier-mâché heads and ungusseted kid bodies, 16" (40.5 cm) tall; human hair wigs. He wears a black wool suit and she, a silk taffeta and velvet dress, both c.1840. At right, young woman with head of wax over composition and human hair ringlets, c.1850; jointed cloth body, 18" (45.5 cm) tall; warp print silk dress.*
COURTESY OF YESTERYEARS.

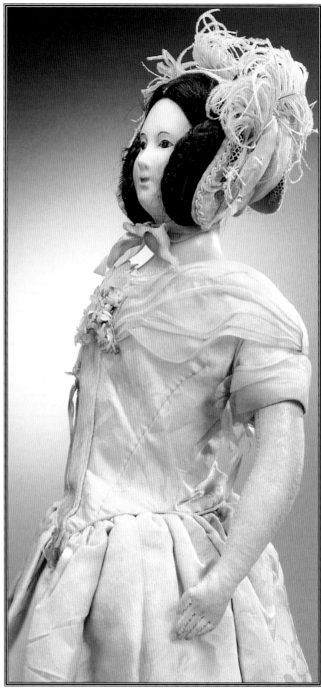

Plate 7. *Lady with papier-mâché head, kid arms, and cloth body; human hair wig elaborately arranged in heavy braids, wearing gauze and net bonnet and silk evening gown, c.1845.*
COURTESY OF YESTERYEARS.

Plate 8. *Typical 1840s china doll, from the original IDC collection. The style of her gown suggests that she was re-dressed about 1865; old records indicate that her costume was supposed to represent a woman of southern Italy.*
COURTESY OF THE WENHAM MUSEUM.

Plate 9. *Left, large child doll by Greiner; papier-mâché head, homemade cloth body; cotton print dress and crisp lawn apron. Right, large child doll with china head and homemade leather body; cotton print dress. Both c.1850.* COURTESY OF YESTERYEARS.

Plate 10. *Young woman, 9" (23 cm) tall, with china head and limbs and cloth body; gauze dress, c.1850.* COURTESY OF YESTERYEARS.

Plate 11. *Four "plain janes," c.1850–60. Left, pink lustre china head, with homemade cloth body, c.1850, 22" (56 cm) tall. She was the childhood toy of Elizabeth Richards Horton. Center front, "milliner's model" with papier-mâché head, wooden limbs, and cloth body, c.1856, 12" (30.5 cm) tall. Center rear, china head, c.1855, with homemade cloth body, 14" (35.5 cm) tall. Right, wax over composition lady with set-in glass eyes with exterior wire mechanism, wooden limbs, and cloth body with squeak box, c.1855–60, 16" (40.5 cm) tall.*
COURTESY OF THE WENHAM MUSEUM.

MRS. HORTON

THE nucleus of the doll collection at the Wenham Museum is the International Doll Collection (IDC) assembled in the late 1890s and early 1900s by Elizabeth Richards Horton to raise money for children's charities. Mrs. Horton was not a doll collector in the conventional sense; her collection was assembled solely to aid a worthy cause. Her dolls comprise one of the few such collections in the world that have survived untouched for almost 100 years.

Born in Wenham, Massachusetts, in 1837, Elizabeth was well educated in local schools and a year after finishing high school was admitted to Salem Normal School (now Salem State College) in September, 1854. She graduated in the first class in 1856.

The same year, she was asked to go to Ohio to teach. In Pomeroy, Ohio, she met Thayer Horton whom she married in 1858. They lived in Pomeroy until Mr. Horton's death in 1887. Mrs. Horton, always proud of her New England lineage, which could be traced back to 1630, returned to Massachusetts to live.

Once back in Boston, she embarked on the project that would absorb her formidable energy and organizing skills for years to come. When she decided to collect dolls for her cause it was on a worldwide scale. The first public exhibition of the dolls was in 1896 at a Christmas fair

Plate 12. *Elizabeth Richards Horton, photographed with her daughters about 1880.*

to benefit the New England Peabody Home for Crippled Children. In 1897 alone the collection traveled 1900 miles and raised over $1000 after expenses for thirteen charities, which included free kindergartens, day nurseries, and various homes for boys and girls. By December of 1897, the number of dolls had grown to over 250 and they were being sent from as far away as Alaska, Austria, and Ireland. At her own expense, Mrs. Horton

packed the dolls in huge traveling trunks and planned the itineraries; the only expense to the charity was transportation. Her greatest triumph was Miss Columbia, the cloth doll that actually traveled alone around the world promoting children's charities and the IDC.

Elizabeth Horton continued to pack and ship the dolls until 1914 when the project became too much of a burden. For several years the collection was in and out of storage. In 1952 the Museum addition was built adjoining the Claflin-Richards House where Mrs. Horton spent her childhood, and for the first time these little figures with so much history could be properly displayed. Elizabeth Horton died in Danvers, Massachusetts, on August 23, 1928, a few weeks short of her 91st birthday.

Thanks to generous donations over the years, the collection has grown to around 5,000 dolls, dollhouses, toys, and miniatures. We like to think that Mrs. Horton would be pleased to know that Miss Columbia is still one of the most famous dolls in the world and that the traditional dolls she collected 100 years ago are now preservers of vanishing cultures and a priceless legacy to future generations.

Diane D. Buck
CURATOR OF DOLLS (1987-1994)

Plate 13. *Left, young girl with head of china and homemade cloth body with leather arms, 18" (45.5 cm) tall, c.1855; wool and cotton dress. Right, young woman with head and limbs of china, c.1855; elaborate molded and gilt hair net and bows; calico dress. Dresser, mid-Victorian, with pink lustreware vanity set. Old braided rug.* COURTESY OF YESTERYEARS.

Plate 14. *A tall china doll of the type known as "Jenny Lind" from her supposed resemblance to the fabulously popular singer. Her gown is a skillful reproduction made, probably, in the early 1960s. The necklace and undergarments, including a crinoline made of steamed bamboo, appear to be authentic.* COURTESY OF YESTERYEARS.

At right, a bonnet of pink silk drawn on wire, with very full self-fabric bavolet, trimmed with pleated netting around the face and tied with broad pink ribbons. COURTESY OF THE WENHAM MUSEUM.

Plate 15. *Young woman, c.1855, china head and limbs, cloth body, 8" (20.5 cm) tall; dress of wool and silk, watch-spring hoops covered with tape.* COURTESY OF THE WENHAM MUSEUM

Plate 16. *A rather matronly Parian lady with upswept hair and pierced ears, and homemade cloth body with leather arms, c.1860, 16" (40.5 cm) tall; wearing a taffeta dinner dress of deep green. Homemade dolls' dresser, mid-Victorian.* COURTESY OF YESTERYEARS.

The dresser bears a collection of mid-to-late Victorian dolls' tablewear, including a sugar bowl and porringer of lead, grape-pattern glass decanter with etched stopper, a pair of painted china urns, and an elaborate clock with a mechanism that once kept time. The copper pots and pans are from a contemporary "Nuremberg kitchen," which was provided with all the modern conveniences, including an outside reservoir for running water. COURTESY OF THE WENHAM MUSEUM. *Whitework table doily, privately owned.*

Plate 17. *Left, Parian doll c.1860, 23" (58.5 cm) tall; leather arms and homemade jointed cloth body. Right, Parian doll c.1860; 22" (56 cm) tall; leather arms and homemade cloth body. Background, mid-Victorian patchwork quilt top.* ALL COURTESY OF THE WENHAM MUSEUM.

Plate 18. *Young woman by Rohmer, Parian head and arms, articulated body of wood, early 1860s, 16" (40.5 cm) tall; blond skin wig; dress of glazed cotton and gauze. Her hat, which is charming but somewhat inaccurate, was made by Eloise Thomas, who assembled the original collection at Yesteryears.* COURTESY OF YESTERYEARS.

Plate 19. *"French fashion" type of unknown manufacture, with bisque head, leather body, and sheepskin wig, 13" (33 cm) tall; dressed in the early 1860s. Background, Japanese hat, c.1867.*
COURTESY OF THE WENHAM MUSEUM.

Plate 20. *French fashion doll of unknown manufacture, bisque head, kid body, skin wig, 14" (35.5 cm) tall. She was the gift of Queen Elizabeth of Romania to Mrs. Horton's project in 1901. As her collection became known, Mrs. Horton began to approach famous people and heads of state for contributions.*
COURTESY OF THE WENHAM MUSEUM.

Plate 21. *French fashion doll of unknown manufacture, bisque head and hands, articulated kid over wood body, and mohair wig; 18" (45.5 cm) tall; c.1865. She wears a cotton faille seaside costume and black velvet bonnet. At front, her walking costume of satin-striped silk and umbrella. Background, vanity top with mirror and drawer, c.1825; painted c.1840–50.* COURTESY OF THE WENHAM MUSEUM.

Gallery

Plate 22. *French fashion lady, 18" (45.5 cm) tall, bisque head and gusseted kid body; human hair wig; silk dinner gown, c.1865. The velvet covered chairs, marble top sideboy, and gilt coffee service are somewhat later.* ALL COURTESY OF YESTERYEARS.

Plates 1. & 2.

Trousseau, 1828-1837. This papier-mâché doll was provided with an exquisitely made trousseau by the great-grandmother of the donor. The head has required substantial repair to halt deterioration of the papier-mâché, but the body of brown, ungusseted kid is in very fine condition. Her hands are interesting, the fingers made of separate rolls of leather stitched into the mitten, which forms the palm. This lady is a good example of the naturalistic modeling found on high-quality papier-mâchés of this period, carefully made with inset glass eyes, real hair wig, and well-proportioned body. This style of doll is usually known as a "French papier-mâché," but the heads were probably made in Germany.

The earliest dress of the trousseau, at left, is the green print afternoon gown she is wearing. It was made in 1828, and shows the style of the period just preceding Queen Victoria's accession to the throne. The skirt is rather narrow, but the bodice has gigantic outspreading sleeves, made to seem even larger when topped by the pelerine provided for outdoor wear. The fabric appears a soft, mossy green, but this is the result of fading. The original color was a brilliant iridescent green mixed with mustard yellow. The silk is printed with green, blue, and reddish-brown floral sprays. The cording that finishes the seams is a dark, dull maroon.

The skirt is interlined with soft, coarse cotton fabric, giving the thin silk a luxurious hand. This was a common practice throughout much of the 19th century. The bodice and sleeves are lined with a stiffer, but similar cotton fabric. The hem is deep, and is caught only to the interlining. The skirt's modest fullness is set to the round waistband in rather large pleats. The join is covered by a separate belt with large gold buckle, but it is a "fake," closed with a set of hidden hooks and eyelets made in the belt.

A focus of fashion interest at this period was in the arrangement of the bodice and the immense gigot sleeve. The number of fashion terminologies for these details is legion, many extremely exotic and reflecting the romantic age that was drawing to a close in the mid-1830s. The neckline is filled in with a net chemisette having the characteristic spreading collar then fashionable, trimmed with a worked edging of lace. The bodice is criss-crossed with a set of pleated sashes laid onto the surface. Armhole, neckline, and sleeve are finished with maroon cording. The cuff is closed with a hidden loop and mother-of-pearl button, and trimmed with a turnback of lace-edged muslin lightly embroidered along its length. At the cuff and head of the sleeve, deep pleats are held in place by sets of long chain stitches. The head of the sleeve is also supported by a supplementary piece of interlining which is quite stiff, to prevent the top of the sleeve from collapsing.

The pelerine completes the ensemble. The pelerine hangs to the waist in back and is lined to the edge with plain cotton that was probably once white, and corded all around the edge in maroon. To be correctly dressed outdoors, women covered their dresses with some sort of capelet or mantle, even in summer. The green silk dress is provided with an alternative pelerine of semi-transparent muslin, delicately finished along its scalloped edges with minute buttonhole stitches.

Matching the green silk dress is a bonnet of dark green velvet with very tall crown and deep brim, presenting a long, narrow silhouette. The front edge of the brim has a dark green net veil, which is cut straight and hangs just below the nose in the center, its length trailing off to the sides. A veil of this type might be worn covering the face, or thrown back and gracefully arranged over the bonnet. The brim is lined to the crown with self-fabric, but the crown itself is unlined. Most bonnets of this period are made in this fashion. The buckram foundation is thin but coarse and yellowish in color. The bonnet is trimmed conservatively with self-colored silk ribbon.

The green silk dress is supported by a petticoat striped with white thread and fastened with a wide waist drawstring, and by a very plain chemise reaching to the knees. The modest lace trim at the neck is just visible at the edge of the corsage. The lady wears no drawers. Drawers had been introduced around the turn of the 19th century, but only "fast" women wore them. The idea of women wearing anything remotely like men's trousers, even if they were completely invisible, was repugnant to most people, but doctors and some social innovators recommended them for warmth and convenience. Their use remained controversial until the 1840s. The doll is also provided with a well-made corset of white jean, which has old-fashioned shoulder straps fastening in front with brass hooks (**PLATE 2**). This style of corset went out of fashion about 1830. Two elegantly shaped gussets are let into each hip; the front and back are boned stoutly, and the corset has 22 eyelets to lace up the back.

The second dress, at center, was probably made about 1836, the year before Victoria's accession to the throne, when, in the middle of the fashion year, the fullness of the sleeve suddenly collapsed and was displaced onto the arm. This type of narrow sleeve with fussy detail at the upper arm and elbow is a telltale form of 1836 and 1837, as is the bodice ornament of pleated or gathered self-fabric arranged across the breast of the garment and gathered into a central band or knot. The pointed waist also became popular in the 1830s, although the round waist did not disappear entirely. The basic form of this dress, modest, graceful, and feminine, remained fashionable for more than 20 years, changing only in detail, until the revolution of the middle 1850s, when the so-called "artificial" crinoline and then the gored skirt appeared.

The pink dress evidences a trend that continued with a passion into the 1850s, to wit, the ever-increasing girth of the skirt. This one's hem measures 7½ times the waist. The dressmaker used the selvages of her narrow cotton for a clean finish inside the skirt, placing them at the side seams. The placket is a rolled and whipped slash in the center back. The skirt is mounted with tiny laid gathers to a piece of tape, which was then stitched into the lower bodice with a set of vertical worked bars.

The bodice is fully lined with white cotton drill and is decorated at the seams with narrow self-fabric covered cord. The unlined sleeves are set plain into the armhole and trimmed with a pair of flounces. The cuffs are hemmed with a cord facing. The neckline, also finished with a cord facing, is filled with a chemisette of windowpane thread-check cotton. Chemisettes continued to be worn through the 1830s, but in the 1840s it became acceptable for women to wear a "half-high" day bodice such as this one without covering up.

The pink dress is assembled entirely with small running stitches. The turnings and seams are all very fine, the only exception being the closure at center back—a set of large brass hooks and eyes roughly stitched in with thick cotton thread like crochet cotton carried from hook to hook rather than being tied off at each one. As this is the latest dress in the trousseau, it may have been finished by another needlewoman with a less fine finishing style. The "eyes" are advanced slightly past the edge on one side and the hooks set slightly back on the other to form a narrow lap.

Instructions for the pink cotton dress are found in Chapter I.

The pink satin bonnet at far right shows the evolution of the bonnet shape through the 1830s toward a rounder, shallower silhouette. It is made in the identical fashion as the green velvet hat, and trimmed likewise with self-colored ribbon. Next to the bonnet is a white day cap matching the checked chemisette. It is made from one piece of fabric, cunningly drawn up to create the round shape, and trimmed with self-fabric strips formed into the bows and ties. The edges are trimmed with ruffles of netting edged with narrow lace.

Plate 3.

ILLUSTRATED here is the next development in bonnet shape, typical of the mid–to late 1840s. The brim and crown are made in one, the so-called "poke" bonnet. This very modest bonnet completely surrounds the lady's face, so that she can see and be seen only directly from the front. This elegant example is made on a wired buckram frame and covered with silk damask in the dark mustard gold so popular at this time. The edge of the tip is defined with two narrow pleats of fabric. The crown is wrapped with striped ribbon whose crumpled length indicates that it once may have been a rosette. The front edge and the bavolet are outlined with a double line of cord. The edge of the bavolet is gathered onto the outside of the brim over the bound neck edge and blind stitched to join; the join itself is covered and decorated with a bow of striped silk ribbon.

The inside of the brim is lined with brilliant yellow silk, the crown with cotton. As was usual at this time, the very top of the crown's inside is unfinished. Most ladies of this period would have worn a cap under a bonnet.

Plates 4. & 5.

A GROUP of pretty German papier-mâché dolls of the 1830s and 1840s. At left is a delicate young woman called "Abigail" with a rather wan complexion, set-in pupilless black eyes of glass, and a body of ungusseted kid. Her wig, which is now rather thin, shows the fine detail of its construction at the hairline.

Her dress of plain white cotton appears earlier than it is because of its narrow silhouette and rather high waist, but that is principally a function of the shape of the doll. The dressmaker clearly had the skill to copy the style of her day exactly, and seems to have chosen to save fabric instead by making the skirt much narrower than was then fashionable. It is made of one breadth of cotton, rather than two; there are no side seams, and the placket is simply formed at the center back by rolling back the selvage edges. In all other respects, it is a very fine interpretation of the style prevailing at the end of the 1830s. Although plain, the dress is beautifully detailed and sewn.

The bodice is fully lined and has a corded center front seam. This seam was usually cut on the selvage at this period, so it is generally an ornamental rather than shaping seam. The pointed waist, armholes, and neckline are also finished with covered cord. The dress has fashionable "bishop" sleeves, gathered into the armhole. The sleeves are full for their entire length, but the fullness is controlled at the top with a series of gathering stitches like the preparation for smocking. Two lines of gathering are placed around the upper arm, and a pair of short, upstanding flounces gathered on cord are mounted across the lines of gathering. The heads of the flounces are left raw underneath. The sleeve then billows over the arm and is gathered into a cuff closed with a tiny hook and loop. The cuff is also defined with cord. When this type of sleeve became fashionable, women often made over their old gigot sleeve dresses by unpicking the sleeve from the armhole, stitching down its fullness at the top, and resetting it into the bodice.

The skirt is supported by a plain, straight petticoat, under which the doll wears a pair of straight-leg drawers finished with a series of tucks and a line of whipped-on lace at the hem. Abby is also wearing a well-made corset with details as finely executed as those of her dress. The front is stiffened with a stout metal busk. A pair of gussets are let into at the hips at the side. The lace holes, of which there appear to be eighteen, are hand-executed behind a narrow metal stiffener that reinforces each center back edge. (Metal eyelets were invented in 1828, so Abby's corsetiere is a trifle behind the times.)

Abigail is wearing a bonnet of silk drawn on wires. It was once a light celery green. It has a separate, stiffened crown to which the drawn silk is sewn. It is decorated with a rosette of matching green silk ribbon on one side, and a small rosette of pink silk on the other. The bavolet is mounted onto the back with small thread tacks. The bonnet ties under the chin with self-colored silk ribbon.

The outfit is completed with black silk ballet slippers tied around the ankle with hanks of thread. The slippers have brown kid soles.

At right is another pretty doll of the mid 1830s, this one with the high color and extravagant, upstanding "giraffe" coiffure associated with the earlier part of the decade. Women wore a great deal of artificial hair during much of the 19th century. The bunches of curls hanging on the cheeks like spaniel's ears, which we associate with the 1830s and early 1840s, were often false, supported by a wire running across the top of the head and covered by the cap or headdress. Braids of the type worn by this doll, who is dressed in the style of about 1837, were also worn as hairpieces; like the doll's, the braids were wired for support. The doll's coiffure is decorated with a small rosette of green silk ribbon. She has brilliant, painted blue eyes and very detailed hands decorated like gloves with lines of turquoise stitching on the backs and beautifully formed little thumbs.

Her dress is made of very fine, nearly transparent wool challis, printed with reddish brown and turquoise blot-like sprigs. It is trimmed across the breast with a set of pleats decorated with a knot of ivory satin and a rosette of turquoise silk ribbon. The neckline is finished with a wide bias band of the same ivory silk. The fully lined bodice is shaped to the body with a pair of front darts and finished at the pointed waist and the armscye with self-fabric covered cord. Unfortunately, the back of this dress is completely disintegrated. The disappearance of the fabric has, however, exposed a pair of light wooden stiffeners, very slender and springy, which originally reinforced the center back under the hooks. These reinforcements acted like a light busk down the center of the gown. They are worked into the center back opening edge; the hooks or eyelets are made against them so that the strain of the tightly laced bodice would be borne by the busk, not the delicate fabric of the dress.

The very full sleeves are gathered into the armhole and corded cuff. A puff of gathering decorates the upper arm. The cuff is also decorated with an extravagant frill of gathered net; like much of the fragile netting of this period, this lady's frills are disappearing. A bow of turquoise ribbon is mounted at the elbow in back; its streamers fall to the fingers.

The skirt is softly pleated into the waist. It is heavily decorated at the hem, finished with a gathered knee-deep flounce and three rows of cord mounted onto the surface of the skirt, which helps it stand away from the body. The head of the flounce is raw inside. The hem itself is finished with a ¼" (.5 cm) bias binding.

The dress is supported by a plain petticoat and pair of long and loose drawers trimmed with an edging of whipped-on lace. The shoes are tan leather with dark soles, bound with blue silk ribbons tied around the ankle.

At center is a doll called "Annabelle," dressed as an adolescent in a plain, but finely made dress. The details of the shoulders and the bonnet date it at about 1845–50.

Although dolls modeled as children were not unknown before this time, it was during the 1850s that they became common and popular, so popular, in fact, that within a generation bébé types dominated the market. It had long been recognized that childhood is a territory all its own. Many 18th century philosophers, in particular those whose "natural rights" theories inspired the founders of the American republic, argued that children were innocent and that parents had the obligation to nurture their children's talents. The idealization of childhood became central to concepts of family life. Instead of viewing infancy and childhood as a difficult period simply to be got through, childhood was viewed as a precious time of growth and learning. In the doll world, the culmination of this approach is, perhaps, the French bébé, who looks like no child who ever lived. Annabelle therefore represents the beginning of a trend in doll design. It was a fairly common practice for dolls modeled as ladies to be dressed as children, as well. Plate 13 is an example of a mature, even glamorous, china shoulder plate doll dressed as an adolescent in a calico frock.

Annabelle's head and plump little hands are made of papier-mâché. She has a commercially assembled cloth body that is jointed by stitching across at the hips and knees, human hair wig, and black, set-in, pupilless glass eyes. The modeling is naturalistic and sensitive.

She is wearing a dress of ivory cotton, delicately printed with sprigs of moss green, two shades of rose pink, brown, and yellow. The low neckline is finished with cord with a lightly gathered frill of cotton lace tacked behind it. The bodice is also detailed with cording, which outlines the yoke and then continues around the top of the armhole—the lower curve of the armscye is not corded. The elbow-length sleeves are set plain into the armhole and finished with a straight piece of lace whipped to the hem.

The pinafore or apron is of thread-striped cotton finished all around with a ⅛" (.3 cm) turn-back. The skirt is gathered; otherwise it is quite plain. The shoulder straps join the waistband/tie at the back. The waist closes with a bow-tie.

The dress is supported by a chemise, a plain petticoat, and a pair of bloomers gathered at the knee. She wears a pair of rather heavy knit stockings and a very pointed pair of black kid shoes bound at the ankle with black silk ribbon. The soles are extremely narrow, nearly straight, and cut from white kid.

Annabelle's outfit is completed with a fine straw bonnet and pretty cap (**PLATE 5**). The front is shaped to meet under the chin and ties with tape. A narrow frill of lace frames the face and goes all around the bottom to the back in one continuous line. The crown is shaped with a piece of very narrow tape drawn close at the nape. Its bow and trailing ties mingle with a wisp of fine brown hair at the back of her neck.

The bonnet is a familiar shape of this period. It is started with a plaque of straw at the crown. Where the brim begins, the braids of straw are cut and lapped. The last braid of straw at the front is lapped underneath around the face, but then drawn up and over the cut ends at the sides. Its own cut ends are hidden beneath the bavolet of satin-striped pink silk tacked at the lower edge of the crown. The bavolet and the inner lining of pink silk (which hides the work inside) are trimmed with a single very narrow braid of straw tacked on like a plain edging of passementerie. The crown is half lined with plain white muslin. Two ribbons matching the ties under her chin are wrapped around the brim.

Plate 6.

AT left, an interesting pair of dolls, clearly meant for each other—a pair of papier-mâchés with set-in, pupilless black glass eyes and well-detailed human hair wigs. The lady wears a simple and elegant bun loosely coiled at the nape of her neck. The gentleman's hair is combed back from a central part. His nose has apparently been augmented to give him a more "masculine" expression, but his head is clearly made from the same mold. The only other apparent difference between the two is the construction of the hands—his are well-formed separate fingers; she has a dainty mitten. Their bodies are of ungusseted kid.

The gentleman's svelte figure draws to mind young Queen Victoria emoting into her diary on the beauties of Albert's slender waist. This gentleman is wearing a lightweight black melton frock coat with matching pantaloons strapped under the instep. He is sewn into his clothes; the "fly" is a fake, formed by a small pleat. The coat has a seam all around the waist to join the full, pleated skirt to the body (in fact, a style that would later evolve into the "Prince Albert"). It has a single, center back seam to shape to the body, and is cut rather narrow in front to display the butter-colored waistcoat closed with small gold buttons, the only bright detail remaining to men's dress in the middle decades of the 19th century. The front of a man's dress shirt is suggested by an edging of narrow broderie anglaise down the center; he wears a high collar with modest points and a tall, neatly arranged black silk stock. (The shadow across the breast of his shirt indicates the lower edge of his substantial shoulder plate.)

The bride is dressed in an ivory taffeta gown with self-colored velvet bodice. Both fabrics are quite wonderful, still soft and in good condition. The velvet is so fine it almost has to be touched before the texture is noticeable. The gown is well cut and shaped close to the figure; the center front seam is outlined with cord that was probably covered in the taffeta but is now hanging loose. Although the inside of the bodice is inaccessible, a bodice of this type would normally be lined with a stout cotton fabric such as a lightweight twill. The bodice has a long, pointed waist finished with taffeta-covered cord. This gown and the one following (Plate 7) show the trend of bodice styles in the 1840s. A long-waisted figure was admired and gowns were cut to suggest this by displacing the waist seam slightly downward. It was a long, rather than dropped, waist that was desired. Deeply pointed center front and, sometimes, center back, seams enhanced the illusion. This style prevailed until the introduction of the crinoline in 1856, when the waist became visibly short, and would remain so for about 20 years, well into the bustle period.

The gown's modest neckline has a wide, Peter Pan-shaped bertha covering the shoulder seams. The bertha is covered with embroidered netting and edged with ruching of disintegrating netting. The upper edge of the neckline is raw, but was probably once covered with a detail that has fallen away. The sleeves are velvet and set in plain, trimmed with several pleats of silk and a netting ruffle.

The unlined skirt has a central back placket which is let into the breadth of the silk. One of the side seams is finished with the selvage edge; the other is left raw. Both seams and placket are executed with fine running stitches. The skirt is joined to the bodice with pleats in the front, but it is closely gathered in back. The bodice is closed at the back with a set of tiny enameled hooks, which may be replacements.

At right, a wax-over-composition girl is acting as the bridesmaid. She has black, pupilless, set-in glass eyes and a beautiful wig of soft curls. This little charmer is in much better condition than is usual for this type of doll. Introduced in an attempt to add lifelike translucency to an inexpensive composition doll, wax-over-composition is perishable and difficult to repair. In addition to the inherent fragility of the wax coat, it tends to separate from the composition base and crack.

The bridesmaid was dressed about 1850. She is wearing a low-cut gown of ivory silk, warp-printed in stripes and roses of celery green and pink. The waist is pointed front and back, and finished with self-fabric covered cord. The front bodice is made in three pieces, fitted close to the body; the back is in four pieces. The bodice is trimmed along the top edge by a ruched band of scalloped self-fabric. The sleeves apparently have disintegrated; her upper arms are now covered only by the short sleeves of her well-detailed chemise. The chemise is finely gathered into narrow cuff bands finished with a strip of fine, whipped-on lace. The upper edge of the chemise is covered by the bodice trimming, but it too is finished with lace whipped onto the edge. It is hemmed with small running stitches and trimmed with a frill about ¾" (2 cm) deep whipped onto the edge. The hem of the skirt is also closed with running stitches. There is no back closure; the doll is sewn into her dress.

The doll is wearing a pair of narrow drawers with an elaborate set of tucks of varying widths at the bottom of the leg, finished with narrow lace whipped to the hem. The general trend in undergarments, until the First World War, was for ever-increasing decorative detail as well as the use of finer and more varied fabrics and trims. The bridesmaid's stockings are knitted lace. She also wears a pair of lavender silk shoes tied around the ankle with silk cord and trimmed at the toes with matching knots of silk.

Her short petticoat is cream-colored wool flannel, trimmed all around with feather stitching in a variegated dull gold silk to close the hem, which is about 1" (2.5 cm) deep. Wool flannel petticoats were worn throughout this period (1830-1860) for warmth, although it is somewhat surprising to find one under this elegant gown.

The bridesmaid is wearing a lovely cap of net with a pair of hanging lappets, which were formed by fulling up a piece of lace to form a U-turn and then whipping the edges together in the center where they meet. The lappets are joined at the crown to a band formed of a piece of twisted pink ribbon. A bunch of pink silk flowers sits over each ear; a frill frames the face. The crown itself is formed by ribbon and lace whipped together in rows to form a fabric from which the circular crown was then cut.

Plate 7.

ANOTHER bonnet of the late 1840s. It foreshadows the bonnets of the mid-1850s and 1860s, which are off the face. The doll is papier-mâché with leather arms and a cloth body. She has an elaborate coiffure of real hair with heavy braids covering her ears. The details of her evening dress are very similar to that of the bride (Plate 6), except that hers is of silk damask trimmed with contrast fabrics and rather elaborate ribbon and flower garnishes. The center front has a self-covered cord in the seam and long curved darts that run almost to the armhole. Her bonnet of netting and gauze over a wire frame is just as elaborate. Decorative cording defines the edges and outlines the shape. Several realistic ribbon rosebuds nestle in the ostrich plumes covering the brim. One can sense what women's rights advocates faced: this dainty, intensely feminine style of dress, so evocative of conventional notions of proper "womanhood," was fashionable the very year (1848) the Seneca Falls convention launched the organized feminist movement in the United States.

Plate 8.

A CHINA doll of the 1840s. She apparently was re-dressed about 1860 in an afternoon dress of blue striped silk and cravat with a dainty tatted border. Her features and general modeling are influenced by classical motifs fashionable in the 1830s, but a hint of things to come can be seen in her delicate, idealized features. China dolls evolved from expensive luxury items in the 1840s to a ubiquitous childhood standard by the late 1850s. They were made in enormous numbers and sold not only as complete figures but also as separate heads that could be assembled to homemade bodies. Like fabrics and books, ceramics of all kinds suddenly became affordable to people of moderate means in the 1840s and 1850s. It is not surprising that quality declined as china heads became cheaper and less fashionable. While they did not actually go out of production until the 1920s, early chinas are of far better quality, not only in their fresh and elegant designs but in the execution as well. Nevertheless, many late Victorian chinas that are otherwise undistinguished retain a sentimental period charm.

Dollmaking became a large factory-based industry in the mid-19th century, most importantly in what is now Germany. Firms that manufactured dolls' heads often made a variety of other domestic ceramic objects as well. It is one of the ironies of the period, not lost on contemporaries, that the dolls bought for middle class children who spent their days in school were made by workers who were often also children. Much of what we know about the effects of urban industrialization was written by mid-Victorian observers who were horrified by its social consequences. They often did not perceive, however, that the children of the poor had to work wherever they lived. When peasant children went without schooling or shoes in villages far from a rail line or newspaper office, it often went unnoticed. It was the restless and vocal city proletariat that had editors alarmed. The anxiety that industrialization and its attendant social disruption caused led many writers to idealize traditional, pre-industrial life; their sense of loss in the disappearance of that way of life is a recurring theme throughout the 19th century.

Plate 9.

A PAIR of dolls representing young girls. Aside from the short length of their skirts, they were dressed in the mid-1850s like young women spending the morning at home.

At right, a large china doll with unusual brown eyes and an attractive, homemade cloth body with leather arms. Her dress is a characteristically neat and tiny printed cotton check in shades of red and rose. A small pink sprig is printed into the white part of the check pattern. The skirt is finished by a wide strip enclosing the raw hem of the dress. This may have been to cover a cutting error, although "false hems" of cotton, sometimes entirely unrelated to the design of the dress, were frequently used to reinforce silks or to save the cost of a deep turn-back. Another characteristic detail is the precisely executed design carried out in ordinary white tape on the hem (and a related pattern on the sleeve). Passementerie of various types went in and out of fashion for the next 60 years. (Compare, for example, the visiting dress in Plate 29 at left, the seaside costume in Plate 21 at the rear, and the French suit in Plate 45 at left.) Two wide tucks are executed over the tape.

The skirt and bodice are closely gauged into the wide waistband. The very low neckline is finished with a ¼" (.5 cm) bias strip that rests right at the base of the shoulder plate. Grown women might have filled in this low neck during the day with a chemisette or tucker of some sort, although it was acceptable in the late 1840s and 1850s for women to forego this with a moderately low day bodice. Although it is often difficult to associate a specific style with a particular cultural preoccupation, the 1850s practice of dressing children of both sexes nearly identically in low-necked dresses with pantaloons or pantelettes underneath may be related to the mid-Victorian concern that children remain sexually innocent as long as possible. They were dressed, therefore, so as to blur sexual differences until little boys were old enough to be breeched.

The skirt is supported by a petticoat with one deep tuck over a substantial hem (about ¾" or 2 cm). A chemise whose neckline is shaped like the dress is hemmed like the petticoat. The drawers are wide and short, with a finely finished narrow flounce let into the hem with a narrow facing. The flat brown shoes have straps that button at the ankle.

At left, a rare and charming head by Greiner with set-in glass eyes and heavy homemade body of wonderful individuality. She has the muscular forearms of a professional laundress, and her hands seem to have been set on backwards. Unlike the large china dolls of this period, whose heads, while pretty, are unnaturally heavy, these homely old Greiners, with their papier-mâché heads and substantial bodies, give one the sensation of picking up a small child when they are cuddled. She was dressed in the mid-1850s.

The dress of red-printed calico is styled for a child, but is modeled after the fashion for young women. It was sewn entirely by hand. The dress is unlined and the seams are raw except where they have been cut on the selvage. The low bodice is finished with a narrow binding at the neckline and reveals the edging of narrow lace that trims the chemise. The sleeves are interesting and unusual—not only are they seamed into the neckline (rather than being set into the armhole), but they are made like a beret sleeve with no underarm seam. The cuff was shaped into shallow dentelles by cutting the opening in the shape of a cross, then turning the edges back narrowly to hem and covering the hems with white rick-rack. The finely gathered bodice and skirt are both sewn into the waistband with a very small hem stitch. The bodice closes at center back with hooks and eyes.

The skirt seams are finished with the selvage edges. The hem is closed with the same fine hem stitch and decorated with a tuck of about ½" (1.5 cm).

The pretty apron was sewn principally on a chain stitch machine, and is probably a bit later than the doll and red dress. It is made of fine, nearly transparent crispy lawn. The shoulder straps are finished with a hand-scalloped frill and secured at the back with a large bow. The wide hem is made with drawn thread work and decorated with a tuck made by machine.

The dress is supported by a plain chemise, drawers, and petticoat, all simply trimmed with edging or narrow lace. Her half boots are made of tan cotton twill with leather toes. Altogether, she is an original character of great personality.

Plate 10.

A VERY small doll representing a young teenager, with chipmunk cheeks rather hectically colored, and small, quickly executed features. Her limbs are china, and the feet are molded with neat little black boots without heels. She was dressed in the late 1850s.

The fabric of her day dress may originally have been white or cream-colored; it is now light brown. It is a cotton gauze printed with pink and red flowers. The hem and the six little tucks over it were executed with a lock stitch machine. The rest of the work was done by hand.

The bodice and skirt are gathered into the waistband; the bodice gathers have been carefully organized to distribute fullness over the bosom. A not very neat turn-back at the neck encloses a string that was used to draw up the neckline ("en coulisse") to the shoulder plate. Little sets of gathers draw the sleeves up into a row of puffs, the last terminating in a flounce to the elbow.

The doll's petticoat is made of black silk taffeta, but is trimmed with a rather surprising flounce lined with substantial red wool to support the skirt. Her drawers were made from three tiny, different scraps of fabric—the waist-to-crotch section of coarse yellowish muslin, and one leg each from a plain and a thread-checked white cotton. They are simply two tubes, untrimmed and not open at the crotch as real drawers would be.

Plate 11.

A GROUP of playthings from the mid-19th century, of several different media. All of these dolls were made in large numbers and sold at moderate prices for a growing middle-class market. They were all apparently dressed "at home," their dresses the product of some busy person's plain but neat and practical sewing skills.

The large doll at left was one of the first dolls to come into the collection at the Wenham Museum. She was named "Phoebe Ann Elizabeth Tilton Abbot Church Richards" by her owner, Elizabeth Richards Horton (see Plate 12), who began the collection at Wenham as a means of raising money for children's charities. Mrs. Horton's mother was a Putnam, and the family believed that the fabric with which the doll is dressed dated from the mid-18th century, having come down to them from the descendants of General Putnam, the Revolutionary War hero.

The doll, representing a young woman, is a common early china of the "pink lustre" variety. She has a nicely proportioned home-made leather body.

The dress is very simply made. The skirt is roughly gathered into the round waist. The bodice is gauged to the center front; the fullness then radiates across the bosom. She wears a high neckline finished with bias binding. The one-piece sleeves are pleated into the armhole and finished with a flounce formed by the thread that gathers up the cuffs.

The dress is supported by two plain petticoats and a pair of drawers. She wears plain black stockings and flat leather shoes that button at the ankle.

Her cloak is a typical piece of doll haberdashery made from commercial instructions, formed of a rounded square of wool whose edges are scalloped and left raw. One corner forms the hood, which is outlined with a narrow piece of cord sewn into the edge. The cloak is lined with white china silk, cut about ½" (1.5 cm) shorter all around and left loose.

Next to Phoebe Ann is a small papier-mâché with wooden limbs and kid body, representing a young girl (center front) . She has the very typical spoon-type hand and extremely narrow feet of the so-called "milliners' model." Her dress can be very accurately dated, as it was the school project of a child who dressed her small friend in 1856.

The very full skirt is joined to the round waist with a close set of gathers. The hem is conventionally closed with a hem stitch. All her underclothes are very plain but meticulously made; they consist of drawers, chemise, short wool flannel petticoat and longer cotton petticoat.

The rather low corsage is gathered and joined to a bit of narrow, self-covered cording. A strip of lace wrapped around her neck and crossed over the breast covers her shoulders. The top of the chemise is just visible at the neck edge. The gathered elbow-length sleeves are finished with turned cuffs.

Her little apron of brown, spotted cotton is finished at the front, but the ties are simply a pair of tapes secured around her waist. The apron is topstitched all over, surprisingly, in white.

At rear center is another familiar face of the 1850s, a china shoulderplate with smoothly drawn back hair, exposing the lower ear. Her homemade body is cloth, the hands represented by plump mittens.

Her dress is familiar as well, a commonly found style for young girls. The unlined bodice is gathered into a low neckband and a waistband, to which the skirt is also joined. The closure is at the back with hooks and worked loops. The only ornament to this plain gown is a row of narrow, embroidered picots around the hem of the loose sleeve, and the gathering at the top, which is achieved through a bit of gauging at the head.

On the far right is a wax-over-composition lady in a very fair state of preservation; she has wooden limbs. She may be a bit earlier than her gown, which dates from the early 1860s. The dress is sewn entirely by hand.

The dress shows the transition from the skirt cut straight, whose fullness was controlled entirely through gathers, to the skirt cut with gores. This brown home dress or wrapper of striped calico is gored from the waist to the knee and finished with a deep, lightly gathered flounce. The joining seam is made with self-fabric covered cord and trimmed above with a single stripe cut from the dress fabric. As the stripe runs on the straight, it has been eased where necessary to conform to the curving shape of the seam. The same trimming finishes the collar and cuffs.

The bodice was fitted with a pair of pleats at side back and side front. A pleat was taken in the neckline; it may have been necessitated by a cutting mistake. The back and front are each cut in two pieces; the closure is by buttons down the front. The two-piece sleeves are set plain into the corded armhole; the cuffs are finished with a stripe of calico.

This doll is wearing a commercially designed apron, of which many examples are extant. They were sold uncut, the design stamped or printed on the cotton, to be finished at home.

Plate 13.

A PAIR of china dolls dressed in the early to mid-1850s. Standing at right, a doll representing a young woman. Her elaborate coiffure is caught in a gilt hair net and decorated with side bows also painted gold. Although the doll's sophisticated hair arrangement and shapely body are obviously designed to represent an adult, she was dressed as an adolescent in a calf-length day dress. This appealing style would be appropriate for a young woman if made floor-length. Many homesewers of the mid-century chose a similar approach in dressing their children's dolls.

The fabric is a cotton printed with brown geometric flowers on a tan ground; the trim is shrimp-colored, printed with naturalistic sprigs. The combination is a characteristic mid-19th century way of using color. The dress has a shaped, narrow yoke that is finished at the neck edge with contrast cord. The bodice is gathered into the yoke and the waistband, which is finished only on the lower edge with contrast cord. The bell-shaped open sleeves are set plain into the low armholes, which are finished all around with contrast cord. The hem of the sleeve is made with a contrast bias binding.

The skirt is calf-length and decorated at the hem with a flat applied band of the contrast trim. It is supported by a plain petticoat with one ½" (1.5 cm) tuck and a set of plain drawers trimmed with one ¼" (.5 cm) tuck.

Seated at left is a young girl dressed in a short style, but one that would be appropriate for a woman if made floor-length. Both the doll and dress are a bit earlier than her friend at right. At the end of the 1840s, ladies' sleeves were made to fit the upper arm closely; the mass of fabric and decorative work was placed on the forearm. About 1850 these bottom-heavy sleeves were opened. The first pagoda sleeve was a loose sleeve with a series of flounces mounted on it, which looked somewhat like the series of roofs on an idealized pagoda. The term "pagoda," however, soon came to refer to any kind of long, open sleeve. The pagoda sleeve was always worn with an undersleeve tacked or tied into the armscye. The undersleeve (or "engageante") was white cotton or lace for day; evening styles might have an undersleeve of black lace.

This beautifully made dress is of rather stout celery-colored cotton and wool fabric printed with a pattern of pomegranates. Some are orange; others, now gray, were once lilac-colored. Although the dressmaker did a good job fitting the dress to the doll, the perfectly molded fit of the bodice is due to the swelling of the doll's sawdust stuffing.

The low neck is finished with a narrow self-fabric cord, as are the low armholes. The bodice is fully lined and smoothly fitted with two curved seams at the side back and a pair of darts at the front. The black buttons merely decorate the front; the center back closes with four pearl buttons and a set of hand-worked buttonholes.

The wide, open sleeves are set to the armhole with several box pleats decorated with small black buttons. The sleeves are trimmed with a flat braided strip that was apparently made by braiding several lengths of plain cord trimming. Although it is now faded to a dull ivory color, it once matched the lilac color in the dress fabric.

The skirt is pleated to the round waist and finished with self-covered cord. The hem is a 1" (2.5 cm) turn-back, and around the bottom is a deep tuck to make the skirt stand away from the body. It is gathered with cartridge pleats at the back.

The skirt is supported by a petticoat that is exquisitely simple, with very fine gauging overcast to the waistband. The chemise is also plain. The drawers, however, although plain in style, are made from a cotton damask fabric patterned with woven sprigs.

The young lady is wearing a pair of very finely knit patterned socks and flat ankle strap shoes with a soft, seamed sole.

Instructions for the pagoda-sleeve day dress are found in Chapter II.
Instructions for the yoke bodice day dress are found in Chapter III.

Plate 15.

A COMMON china doll of the 1850s, which has suffered some traumatic damage in her long life. She is interesting principally because of the well-detailed hoops with which she was provided. They were formed by wrapping tape around a set of springy flat metal rings, which were then sewn to a set of tapes hanging from her waist, just like the life-size ones.

The "artificial" crinoline, introduced in 1856, freed women from the weight of the many petticoats needed to support their wide skirts. Moreover, the width of the crinoline skirt made almost everyone's waist look small by comparison, so in the age of the crinoline, women abandoned long, tight corsets for shorter, more comfortable ones. Judging by the number sold, which was in the many millions, the crinoline was an instant and enormous success. Men hated it. Despite being made, with the manic ingenuity for which the Victorians are known, to collapse or fold up in various ways, the crinoline's springy instability made it a nuisance wherever it went. Employers complained that factory girls wanted to wear them to work. Papers frequently reported women being dragged to death when their hoops were caught in carriage wheels or burned when they caught fire. Worse yet, crinolines were always liable to be tipped up by wind or ordinary movement, causing one social critic to complain that the term "ankle" was now by courtesy extended to half the leg. [Alison Gernsheim, *Victorian and Edwardian Fashion: A Photographic Survey*, 1981, p.46, quoting *The Illustrated News of the World*, 1863, London.] This propensity led immediately to a fashion in colored petticoats, elaborately trimmed drawers, and fancy patterned stockings. Conservatives condemned the crinoline as vulgar, not merely because of its evident immodesty but for the cost of the display, since the crinoline required many yards of fabric to cover. Nevertheless, the crinoline remained fashionable in one form or another until the late 1860s, when it was replaced by the bustle.

Her dress is nicely detailed for so small a design. The fabric is a wool and cotton twill plaid of subdued olive, blue, and cream. The bodice was very carefully fitted with a set of darts radiating from the center front waist. The waist seam is defined with narrow, self-covered cord. The bell sleeves are also finished with cording at the cuff and armhole. They are trimmed with silk ribbon woven in alternating grosgrain and velvet bands. The neckline is filled in with two rows of lace.

Her underwear received the same careful attention to detail. Under her hoops, she wears a set of drawers and petticoat, both meticulously decorated with sets of tiny tucks.

Plate 16.

A PARIAN lady of around 1855-1860. Genuine Parian is a rather expensive medium used for minor art objects. "Parian" dolls, popular from the mid-1850s to the mid-1880s, are actually made of a white "biscuit" porcelain; their modeling does, however, relate to the contemporary fashion for white parlor ornaments decorated with painted or gilt details. Parian dolls are noted for their detailed modeling, including molded lace chemisettes and ensembles of jewelry; blonde or brown hair is common, and the coiffure is frequently decorated with delicate posies of flowers. Like china dolls, they were sold fully assembled or by the shoulderplate alone, and were a less costly alternative to the more realistically representational French fashion dolls.

This doll has a homemade cloth body and leather arms with carefully made and amusingly shaped hands. Her ears are pierced into her head. Her slightly faded silk taffeta dinner dress is brilliant green. The dress may have been made from a scrap of commercially scalloped trimming. The dressmaker used one simple technique—gathering—in various combinations to form the entire gown.

The skirt and bodice are gathered using an enclosed cord to simulate gauging. The pieces were then overcast onto the waistband. The skirt has several large applied ruffles blind stitched like branches of foliage onto its surface. They are made of the scalloped edging drawn on cord. The turned-under top edges are left raw.

The bodice is trimmed with a bertha of the scalloped edging, doubled at the top to finish the neckline and gathered several times to make the appearance of gauging. The top set of gathers encloses a cord. The whole construction was then stitched into place over the shoulders. The lines of gathering permit the shaping as the cord was drawn up around the shoulderplate. The scalloped edging has been backed by a piece of lace. A large filigree brooch decorates one shoulder.

The sleeves were similarly formed by gathering into the armhole. The cuffs are formed of the scalloped edge gathered like the bertha with a piece of lace underneath.

The dress is supported by a chemise with plain hem and knee-length petticoat trimmed with one bit of edging lace whipped onto the fold of the hem and another applied flat above it. A second, floor-length petticoat has a flounce of lace let into a small tuck taken in the hem, which is about 2" (5 cm) deep. The doll's drawers are straight, trimmed with two tucks and a whipped-on edging of lace. Although they have a center seam, they are not slit.

Plate 17.

Two typical Parian ladies of about 1860. At left, a doll much like china dolls of the same period, with a good deal of detail, but very simply rendered. (Compare, for example, Plate 13.) This lady's snood and side bows, as well as her facial features, are modeled rather flatly and painted with a minimum of fuss over the details. Her body is homemade, with leather arms and jointed cloth body.

Her day dress of claret-colored wool printed with small black chevrons is entirely handsewn, rather roughly, but is well-designed. Its pretty lines have been sabotaged by the proportions of its wearer.

The bodice and sleeves are lined with coarse, soft cotton. The low neckline is finished with a narrow black velvet ribbon folded over the edge and stitched down. Fullness at the waist is gathered into the waistband, which is raw inside. The closure is at the back with small faceted jet half-ball buttons. The bell sleeves are pleated into the armhole.

The skirt is unlined and rather narrower than was then fashionable. The dress may have been made from a scrap. The skirt's fullness is distributed with double inverted box pleats set over each front hip. This is a very common style of the period and may be found on early French fashion dolls as well. (See Plates 19 and 20, for instance.) It presages the gored skirts of the 1860s. The skirt back has a double knife pleat at each side of the center back seam,

which in effect repeats the double box pleat pattern. The "placket" at center back is the unsewn top of the seam. It and the two side seams are left raw inside.

The dress is supported by a mid-thigh chemise and knee-length petticoat trimmed with narrow embroidery much like rick-rack and inserted into the seam of a wide, applied facing. She wears a pair of eyelet-trimmed drawers which extend to the mid-calf. There is no long petticoat.

Completing the outfit are a pair of plain white socks and very dark green leather ankle-strap shoes sewn like a child's bootie with a turned seam. They are lined with white cotton. The soles are tan, and the whole shoe is bound with green silk. The straps fasten at the center with a button.

At right is another Parian doll of much superior quality. Her carefully styled hair has individual strands modeled in it, and her face, although not conventionally pretty, is individual and intelligent. I include her in the selection because all of her various components are approximately contemporaneous; however, she has been assembled from odd elements in the Wenham Museum's collection. The principal reason for choosing her is the simple and very smart wrapper. The homemade cloth body is proportionate and neatly made.

The cream-colored cotton wrapper is printed with a small square blot design like stylized flower pots. Although slightly stained, the fabric retains its crispness. The wrapper is trimmed all over with flat cotton braid-like tape, which has begun to deteriorate in places, but is still bright.

The bodice, gathered into the waistband, closes down the front with buttons. Only the bodice and waistband have functional buttonholes. The neckline is trimmed with a narrow frill of lace. The waistband is carefully finished to enclose the raw bottom edge of the bodice; the skirt is gathered neatly but left raw inside. The dress has the flat, two-piece coat sleeve typical of the period trimmed at the cuff with braid and a narrow frill of lace. It is set plain into the low armhole.

The skirt is gently gored as well as gathered and is slightly longer in back than in front, a glimpse of things to come. The lower buttons on the skirt are "fakes"—the bottom two are sewn through and through (with no buttonhole) and the next two are sewn through the top fabric only. The skirt is decorated with a pair of round patch pockets trimmed with tape.

The skirt is supported by a pair of loose, lace-edged drawers that extend to mid-calf. Over them is a plain cotton petticoat with a deep (1½" or 4 cm) hem and plain lace edging. Her upper petticoat is a handsome crisp cotton faille whose ribbed texture is covered with closely executed, exuberantly designed floral motifs extending to the knee. The hem is finished with buttonholed scallops. As was frequently done in "real life," the beautiful fabric that might occasionally show when the skirt hem was lifted was sewn to a hip yoke of lesser, plain white cotton gathered onto the waistband.

Instructions for the 1860 wrapper are found in Chapter IV.

Plate 23. *"Portrait Jumeau," 20" (51 cm) tall, bisque head and arms, articulated wood body; mohair wig; dressed in a ball gown, c.1865–70. Writing desk with a collection of miniature Limoges.* ALL COURTESY OF YESTERYEARS.

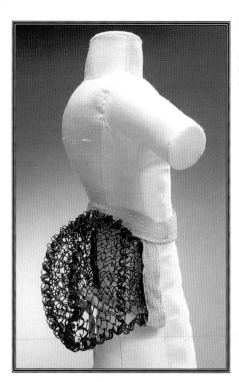

Plate 24.
Wire "health bustle," c.1870.
COURTESY OF
YESTERYEARS.

Plate 26. *French fashion lady, 23" (58.5 cm) tall, with gusseted kid body and articulated wooden arms; human hair wig; muslin walking dress, c.1875.* COURTESY OF YESTERYEARS.

Plate 25.
"Crinolette" of canvas and steels, c.1880–1885. The shape of the silhouette was controlled by a set of interior laces that could be used to draw the bustle into a more or less protruding shape.
COURTESY OF THE
WENHAM MUSEUM.

Plate 27. *French fashion lady by F.G., 18" (45.5 cm) tall, bisque head and articulated wood body; human hair wig; walking costume, c.1873–1875. Mid-Victorian dresser with marble top and collection of miniature Limoges.* COURTESY OF YESTERYEARS.

Background, silk fan, c.1870. COURTESY OF THE WENHAM MUSEUM.

Plate 28
*French fashion lady,
20" (51 cm) tall,
with kid body and
blond mohair wig,
silk promenade dress,
c.1873–1875.*
COURTESY OF THE
WENHAM MUSEUM.

Plate 29. *Right, French fashion lady, 15" (38 cm) tall, with fully articulated kid-covered wood body; porcelain hands; human hair wig; dress of spotted muslin, c.1872. Left, French fashion type (the head has been lost); gusseted kid body and bisque hands; calling costume, black silk and velvet, trimmed with jet beads and braid, c.1870–75. Dresser and cheval mirror, late 19th century. Background, silk fan, c.1870.*
ALL COURTESY OF THE WENHAM MUSEUM.

Plate 30. *French fashion lady, 12" (30.5 cm) tall; gusseted kid body;
black silk dress, c.1875.* COURTESY OF YESTERYEARS.

Plate 31. *Lady with Parian head and elaborately molded hair and necklace, homemade cloth body with leather arms; 13" (33 cm) tall. She is wearing a cotton polonaise style called the "Dolly Varden," fashionable about 1873, probably a reproduction made in the 1940s or 1950s. Although very charming, the Dolly Varden was considered rather declassé in the mid-1870s. Parian dolls were popular with collectors of the 1940s, and their reproduced clothing, 50 years hence, can look very convincing if it is well made.* COURTESY OF THE WENHAM MUSEUM.

Plate 32. *Morning gown, c.1875, probably French, of white cotton fabric and machine-made lace.* COURTESY OF THE WENHAM MUSEUM.

Plate 33. *French fashion lady, 9½" (24 cm) tall, with gusseted kid body; silk traveling costume and straw hat, c.1874. She is accompanied by her trunk full of clothes.* ALL COURTESY OF THE WENHAM MUSEUM.

Plate 18.

A pensive young woman by Rohmer. This little sweetheart with painted eyes and blond skin wig is wearing a gauze afternoon dress tastefully trimmed with lace-edged flounces. While most French dollmakers were turning to more realistic tinted bisque, Mlle. Rohmer employed white china or Parian for the modeling of her dolls' heads. They are among the most charming and distinctive of late Victorian dolls.

The dress foundation is a rather coarse, glazed white cotton. The bodice lining is sewn in one with the gauze shell; they are shaped with two front darts. The neckline and the waist are finished with narrow cord. The sleeves are transparent, three-quarter length, and gathered into poufs with a drawn thread. They are finished with a pair of flounces edged with lace to match the skirt.

The overskirt has three lightly gathered flounces whose hems are edged with narrow medallion lace. The header of the topmost flounce is covered with the same lace. The skirt is supported by a pair of petticoats, one with six narrow tucks, the other twelve. The first petticoat is edged simply with a strip of whipped-on lace. The second, shorter one is more elaborately trimmed with a narrow strip of fabric rolled, whipped, and gathered to the hem. The outer edge of the trimming has a design of lace-like crochet edging woven to it. The doll has no drawers.

Her shoes are of white kid edged with blue silk ribbon and decorated on the toes with a rather elaborate rosette of the same ribbon.

To finish her outfit, posies of flowers are pinned to the dress and to the blue silk ribbon in her curls. She also wears several bracelets of turquoise and faceted gold beads, and a matching necklace.

In the 1860s, a revolutionary product began appearing on the toy market, the so-called "French fashion" doll or Parisienne. The heads were made of realistically tinted bisque. Most had large, set-in glass eyes and meticulously styled wigs of hair—typically, blue eyes and blond hair. The classic body for this type of doll is elaborately gusseted kid, but less commonly they may be found with arms of china or wood on a kid body, or even a fully articulated body of painted wood or wood covered with kid shrunk to its surface. Hands and limbs were experimentally offered in gutta percha and metal. Dolls of more conventional materials like china, Parian, and papier-mâché continued to be marketed in large numbers, but the worldly and fashionable Parisienne became the doll of little girls' dreams. Nearly any item imaginable could be had for them, from boots, gloves, and parasols to railway rugs and letter paper. Many were apparently made just to be looked at, their clothing detail secured with glue and garments stitched onto the doll. The French fashion doll is an iconic product of the "gilded age"—cheerfully vulgar, intensely detailed and beautifully made, she was sold with the aid of saturation marketing campaigns aimed directly at the ultimate consumer, the child.

In her design, the French fashion doll refers indirectly to the trend toward dolls modeled as children. The French dollmakers who designed her were also producing another classic at this time, the bébé. Some Parisiennes are meant to represent adolescents, but many clearly are intended to be young women, and, although the bodies are often mature, the faces are young, like the sentimentalized images of children in contemporary prints, with large eyes, rosebud mouth, and plump, rosy cheeks.

Plate 19.

A pretty doll representing an adolescent wearing a typical look of the early 1860s. Her jumper is a gray cotton and silk mixture. The texture is quite smooth, with an interesting black fleck woven into it. The surface of the dress is decorated with appliqué bows of blue silk ribbon, which was folded into the bow-shaped motif and then stitched down with tiny running stitches. The bodice is decorated with lines of velvet ribbon in matching blue. All of the interior seams of this dress are unfinished.

The full skirt is joined directly to the bodice with a series of double inverted box pleats. The effect of a waistband is simulated with rows of velvet ribbon trim. Despite the short length, it is cut as though to take a modest crinoline, slightly longer in back than in front.

The bodice is closed at center back with a set of brass hooks. It is fully interlined with cotton. The striping is carried out around the neck and the short jockeys at the armhole.

Her blouse, or "waist," is of sheer batiste. It is vertically tucked and then gathered into a waistband that closes with a single hook. One button at about the shoulder blades and one in the neckband close the center back. A band of machine-worked embroidery is mitered and whipped to the top of the bodice to form a yoke. The inner edge is gathered up to form the actual neckhole, to which a second band is whipped to form a standing collar, trimmed with lace. The cuffs are similarly formed. The sleeve end is rolled, whipped, and gathered to fit.

The skirt is supported by a plain petticoat on a drawstring and a plain chemise. Both are trimmed with lace. The doll has no drawers. Her shoes are of blue kid sewn like a baby shoe with turned sole and no heel. They are bound with light blue silk ribbon, and trimmed with a flat bow in a silver buckle.

Her fashionable "Japanese" straw hat with velvet trimmings is slightly later than her dress. This type of hat, stylish in 1867, was woven in one continuous round with string weft.

Plate 20.

This young woman is wearing a particularly smart blouse of untrimmed batiste. It is tucked across both front and back; the shoulders are closed with a corded seam. The closure at center back is with a set of tiny, fabric-covered buttons; the neckband and collar also have a pair of buttons. The collar, split at the front as well, is joined to the neck by a narrow facing. The poet-style sleeve, actually a loose bishop sleeve, is pleated into the armhole, but rolled, whipped, and gathered into French turn-back cuffs. The cuff is topstitched and closed with a button and loop. This type of very full sleeve was fashionable from about 1855–1865.

The bodice of this dress is joined directly to the skirt, whose fullness has been made into sets of double inverted box pleats. The "waistband" is actually a separate belt, which closes at the back with a broad, petal-shaped sash and round bow.

She is wearing a stylish garrison cap, another signature piece of this period in which military motifs were very popular for ladies' wear. Garrison caps for dolls were made in all sorts of materials, from this one of tartan velvet to straw. The front is ornamented with a thistle medallion and tuft of parti-colored ostrich.

WOMEN'S RIGHTS

"Men, their rights and nothing more; women, their rights and nothing less."
MASTHEAD OF "THE REVOLUTION," 1868

When the dresses shown in Plate 21 were made, it had been nearly 20 years since the 1848 convention at Seneca Falls, New York, had inaugurated the organized women's rights movement in the United States. Upstate New York was the locus of intense reform activity in the second quarter of the 19th century, from religious enthusiasm to agitation for the abolition of slavery. In the beginning, the women's suffrage movement in the United States was closely associated with the abolition movement, a general effort to extend the benefits of the Constitution to people who were as yet unenfranchised. In her youth, Susan B. Anthony worked on behalf of both causes.

Immediately following the Civil War, women activists were disappointed to learn that the Fourteenth and Fifteenth Amendments would extend benefits to males only. A bitter controversy erupted within the two movements, one side arguing that blacks should hold out until women were given the vote, and the other side that holding black suffrage hostage to women's would mean that neither would enjoy the franchise. Eventually, those arguing that it was the "Negro's hour" prevailed; the women's suffrage movement was split, and would remain split for nearly two generations. Suffrage activists were occasionally embarrassed by state-sponsored referenda in which women indicated by comfortable majorities that they preferred not to have the vote—they, too, felt this was the perquisite of men.

The "woman question" was a central issue for the later Victorians. In their complex and fast-changing society, there was no single answer. Like a social guerrilla movement, however, women gradually insinuated themselves further and further into public life by redefining what the terms of "domestic" management should be.

In the third quarter of the 19th century, teaching and social work became largely female occupations, filled with young women earning college degrees despite warnings from conservative doctors that concentrated study would deprive them of needed vitality for childbearing. Women often gravitated toward professions that were new and therefore without an established hierarchy of men. Social work was one; photography and spiritualism also provided venues for creative women. Women writers dominated a vast sub-genre of sentimental domestic novels in which women's viewpoints and concerns could be discussed through the medium of fictional situations. Advice writers of the period began to suggest that to marry a man one did not love simply to get a home was not merely contemptible, but morally repellent.

The first women's clubs date from the post-war period, when it was still controversial for women to have lunch in public unaccompanied by men. A movement like temperance, in which women organized essentially to stop men from drinking, can be seen as a proxy for discussion of deeper issues between the sexes. The roots of the progressivist agenda lie in the late 19th century, with networks of unenfranchised women organizing to bring their influence to bear in public life. Ironically, their moral authority was derived from Victorian notions of female purity and the extension of feminized domestic life to the public, political world.

Plate 21.

Two dresses of the middle 1860s. This pale bisque doll is a relatively unusual type, made of fully articulated, kid-covered wood with Parian hands. She is wearing a rather advanced style of the early 1860s, a cotton faille costume made to be worn at the seaside resorts so popular with all classes of Victorians. It is cut short for a not-quite-mature young woman. Her second costume, a well-cut silk walking suit, was presumably made for her coming out.

The angular style and smart tailoring that characterize the fashionable ladies' clothing of the late 1860s perhaps reflect not only a general trend toward a more "engineered" world, but women's changing place in it. Both the faille seaside costume and the silk walking suit well illustrate the new fashion line with its crisp gored skirts and jacket bodices.

The white faille ensemble consists of a dress with double skirt and a matching jacket, both trimmed with a design in narrow white tape. At this date, an ensemble consisting of separate pieces in the same fabric was called a "costume." This one was probably commercially made. None of the seams in the tightly woven cotton fabric have been finished, but this beautifully made fabric more or less refuses to ravel.

The bodice of the dress is fitted at the front with a pair of side front seams. The back is made in two pieces. The corsage is modestly low. The neckline is finished with a narrow cording of plain white cotton and decorated with a narrow design of tape arabesques. Because the doll's joints are frozen, some of the interior detail is inaccessible, but pulling the jacket down reveals the tape trim of the short sleeves. The sleeve hem is turned with cord facing. The bodice closure is at the center back, but, although the placket is cleanly finished, there are no fasteners.

The double five-gore skirt is sewn as one to the bodice. Both of the skirt hems, which are simply turned up, are decorated with an elaborate line of passementerie in white tape. All of the skirt shaping is done with goring; there is no gathering or pleating. The skirt is slightly longer at the back than the front and is supported by a short, stiff, petticoat of gray horsehair fabric and striped with white cotton, cord-like threads. (A short crinoline is now under the green silk dress on its form.) Under her petticoat, she wears a pair of plain white drawers and a white cotton chemise.

The unlined jacket is a gentle trapeze shape meant to be worn open. The neckline is finished with plain white cotton cord. The two-piece coat sleeves are set plain into the low armholes. Tape trimming was applied over the finished seams of the sleeve and jacket side seams; however, at the shoulders, the tape was applied first and then the shoulder seam closed, interrupting the design.

The second costume, although well cut, is not very well made. The inside is rough and unfinished. It is supported by an elaborate crinoline which probably belongs to the white faille ensemble. The hoops are threaded through a shaped network of mesh, to give the appropriate, elliptical cone shape to the skirt.

The skirt has six gores, one each at center front and back, and two on each side. The closure at the left side of the center back gore was with a hook (now missing). The wide center back gore is made with deep cartridge pleats at the waist. The skirt is unlined and the seams are raw except where the leading edges of the gores have been cut with the selvage. The hem is finished with a 2" (5 cm) wide bias facing.

The jacket is styled with a pair of basques in front; the deeply shaped hem, accommodating the fullness of the skirt at the sides, terminates in back with a complementary tail. The actual hem is finished by turning the raw edge out to the front side, where it is covered by the trim, a two-edged lace sewn with jet beads in the center. Curved darts shape the front. The buttons at center front, of black jet on a metal shank, are "fakes"; the actual closure is a set of hooks and loops. The neckline is finished with a piece of the black lace folded over the edge. A frill of white lace is set behind it. The back is made in three pieces; the side body seam runs into the lower part of the armhole on each side. Like the skirt, the bodice is unlined, but the dressmaker did trouble to overcast the long seams of the bodice to neaten them.

The two-piece coat sleeve is eased into the armhole at the head, where it is covered by shoulderboards of lace. Military-style trimmings enjoyed a vogue at this time, although many suggest the uniforms of the 18th century rather than the 19th century. The top sleeve is cut on the bias, with the stripe running diagonally down the arm; the undersleeve is cut on the crosswise straight with the stripes running horizontally.

The doll's little velvet bonnet probably was bought to go with this silk ensemble. Her functional black umbrella with green handle is leaning against the vanity.

Instructions for the silk walking suit are found in Chapter V.

Plate 22.

A French fashion doll with piled hair and long trailing ringlets wearing a superlatively cut dinner gown. Although it now appears to be a mellow French blue, the unfaded interior is actually a vivid purplish cobalt color. The silk taffeta is patterned with raised velvet coin dots, themselves decorated with pin dots of blue. The fabric is disintegrating in places.

Chemical dyes were introduced to the fashion world in the 1850s. Colors as brilliant in name as in hue—mauvine, solferino,

and magenta, for example—suddenly became very chic. Although they look garish to a contemporary eye, their vivid brightness was a delightful novelty when they were introduced.

In addition to the sewing machine and the commercial paper pattern, which allowed women of modest skills and means to turn out fashionable, well-fitting clothing, manufacturers offered many highly processed materials designed to resemble expensive goods at relatively low prices. One of the most common practices, which conservators everywhere regret, was the "weighting" of silk, so that it appeared to be of much heavier, and, therefore, more expensive, quality. This was done by soaking the fabric in baths of metal salts, which were absorbed into the fabric sometimes to two or three times the weight of the original material. The exciting new colors were often made of chemicals that were, in addition to being toxic, relatively perishable. Arsenic was used to make green, for example, and even then it was believed that library book borrowers had been poisoned by the fabrics covering books. For the modern collector or conservator, the problem is that when these primitive chemicals break down, they take the fabric with them, and late Victorian and Edwardian clothing is often falling apart right before one's eyes.

The dinner dress has a functional yoke to which the princess-seamed body of the dress is attached. The seam is hidden under a tasteful little flounce of lace laid around the shoulders, gathered very lightly, and the header oversewn with two lines of faceted black beads. The high neckline has a narrow frill of white lace. The front closure is a row of tiny hooks and worked loops. The dress has a fashionable two-piece coat sleeve set plain into the armhole. The cuffs are trimmed with the same lace and bead flouncing.

The gown has a long train whose fullness is achieved through a deep box pleat. The back is made in three pieces, the front in four. The bodice is lined to the hip. The skirt hem is finished with a straight piece of glazed cotton about 1¼" (3 cm) wide, which is laid straight on around the edge with a small running stitch. Little tucks are taken at the top to conform it to the curve of the skirt.

This lady is wearing one rather plain petticoat, not shaped to the dress, with six tucks and a deep hem trimmed with lace whipped to the edge. The doll's look is completed with a gold cross bearing several tiny lavender cabochons.

Plate 23.

A "portrait Jumeau" wearing a brilliant apple green evening gown trimmed with black velvet ribbon and ivory lace. (The back of this dress is pictured on the cover.) Her curls of yellow mohair are dressed with a posey of pink roses. Her ears are pierced into her head, and she is wearing a pair of long crystal drops.

This dress, probably commercially made, is similar in cut to the fashions in Plate 21 and Plate 22, but shows the developing bustle. The silk is unlined and some of the carefully cut details are not functional. This doll was meant only to be looked at, not played with. The skirt has seven gores: two at center back, two at side back, two at the side front, and one central front gore. Pleats at the back are deep and full. From the side front gores, the skirt spreads into an extravagant train. The hem is finished with a wide shaped facing of coarse cotton to which is sewn a narrower double frill of netting around the edge. Two flounces made with minimal fullness are mounted on the surface of the skirt, both trimmed at the lower edge with ivory lace. The top edge of the lower flounce, which is hidden by the lace of the upper flounce, has been left raw. The upper flounce is formed with an inserted cord and trimmed at the top edge as well with ivory lace.

The jacket is cut with short basques. Fullness at the center back is achieved with a double pleat let into a short waist seam across the small of the back. A bunch of lace let into the seam increases the apparent size and fullness of the bustle. It is a four-piece back; the two-piece front is shaped by a pair of darts. Five buttons at the front closure go only to the bottom of the bertha.

The sleeve is gathered into the armscye. Midway down, the outer portion has been gathered to form a pouf or half-flounce. The hem is decorated with ivory lace and a net "undersleeve."

The bertha is formed simply from a set of tucks mounted onto a netting foundation, alternating with rows of lace. It is laid over the shoulders of the dress like a necklace, having no attachment to the neckline and no functional closure. The neck edge is drawn up with a piece of very narrow black velvet ribbon. A posey of pink roses decorates the breast. The doll is also wearing a watch with a turquoise fob.

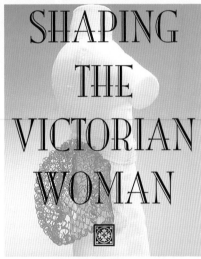

SHAPING THE VICTORIAN WOMAN

Around 1860, the shape of fashionable skirts began to change. Although they remained very full, the round, dome-shaped skirt was becoming elliptical, the fullness slipping to the back. At first, this was done through the use of pleats, which allowed the front of the skirt to drape straight down the figure, while the longer back breadths spread out behind. In the early 1860s, goring was introduced. Initially, it was used to increase the girth of the hem while reducing bulk at the waistline. But the gores soon became very asymmetrical, throwing more of the fullness of the skirt to the back. In the late 1860s gores too began to be cut with a great deal of fullness to be pleated or gathered at the waist, which was artfully arranged in draperies supported by the bustle. Although bustles, "bum rolls," and hip pads had been worn for centuries, the new silhouette was an extreme shape that required a great deal of structural support. For about fifteen years, until the early 1880s, fashionable women wore one incarnation after another of this rather bizarre form. The bustle enjoyed a brief revival in the mid-1880s.

Plates 24 and 25

PICTURED here is the progressive "Wire Health Bustle," "Light, Flexible, Strong, Durable, Perfect, Recommended by Leading Physicians as being less heating to the spine than any others." [James Laver, *The Concise History of Costume and Fashion*, 1969, p. 201.] Advertisements assured ladies that they would never be "mortified" by the bustle's being crushed into a "ridiculous shape" and that it was capable of "sustaining the heaviest drapery." [Alison Carter, *Underwear, The Fashion History*, 1992, p.60.] The bustle generally was worn over the petticoat, although some dresses were designed for the bustle to be worn between the main skirt and upper draperies. The various arrangements for achieving the then-fashionable silhouette are amusingly ingenious. **PLATE 25** illustrates the "crinolette," and bustle with half-crinoline at the back. Full-size versions could be adjusted with ties underneath to make the bustle more or less prominent as need be.

This is also the period of the infamous tightlacing controversy. The health and moral effects of wearing corsets had been the subject of debate for years, but reached its crescendo in the era of the bustle, when fashion seemed to advocate a really punishing corset. Nevertheless, it is clear from con-temporary photographs and surviving garments, indeed, from the shape of the fashionable dolls of this time, that very few women must have worn them. It was recommended, for instance, that a woman buy a corset whose waist measure was two inches less than her own "nude waist." However, corsets were not laced so as to meet edge to edge.

The late Victorian world, like other complex cultures, was filled with contradictory messages. Risqué postcards were retouched to make the models' waists narrower. A slender waist was important to a fashionable shape, but the Victorians did not admire a skinny figure. While sports and work were opening to vigorous, healthy women, some women still aspired to an image of extreme delicacy. Physicians in England and France first identified anorexia nervosa as a specific syndrome in the early 1870s. Although few respectable woman would go out without a corset, the agonies suffered by the typical woman to be well dressed have just as certainly been exaggerated. Even manufacturers of corsets advised buying a corset that was "comfortable" and warned against trying to achieve an unnaturally small waist. The often repeated assertion that women had their lower ribs removed in order to lace themselves smaller has never been authenticated. [Valerie Steele, *Fashion and Eroticism, Ideals of Feminine Beauty*, 1985, p.170.]

Plate 26.

A tall French fashion doll, whose long, loose hair emphasizes her youth. This young woman has articulated wooden arms with beautifully modeled, delicate hands, and a gusseted kid body.

The doll wears a two-piece whitework afternoon dress of fine white muslin, probably commercially made about 1870. Its design is simple, although requiring many hours of work to complete, a masterpiece of intense but understated detail.

The skirt is fully lined with a layer of the semi-sheer white muslin, which has an applied flounce to mid-thigh. Both the top and bottom edges of the flounce are hemmed. To form the flounce, the top edge was gathered onto a cord about ½" (1.5 cm) from the top and blind stitched to the actual foundation. The top edge forms a short, upstanding ruffle.

The outer skirt is decorated around the sides and back with ten narrow flounces which are flat-hemmed at the lower edge with a tiny running stitch. The top edge of the top flounce is hemmed, then gathered onto a cord and blind stitched down with a small ruffle, the same as the long underskirt flounce. The lower nine flounces are rolled, whipped, gathered, and blind stitched around, each one slightly lapping the one below. The skirt is cut with a short train. The front panel is gathered up on six little cords stitched into channels.

The bodice has a pair of tails and modest basques, which are finished around the hem with a narrow double flounce also drawn on cord. The jacket is well-tailored to the doll's form with a center back seam, pair of side seams, and two front darts. The center back is decorated with a pair of self-covered buttons at the waist; the same buttons are used to make the front closure. Under the long curls, a medallion of heavy white lace has been let into the seam. As it matches none of the other work, it may have been inserted to correct a cutting error. The two-piece coat sleeves have beautifully detailed cuffs, trimmed all around with the double narrow flounce drawn on cord, and tacked to the sleeves to hold them in position. The modest V-neck also is finished with a ruffle gathered onto cord.

The doll wears a camisole under the jacket, whose short sleeves can be seen through the jacket fabric. Her rather plain drawers are decorated with seven tiny tucks divided by an insertion of broderie anglaise, which also trims the hem. Her petticoat has a knee-deep flounce trimmed with crochet lace and three small tucks. The flounce is joined to the petticoat skirt with a taped seam.

To finish this exquisitely detailed ensemble, the doll wears a complete set of gold and turquoise jewelry, including blossom-shaped drops in her ears, a watch with turquoise fob, and a pair of bracelets. Her small handbag of knitted tiny beads, a wonderful copy of the fashionable full-size item, has a gold chain and working frame and clasp. She wears a pair of buttoned white kid boots, and holds a pair of white kid gloves topstitched in black. To shade her from the sun, she carries a pink silk parasol trimmed with lace. Ribbons decorate the handle, which is shaped like the head of a dog.

Plate 27.

A French fashion doll marked "F.G." with wooden hands, blue glass eyes, pierced-through ears, and fashionable chignon. She is wearing a stylish walking costume of about 1870 of tan wool printed with little stylized sprigs of red, olive, blue, and brown and trimmed with lace and shrimp-colored ribbon. The ensemble consists of separate skirt and jacket with basque and has the rather high waist of the period, required to clear the prominent bustle then being worn.

The jacket is fully lined. The hem is finished with a separate, shaped facing; the flounce and three rows of pink ribbon were then laid on around the edge. The jacket skirt flares at the back to spread gracefully over the bustle. More fullness is introduced at the waist by a reverse pleat on each center panel of the four-piece back. The jacket also has a pair of side seams, and a pair of front darts for shaping. The modest V-neck is trimmed with a ruffle of white lace and a line of ribbon with a bow at center front. The closure is by four small pearl buttons. On her breast, she wears a watch with blue enamel back, chain, and turkey red watch fob (a bead).

The sleeves are set plain into the armhole. They are three-quarter length, finished with a wide ruffle headed by a line of the pink ribbon. One of the flounces has been thriftily pieced to get it out of a tiny scrap of fabric. The actual cuff under the decorative flounce is trimmed with a pleated lace frill.

The skirt is another pattern of ruffles and ribbons. The hem is finished with a shaped facing. The ruffles, finished with plain hems, are mounted on top. The bottom, wide ruffle, is headed by three rows of ribbon. The next two point up, rather than down, with rows of ribbon hiding the join to the skirt.

This doll has an especially charming ensemble of underthings, although no bustle. The skirt is supported by two petticoats. The first, short petticoat is made of strips of lace pieced horizontally with bands of plain fabric to form the length. The hem is finished with a plain flounce. The second, longer petticoat is finished with a deep flounce set into a strip of fabric and headed by a set of four ¼" (.5 cm) tucks, all made by machine.

Her drawers are cut plain, but are trimmed just below the knee with three tucks, a band of puffing, three more tucks, a plain hem, and a flounce that, after running around the lower edge, goes up the outside of the leg for about 2" (5 cm) to suggest a placket before being narrowed to nothing and sewn off.

Her look is completed by a gem of a casquette of brilliant blue satin whose sides are trimmed with two lines of bright pink fringe—one pointing down, the other up. It bears two tea roses mounted coquettishly over her eye, and the whole confection is held in place, tipped onto her forehead, with a pink hatpin.

Plate 28.

A pretty fashion doll of unknown manufacture, with heavy blond mohair wig and kid body. She is dressed in a smart, homemade promenade gown cut at walking length, whose fabrics have been chosen with care and used with exquisite thrift. The arrangement of two contrasting fabrics is characteristic of the early 1870s, as is the very round, prominent bustle shape.

The French blue taffeta skirt is cut very straight; there is almost no shaping at all except with the pleats at the top, which are arranged so as to throw all the fullness of the skirt to the back. A piece of ribbon has been applied with a very narrow seam to hem the bottom; the side seams are equally narrow. The placket at center back was made by hemming back the edges of a slit; the slit is finished in the traditional way with a row of buttonhole stitches around the "V" and a bar tack across the bottom. The skirt is whipped to a waistband of white batiste.

The "apron" overskirt is applied to the waistband over the skirt. It is cut on the straight from ivory taffeta with a small black windowpane check. The front is gathered at the center and pleated at the sides to form the drapery. The bottom edges are finished with blue bias strips. The back is open, decorated with a large blue bow that covers the skirt opening and suggests a "bustle."

The bodice is cut with two pieces in front and two in back. The basques are cut in one with the bodice. The improvisational nature of the ensemble is most evident in the cut of the bodice. Not only is the left and right completely asymmetrical, but the dressmaker did not have enough of her fine blue taffeta to finish the whole design. One of the top sleeves is assembled from several pieces like a crazy quilt, and the undersleeves are cut from the blue ribbon. The sleeves are trimmed with a narrow pleated frill. The bodice is fully lined with white batiste. The basques are split in back and trimmed at the waist with a pair of silk-covered blue buttons. The front closure is by the same blue buttons and buttonholes. The neck is finished with a cord facing, then trimmed with an applied pleated flounce and lace frill.

The doll is wearing two petticoats trimmed with eyelet frills and a pair of wide drawers. Her underbodice is inaccessible because of the fragility of the silk of the bodice. Her stockings are a near match in color to the dress. She is, however, still wearing her bedroom slippers of red worsted embroidered with taupe silk. The soles are turned rather than applied.

To complete her ensemble, this lady is wearing an extremely smart riding hat of black straw rakishly trimmed with ecru silk jacquard ribbon and fabric roses under the brim and on the band. The roses appear to have once been pink. A black ostrich feather has been meticulously stitched along the flue to hold it in place across the crown. On her breast, a watch is decorated with a pair of blue fobs.

Instructions for the promenade dress are found in Chapter VI.

Plate 29.

Two well-dressed French fashion ladies. At right, an unusually fine lady of fully articulated, kid-covered wood with graceful bisque hands. She has a swivel joint above the waist to give move-

ment to her torso. Her wig is rather worn, but she is otherwise in very fine condition. Across her back in the fine script we associate so closely with Victorian elementary schools is written "/Edith/ from Uncle Ben, March 1872. Dressed Christmas 1872."

She is wearing a two-piece afternoon dress of spotted muslin arranged on a stout cotton twill foundation. The jacket is fully lined, and fits the doll's figure like the proverbial glove. It has a modest, lace-trimmed, V-neck front for which no closure has been provided. Perhaps the dressmaker intended a line of little hooks and loops hidden under the lace. Neckline, hem, and sleeves are trimmed with a double line of lightly gathered lace. The sleeves have a V-shaped vent at the back of the elbow.

The skirt is draped onto the foundation. Front and back are formed into billowy, horizontal folds across the body, tacked down at the sides, on the left with a set of narrow, vertical pleats, and on the right with a winding, vertical "flounce." The bottom front is finished with a flounce set onto the surface. The center of the flounce header is formed into a line of puffing; the top edge, characteristically, ruffles up toward the bodice. The back is finished with a loose, flaring ruffle tacked over a short, tongue-shaped train. It is trimmed with a double ruching of lace.

At left is a calling costume carried out entirely in various textures of black. There is quite a lot of interesting and very typical detail in this small ensemble. The doll was originally sewn into her dress, and when the head disappeared, the gown, fortunately, was left undisturbed.

Black was a fashionable, if conservative, "safety" for many middle class women. It was important to look appropriate at all times, and a "good black dress" was the basis for many wardrobes. Moreover, high mortality rates through most of the 19th century meant that women were in mourning often. Mourning rituals were more or less an art form to the Victorians. "Hair jewelry" was worn, made with hair of the deceased. People, including children, were photographed in their coffins. Once past the first, deepest stage of mourning, fashionable black clothes trimmed with jet were a social necessity, so as to enable women to be well turned out at other social events while still observing mourning correctly.

The jacket in Plate 29 has a contrast body, a smart combination of the 1870s. (Compare, for example, Plate 36.) This one uses contrasting textures: the brown appearance of the bodice is the usual result of the fading of black dyes of this period. This ensemble is also a good example of the "upholstery" look of the time, with its stiff flounces, cord, and dense velvet. The high neckline is trimmed with a narrow ruffle of pleated lawn. The necklace with its cross is sewn to the front of the bodice. The beads are of fragile blown glass to simulate turquoise. The jewelry of this period is frequently rather oversized, as can be seen in photo portraits; large, heavy crosses were a popular accessory item. The doll also wears a pair of narrow gold bangle bracelets on her wrists. (Her bright jewelry is an indication that she is not, in fact, in mourning.)

The bodice front is cut in four pieces and styled with basques. The front shaping seams are sewn into the armhole. The hem is finished by turning the raw edges to the right side of the tails and covering them with a wide band of cotton braid-like cording, sewn into a pattern of whorls and picots and covered with a line of jet beads. The back is made in two pieces only.

The skirt consists of a long underskirt with applied petal-like apron drapery. The gored underskirt has the basic shaping. The hem is decorated with an applied knife-pleated flounce finished with braid and beads. The apron part, surprisingly, is cut in one piece and shaped entirely with pleats taken at the sides and center back, where it is seamed. The overskirt hem is also finished by turning it to the right side of the garment and covering the raw edges with the trim, a pleated flounce, and braid design.

The skirt is supported by a plain petticoat finished with a ½" (1.5 cm) frill which is rolled, whipped, and gathered, then whipped to the hemmed lower edge. There are three small tucks above. The lower edge of the frill looks like a very narrow selvage edge. The drawers are finished the same. Additionally, the doll wears a short flannel petticoat hemmed with featherstitching.

The dresser holds an assortment of cosmetics and other toilette accessories. The small canister contains "Poudre d'Or pour le Cheveaux," reflecting a short-lived fashion for powdering the hair with gold flakes, a practice roundly criticized as decadent.

Plate 30.

A small French fashion doll who appears to float with joie de vivre. She has a gusseted kid body and wears a carriage or promenade dress of about 1870, in black silk and silver braid.

The jacket has a full basque with allowance for the bustle. It is lined with brown glazed cotton. The lower edge and the ¾-length, two-piece coat sleeves are trimmed with a scalloped, pleated flounce of silk with a woven stripe running through it. The upper edge is finished with silver braid. The high, round neck is finished with an upstanding "pie crust" frill of lace. The closure is at the front with six small pearl buttons.

The skirt is rather plainly made, its detail coming from the repetition of the pleated flounces, trimmed on the top edge by the same silver braid.

Her look is completed with a black velvet riding hat trimmed with ribbon and silver braid formed into upstanding bows. She wears two rather plain petticoats and drawers trimmed with broderie anglaise.

Plate 32.

A charming morning gown almost certainly commercially made in France. Although it presents the appearance of a classic handwork gown, it is cunningly made almost entirely by machine.

Loose-fitting gowns designed for morning wear at home excited some controversy when they first became fashionable. They were taken by some to indicate that women of means no longer took seriously their responsibilities as managers of the household, presumably because the gown's loose cut allowed ladies to come down to breakfast without a tightly laced corset. It was suggested that if men properly appreciated and paid attention to their wives, they would not come downstairs en deshabille. However, it is hard to see how anyone in his right mind could object to seeing the light of his life seated across the breakfast table in this angelic creation.

The long polonaise-style jacket bodice was made by sewing strips of fine muslin to lace insertion in rows to form a fabric. The backs of the folded strips of fabric are raw. The body of the jacket was artfully shaped by the insertion of strips to form gentle godets where needed. Two long basques in front are balanced by a tail in back hanging almost to the hem. The tail was formed with blocks of lace and embroidery motifs similarly mounted in rows with strips of fabric. The hem is decorated at the back by a narrow ruffle of lace-trimmed lawn finished by hand. The gathered sleeves, trimmed at the shoulders with jockeys of gathered lace, are made into poufs with drawn thread down the length of the arm and finished with a wide lace cuff. There is no front closure—the jacket would have been worn over the ample underwear of the period, probably a set designed to fill in the open front modestly.

The skirt is shaped at the top; the lower portion is made of the same blocks set in rows to form a rectangular piece of fabric. The hem is trimmed with a double ruffle of blocks edged with lace over a gathered flounce of lawn and lace. The skirt is supported by a petticoat shaped to match it.

THE SEWING MACHINE

The sewing machine was invented in 1848 but was not in general use until the late 1850s, when Isaac Singer and his marketing man, Edward Clark, devised a method for selling their relatively expensive machine. They covered it with painted floral designs and decorated their showrooms like a lady's parlor; and they introduced the installment plan. In 1855 they sold 883 machines; the next year, 2,564. The rest, as they say, is history. The role of the sewing machine in the democratization of 19th century life, first by providing women an efficient means to sew at home, and second, by forming the basis for the mass production clothing industry, is a fascinating study in its own right.

An entire secondary industry of patterns made for domestic use sprang up in these years. Madame Demorest, one of the innovators in the field, assured her American readers that, although her designs were based on the latest Paris styles, they had been appropriately altered to be suitable for a republican society. She preferred to hire women as agents to sell her products.

It is not until the 1860s that we typically find clothing put together by machine, although certainly examples exist from the 1850s. Until almost the turn of the century, women continued to do detail work by hand, limiting the use of the machine to long seams. The sleeve set with cord, for instance, was done by hand, as was the finishing of seams inside the garment. It is not uncommon to find whitework gowns and linens from this time with structural seams executed by machine, and the details and trimmings carried out by hand, although variations abound.

Plate 33.

A very small lady dressed in 1874 for travel. There is an amazing amount of casually applied detail to this tiny ensemble, which was probably made commercially. Jacket and overskirt are of light brown damask-pattern silk twill decorated with darker braid of a matching hue and bullion fringe of the self color. Her trunk is stuffed with a trousseau of homemade clothes whose standards of workmanship are quite a bit lower than the gown the doll is now wearing. The inside lid reads "Kate from Aunt Emma. Merry Xmas, 1874."

The V-neck bodice is closed at center front and trimmed with braid, lace, and fringe. The bell-shaped sleeves are similarly trimmed, and also provided with tiny jockeys trimmed with braid and lace. The jacket bodice is fitted by a pair of front darts and seamed at the side. Under it she wears a tiny chemise, whose lace neckline trimming is just visible.

The deep basques are divided at center back to emphasize the shape of the bustle. The apron drapery is trimmed with rows of braid and fringe, and a set of bows at the center front. The bustle itself is formed by a set of pleats into the side seams. The whole is tacked into place on a plain blue silk faille underskirt, which is fully lined.

The doll is wearing a charming mushroom hat of natural straw. It is lined with pleated lace and trimmed round the crown, which is made in one with the brim, with an artfully arranged streamer of lace and blue ribbon twisted together, a posey of velvet blossoms, and an ethereal feather. The turnout is completed with a typical large medallion necklace of oversize beads and matching earrings pierced into her head.

Plate 34.

Two adolescents dressed in shades of blue. At left, a young woman probably by Jumeau, with a wistful, beautifully modeled face and a gusseted kid body. Her wig is a replacement. She was dressed about 1870. Her outfit, with its multi-textured ornamentation of self-colored silk fringe and velvet ribbon on a stout silk faille, is typical of the "upholstery" style of dress of the period. (See Plate 29 and Plate 36 for comparison.) Her ensemble also references military motifs in its details. Her dress is actually only two pieces, a jacket and skirt, but they are arranged to suggest a more complex construction.

The side seams of the jacket are displaced rather far to the back. The front is shaped with two curving darts at each side front. The dressmaker did not leave quite enough room for the lap, although she placed the buttons on the left, as though real buttonholes originally were planned. (I can imagine her trying the jacket on the doll to mark the buttonholes and exclaiming, "Oh, no!")

The jacket is fully lined with a stiff brown cotton; its seams are finished with overcasting. The front turn-back is stitched down with neat little cross stitches. The curving bottom edge is turned back and covered with a shaped facing of self-colored silk taffeta. The round neck is finished with taffeta-covered cording and trimmed with a ruffle of lace.

Allowance is made in the coat tails for a small bustle. Basques at the front are shaped up at the sides; the hem then dips down again at the center back. There is only one back piece, which is deeply pleated from neck to waist, giving the appearance of a seam; the released fullness at the small of the back forms an inverse pleat for the bustle allowance, which is draped in a tail down the back of the skirt. The jacket is trimmed at the back waist with two ball buttons.

The two-piece coat sleeve is trimmed with three buttons and self-colored fringe to suggest a cuff. The fringe also makes a yoke at the shoulders and finishes the hem.

The double skirt is joined as one to the waistband. The under layer is trimmed with an applied ruffle joined to the foundation with top-stitching hidden under the line of velvet ribbon. Lines of velvet ribbon also trim the hem. The underskirt is made in two pieces joined at the side seams, with a placket at the center back breadth. It is somewhat longer in back, to accommodate the bustle.

The overskirt, or apron, drapery repeats the seaming pattern of the jacket, drawn up at the side seam and draped down at center back and center front. The spade-shaped front section is trimmed with velvet ribbon and fringe. The sides are pleated to form the drapery and stitched to the side seam of the back section. The back is actually cut in two pieces. The center back is on the selvage and the placket is made simply by turning the edges back. The drapery is formed by making a set of short tucks across the center back seam and stitching them in place.

The doll's ensemble is completed with a pair of shiny brown boots closed with brass buttons at the side, and decorated with tassels of crinkle-textured silk.

At right a French fashion doll with gusseted kid body whose unknown maker gave her a whimsical, pixie face and long, loose curls. She was called "Emeline." Emeline is wearing a slate blue two-piece afternoon dress of wool and silk consisting of polonaise and separate skirt. (Compare, for example, Plate 36.) In the late 1870s, the whole line of the fashionable dress was becoming longer and leaner, with the fullness slipping lower down the back.

The back of this particular outfit is unfinished and held together with pins. The dressmaker seems to have stopped to deal with a fitting mistake at the center back that was never resolved. The dress was made entirely by machine with the exception of the trimming and the finishing of the seams, which are all overcast by hand.

The front of the princess-style polonaise is in two pieces, seamed at the center front and fitted to the body with long side darts. It is trimmed at the front with a plastron of lace and a set of self-colored silk ribbon bows. Another set of bows trims the shoulders at the corner of the plastron under her curls. The neck edge itself is bound with self-fabric bias binding.

The elbow-length sleeves are cut in two pieces and set plain into the armhole. They are finished with a double self-fabric ruffle over a frill of lace.

There is a conventionally placed side seam under the arm. The two-piece back is also fitted to the body with long side darts. The bustle drapery is formed by deep pleats into the side seams. There is a large, asymmetrical, self-colored grosgrain bow at the bottom of the back opening to suggest the bustle itself. The polonaise hem is gently shaped and finished all around with a bias strip into which sets of pleats are sewn.

The skirt underneath is a plain, five-gore shape trimmed at the hem with a pleated flounce set on by machine. At the extreme right of the photograph, these fussy little pleats, with their characteristic, artfully arranged tops, are visible. Contemporary sewing writers explained dozens of decorative pleating arrangements for this popular style of trimming.

The dress is supported by a plain petticoat. Emeline's drawers are trimmed with lace. She wears brown kid boots.

Plate 34. *Left, a girl attributed to Maison Jumeau, 19½" (49.5 cm) tall, bisque head, kid body; silk walking costume, c.1875. The strawberry human hair wig is a replacement. Right, French fashion doll of unknown manufacture, bisque head, kid body, 16" (40.5 cm) tall, named "Emeline"; wool, or wool and silk, long polonaise with separate skirt, c.1875.* COURTESY OF THE WENHAM MUSEUM.

Plate 35. *French fashion doll of unknown manufacture, bisque swivel shoulderplate, cloth body and kid arms; 20" (51 cm) tall; ivory silk faille dinner gown, c.1875. Center, bureau and mirror with accoutrements, late 19th century.* COURTESY OF THE WENHAM MUSEUM.

Plate 36. *Papier-mâché head by Greiner and body probably by Lacman; dressed about 1876.* COURTESY OF THE WENHAM MUSEUM.

Plate 37. *French fashion doll by Gaultier, with gusseted kid body; 12"* (30.5 cm) tall; c.1880; velvet bonnet. COURTESY OF THE WENHAM MUSEUM.

Plate 38. *Lady with china shoulderplate and hands and Lacman-type body, 21" (53.5 cm) tall; woolen dress, c.1880. "Staffordshire" style pottery, late 19th century. Metal mesh handbag.*
COURTESY OF THE WENHAM MUSEUM.

Plate 39. *French fashion lady with gusseted kid body; 14" (35.5 cm) tall; bustle gown, c.1885. Traveling case and Berlin work pillow, background, dated 1880–86; pillow's back is made of small silk "tumbling blocks."*
ALL COURTESY OF THE WENHAM MUSEUM.

Plate 40. *Poured wax bride, perhaps by Pierotti, 20" (51 cm) tall; human hair wig; silk gown, c.1890. Velvet carpet and sofa.* ALL COURTESY OF YESTERYEARS. *Small pots of "rose medallion" late Victorian Chinese export ware, privately owned.*

Plate 42. *The "Gibson girl," by J.D. Kestner, c.1910; 18" (45.5 cm) tall; wearing a copy of a wedding gown, c.1875. She was apparently dressed as a memento of the original gown, perhaps when it was recut for a later generation.* COURTESY OF THE WENHAM MUSEUM.

Plate 41. *A china doll of the 1890s known to collectors as the "Irish Queen." This doll seems to have been assembled from various unrelated but old elements. She was elegantly dressed by Nellie Perkins, probably in the 1950s. Ms. Perkins was a well-known collector and writer on doll collecting. The dress was apparently assembled from old materials, and is a fine interpretation of the style of about 1895. Ms. Perkins was able to use the molded neckline attractively, always a challenge when dressing this type of doll. She conscientiously labeled her work.* COURTESY OF YESTERYEARS.

Collar of "chemical" lace, c.1890. COURTESY OF THE WENHAM MUSEUM.

The doll is resting upon a copy of "Vivilore: The Pathway to Mental and Physical Perfection, The Twentieth Century Book for Every Woman" by Mary Ries Melendy, M.D., Ph.D., published in 1904. The frontispiece calls it a "Brave and Scholarly Treatment of Sex-Life, Parenthood, Child Training, Beauty Laws and Vital Interests of Women and Men." Aimed at the "new woman," it contains, along with a great deal of turn-of-the-century psychobabble, advice on reproductive health illustrated with very explicit drawings.

Plate 43. *"Lady Betty Modish," a Kestner doll, No.162, 18" (45.5 cm) tall; porcelain head, fully articulated wood and composition lady's body; honey-colored human hair wig; brown eyes. She is wearing her riding habit, made in 1905. At left, the tennis dress, c.1903. Four straw hats from the collection on the stands. Background, straw hat trimmed with brown ostrich and brown velvet ribbon, c.1905.* ALL COURTESY OF THE WENHAM MUSEUM. *Skin horse, c.1900, privately owned.*

Plate 44. *Kestner doll, No.162, c.1901; 18" (45.5 cm) tall; porcelain head, fully articulated wood and composition lady's body; dark brown sleep eyes; dark brown mohair wig; jet ball gown, c.1904, from the Pingree collection. Also from the Pingree trousseau at center, robin's egg blue ballgown, c.1907. Jet fan, c.1900.* COURTESY OF THE WENHAM MUSEUM. *Doll, privately owned.*

Plate 45. *From the Pingree collection, two tailored suits. At left, French suit, c.1904; ostrich trimmed velvet hat, buttoned boots, and umbrella (in its cover). At right, purple velvet suit with matching muff and tricorn. Embroidered handbag, c.1900.*
ALL COURTESY OF THE WENHAM MUSEUM.

Plate 46. *Lady Betty Modish, wearing her lace tea gown, c.1905. On the bed and cane-bottom chair, a set of eyelet trimmed underthings for day wear, the blue silk corset, and the ottoman petticoat. On the chair, her silk knitting bag. Bed, c.1895; silk quilt top, with thousands of dime-sized tiles in the "Grandmother's Flowergarden" pattern, c.1900.* ALL COURTESY OF THE WENHAM MUSEUM.

Plate 47. *Lady Betty's corset, c.1905.* COURTESY OF THE WENHAM MUSEUM.

Plate 49. *Detail of embroidery on the collar of the evening wrap from the Pingree trousseau, c.1906.*
COURTESY OF THE WENHAM MUSEUM.

Plate 48. *Simon & Halbig doll, No.1159, c.1910; 16"
(40.5 cm) tall; porcelain head, fully articulated wood and
composition lady's body; yellow mohair wig; blue sleep eyes;
gown of satin-striped chiffon, c.1905. Right, the chair
supports her fur jacket and matching muff. Left, the
mannequin is wearing the net ballgown and blue velvet
cloak from the Pingree collection, c.1906.*
ALL COURTESY OF THE WENHAM MUSEUM.

Plate 50. *Left, Kestner doll, No. 162, wearing the emerald evening gown from the Pingree trousseau, c.1910, and tiara. The sash is a replacement. Right, the pink satin evening gown, c.1911. Center, beaded silk evening bag, c.1910.*
CLOTHING, COURTESY OF THE WENHAM MUSEUM. *Doll, privately owned.*

Plate 51. *Lady Betty Modish wearing the bridge dress, c.1911. The matching hat is on the stand. Embroidered silk handbag and pink suede lace-up walking shoes.* COURTESY OF THE WENHAM MUSEUM.

Plate 52. *Simon & Halbig doll, No. 1159, c. 1910; 18" (45.5 cm) tall; porcelain head; fully articulated wood and composition body; brown eyes; very full honey-colored human hair wig. Wearing a houndstooth check suit with stole and muff, blue felt hat, knit gloves, umbrella. Her buttoned boots are from the Pingree collection. Background, blue velvet hat with ostrich trim, c.1913. Color lithograph fan dated 1915, "Gloire Aux Allies"; the American flag is absent from among those of the Allies—the United States did not enter the First World War until 1917.*
COURTESY OF THE WENHAM MUSEUM.

Plate 35.

A DOLL of unknown manufacture wearing a dinner gown of ivory silk faille trimmed elaborately with lace. This dress is a good example of the style of the end of the 1870s, when the fullness of the bustle began to slip ever lower on the figure until it disappeared entirely.

The dress is fully lined with soft, coarse cotton. Its seams are left raw. It is cut in the princess style with a center front piece and two side fronts, which are seamed into the front of the armhole. The long side front sections are pieced at the back hem with small triangular sections. The back is a pair of long, trained sections; the balloon-like bustle form is made with pleats into the side seams. Two very long side darts shape the back. Closure at center back is a set of small shell buttons with carefully worked buttonholes.

The long hem of this gown is turned and eased where necessary to accommodate the curve. A visible ruffle of lace-trimmed cotton is attached around the train, beginning on each side. Although the lace of the ruffle matches the rest of the hand-sewn dress, the ruffle itself may be a commercially made-up trim, since it is joined all around the edge by a tiny chain stitch, which is clipped away at the seam, giving the appearance of a rolled and whipped edge at first glance.

The entire gown is trimmed with yards and yards of lace. Interestingly, the lower front lace panel does not follow the seaming exactly. The large bias-design section from knee to hem was worked separately and then attached at its edges to the dress. The rows of lace outlining it meet the structural front seams only at its top, where they continue up to the shoulders and around the neckline. The chevron panel over the breast is also separately worked, and is loose at the bottom edge. Two lines of lace are used to create the outline motif around the seams and hem; the space between them is not bare, but filled with a flat-worked piece of insertion. Three posies pinned to the gown complete the decoration.

The sleeve is one piece, its seam at the lower front of the armhole. It is trimmed with the lines motif, the lowest line of which with its border of insertion is attached to the edge of the cuff and forms a frill. Two more are added above. The sleeve is joined plain into the corded armhole.

To support the long train, the doll is wearing a petticoat with a train of its own. The petticoat's generous fullness has been controlled by a set of gathering stitches pulling it in behind the knee. The petticoat is also attractively trimmed with a tucked broderie anglaise flounce mounted onto the surface, forming a double layer at the hem.

To complete her ensemble, the lady wears a cap of matching ivory silk, rather roughly made but charmingly shaped and trimmed with the same lace. Her hair is dressed with a black velvet ribbon tied in a dainty bow. She wears a small blue enamel brooch shaped like a heart and decorated with a tiny incised star.

Plate 36.

A DOLL of the late 1870s, made by the Greiner Company of Philadelphia. Not only is she an ordinary shoulderplate type, but made of papier-mâché, a somewhat old-fashioned material by the time she was made in the late 1870s. Still, she is well modeled and attractive, and extremely well turned out. She has a Lacman body with boots sewn in one with the legs. The strange pocket detail puts the date of this dress at about 1876 or shortly thereafter.

This two-piece dress, consisting of skirt and long princess-cut "polonaise," shows a typical two-color arrangement fashionable in the late 1870s. Fashion writers of the time complained that the multi-colored and asymmetrical arrangement of ladies' dresses had become so complex that they were impossible to describe. The arrangement of fabrics is characteristic of the fashion, with the bodice made of one fabric and trimmed with another, while the skirt is arranged just the opposite.

The polonaise-style bodice is fitted to the body with a long center front seam and pair of radiating side darts. This dress also has a horizontal seam running at the waist across the side body piece. The back is cut in four pieces with the side body seam running to the shoulder. The bodice is lined to the hip only with dark brown glazed cotton. A placket inserted into the center back seam provides the lap for the closure, which is a set of large steel hooks. The line of ball buttons, made of fine bronze thread crochet over a plain ball foundation, is ornamental only. These would be horribly uncomfortable in a modern dress, but the bustle fashion prevented ladies from relaxing back into a chair—ladies always sat erect—so they would not be bothered by the button shanks digging into them. The plastron and large cuff detail are appliqué trim, finished with ruffles of lace.

The skirt is made principally of the glazed cotton. The silk ruffles were added from the hem to just above the polonaise drapery. This method of construction, with a foundation covered with elaborate arrangements stitched over its surface, is an innovation of the late 1870s. Above the hem ruffle are bands of bias fabric blind stitched in place, two in front, and four across the back. The dressmaker made excellent use of the striped pattern to create the impression of much more detail than there actually is. This would be a desirable object of the dress design of the day.

All of the skirt's fullness is inclined to the back and held in place by a line of stout gathering stitches across the back of the knee. The polonaise drapery was created with a set of small tucks taken into the back side body. The tucks were then drawn together with a set of tapes inside. This is a fashion that would go somewhat out of control in the next few years, with women wearing skirts so tightly tied around their legs that a normal step was difficult. (See Plate 38.)

The lady wears a plain petticoat shaped and drawn in like the skirt, and drawers, both trimmed with broderie anglaise.

Instructions for the princess polonaise are found in Chapter VII.

Plate 37.

THE bonnet of the late 1870s and early 1880s, distinguishable from a "hat" only by its vestigial strings, which at this period are made to run behind the ears to tie under the chin. The headgear of this period is worn perched on the back of the head. This small, pretty fashion doll carries a paper label bearing the name "Miss Susan W. Osgood" in delicate copperplate. She is wearing a charming example of the late Victorian bonnet made of cobalt velvet. It has been blocked with a decorative pleat at the center back, and is shaped as a shallow half orb. The edge is decorated with turquoise ribbon and a strip of very narrow lace. The hat is lined with ruched pink chiffon. Around the crown is a twisted double band of turquoise and pink ribbon. It is festooned with a large rosette of pink and turquoise ribbon and white lace loops dripping over the left ear.

Plate 38.

AN old-fashioned china doll of a type that was made continuously from the 1860s until the 1890s. An inexpensive alternative to more fashionable playthings, her face has been executed so mechanically as to render her almost expressionless. She has a Lacman-type body whose sewn-in boots are a surprising vivid purple decorated with black silk grosgrain bows. Even more surprising is the rather extreme fashion in which this plain jane is attired, a tight, wholly impractical style that would make the come-back of the bustle a few years hence seem comparatively sensible. This dress was put together with considerable panache, but not much skill, about 1880. Upon closer inspection, it reveals a series of improvisations. It is made of dark green wool, which has faded to a brownish olive color. The cameo "buttons" (actually a pair of old earrings whose studs have been bent like screw-in upholstery buttons) were added at a later date.

This one-piece dress is fully lined; the various layers and parts are all assembled on a brown cotton foundation. There is a pieced yoke front and back that is outlined at the neck edge with self-fabric puffing. The neckline is filled in at the front with a lace and net bib. The bodice is decorated with tucks, some of which are folded and executed like conventional tucks; others are separate appliquéd pieces. The one-piece sleeves are seamed at the front of the armhole. The cuff is a set of knife pleats joined to the sleeve under a gathered swath with a lace ruffle underneath.

A pair of pannier-like apron draperies hang from the waistband, covering the front of the hips only. The front of the dress is ruched up in rows, a signature texture of this time. The last row termi-nates in a short flounce; a set of knife pleats is let in underneath to form the hem. Tight, smocking-type gathering came into fashion as a surface treatment about 1881, and remained fashionable in women's clothes until the return of the bustle in 1883.

The back breadth consists of a set of wide tucks tied in at the knee with a large and elaborate self-fabric bow. The back termi-nates with a short train of several knife pleats (carried around from the front) decorated with a ruffle of lace. This dress is closed at the center back with a row of hooks and loops under decorative half ball buttons of steel.

Plate 39.

A plump young thing of unknown manufacture called "Daisy Dell." She was dressed, probably professionally, about 1885, after the return of the bustle. The hard, cuirass-style bodice and horizontal drapery across the hips is the signature look of the time. She is wearing a walking length afternoon dress.

The bodice, rather faded at the front and somewhat deteriorated, is of bright, cherry-colored silk satin. It is stoutly lined and made with a four-piece back and two-piece front fitted with long side darts. The bodice is long; it is pointed front and back and shaped up over the hips at the sides. The bottom edge is finished with a self-fabric binding.

The bodice also has an interesting neckline, cut into a trapezoid at the front. A low standing collar is cut in one with the back shoulders. The sides and back of the neckline are turned under to finish, but the front is separately bound. Collar and front opening are trimmed with a carefully arranged fall of lace that covers the hooks and eyes.

The elbow-length sleeves are finished with a knife-pleated frill of plum-colored satin ribbon trimmed at the top and bottom edges with lace.

The skirt drapery is arranged on a white cotton foundation. A knife-pleated flounce finished with lace is blind stitched to the inside hem. Its lower edge is trimmed with a whipped-on edging of lace. Two flounces of spotted muslin are softly pleated onto the foundation, simply turned under and blind stitched in place. They are hemmed with a running stitch and edged with lace. The apron drapery is formed of a swath of cotton lawn tacked around the hips and arranged in a large, asymmetrical bow at the back left. The interior seams are left raw.

Her heeled boots are quite elaborate, of two-tone leather. The toes and button flaps are dark tan, the boots themselves of medium brown. They close with two steel buttons. On each toe is a star-shaped ornament with a bead at the center and two bunches of fringe peeking out from underneath.

WOMEN'S WORK

My grandfather's mother supported him and herself by rolling cigars, in the days when Boston still had a cigar trade. She always made good money because she was ambidextrous and very quick. At the end of the 19th century, the cigarmakers union was one of only two large unions that admitted women on an equal basis with men. When my great-grandmother read her evening papers in the mid-1880s, she would have learned that a sublime, colossal female figure was being erected in New York harbor as a symbol for the hope of liberty, and that a maniac was butchering women in the streets of London.

It was the kind of information that made many people think it inappropriate for ladies to read the newspapers. It is somehow not surprising that the very correct Victorians gave us, in addition to so much else that we think of as modern, our paradigmatic notion of the random serial killer; nor that they would be unable to recognize his grisly deeds as sex crimes.

Contemporary social workers attempting to reduce prostitution could not understand why women preferred the precarious life of the streets to the restrictions of conventional marriage. As early as 1828 religious women had organized to try to end "the trade," but in large, impersonal cities where almost everything was becoming a commercial transaction, they had little success. From the first, reformers understood that a woman alone had few ways of earning a living.

In our time, critics of the "double standard" have argued that women should have the same perquisites as men; in the Victorian period, reformers aimed to convince men to be chaste. The reformers' success was not registered by a reduction in the demand for paid sex, but in a falling birth rate. One of the truly striking demographic trends of the 19th century is the reduction in the number of children borne by married middle class women, a trend usually explained by the desire to provide a more comfortable and secure life for each child. In an age of very uncertain birth control, the only effective way to accomplish this was abstinence.

Women labor organizers and settlement workers tried with frustratingly little success to secure a "living wage" for women. Many people understood that perfectly blameless women could end up supporting their children alone; in the 19th century it was high mortality rather than divorce that created one-parent families. Women were difficult to organize because even working class women expected to work for only a short time, until they were married. Social conservatives and mainstream labor organizers, who feared that the low wages women were willing to accept would drive down the wages of men, opposed efforts at economic reform. They argued that progressives should work for a "family wage" that would allow men to support their families without the contributions of their wives and children.

Plate 40.

Abride of poured wax with rather high coloring, possibly by Pierrotti. Her dress is a transitional garment, of the neither-here-nor-there style of about 1890.

After its brief revival in the early 1880s, the bustle disappeared never to be seen again. Skirts were rather plain and remained rather short, at a practical walking length for day. Women's clothes were cut rather severely in 1890, but interest was gradually being displaced from the skirt and its draperies to the bodice. This bridal gown's sleeves are gathered into the armhole at the top; a revival of sleeve interest reminiscent of 1830 was almost upon the fashion world when this gown was made.

The two-piece wedding dress was made of a very heavy silk, now hanging in strings in places, covered with stiff worked motifs of lace across the shoulders and breast, down the front, and around the hem. The dress is fully lined with stiff white cotton, and finished at the hem with a shaped facing.

The skirt still shows the narrow shape characteristic of the immediate post-bustle period, but the generous train evidences the beginning of the "fan" shape of the end of the century in its full gores. The fullness is controlled by deep pleats.

The separate bodice is pleated decoratively across the waist under the lace trim; the pleats do not provide any functional fullness. The sleeves, while full, are tightly gathered at the shoulder so that the fullness projects up rather than out. The top of the sleeve is reinforced inside with a stiff interlining. The cuff is finished by delicate ruched lace.

The veil, which is supported by a small cap of lace, is a long narrow piece, finished on both ends. It is gathered in the center to extend to the middle of the doll's back; the remainder floats off to either side. She wears a posey of wax orange blossoms over each ear, and carries one in her hand.

THE EDWARDIAN PERIOD

Edwardian styles for lady dolls are rather over-represented in this book principally because the Wenham Museum owns a fabulous collection of doll clothes made between 1902 and 1911 for a Kestner 162 owned by Mary Weld. The high-fashion turn-outs with which "Lady Betty Modish" was provided were the work of Mary's mother, Hannah Weld, and her aunt, Elizabeth Train. Many of the clothes bear the "house label," "Mere et Tante" ("Mother and Aunt"); they may have been copies of the sisters' own custom-made clothes.

The trousseau is fascinating in the degree to which it tracks the change in fashion over the course of the decade. The Edwardian period is like a baroque footnote to the Victorian age, not inappropriate in view of Edward's having to wait his entire life in the wings in order to sit briefly on the throne in his old age. A sophisticated, worldly, frankly sensual man, he was an apt icon for his time. The haute couture of this period is characterized by brilliant color, rich fabrica-tion, exquisite detail, and shocking costliness. Lady Betty Modish's brilliant wardrobe appears never to have been played with, and it seems likely that the project was in fact an elaborate sampler created for the sisters' own delectation; not the least of its charms is the slightly subversive sense of humor evident in the ladies' observations of the fashions of their day.

It is all the more amusing, given the assumptions evident in the design of the doll. By the turn of the century, moderately priced dolls from Germany dominated the market. Their design was "progressive," often inspired by real children rather than an ethereal ideal. Although many German dolls of the time are quite pretty, few are glamorous.

The Gibson girl is the best known exception, made by Kestner in 1910 and based on the famous drawings. (**PLATE** 42.) Charles Dana Gibson often portrayed his ladies naturally and easily dominating the simple men around them. The Gibson girl is actually something of a "retro" type, made like a French fashion doll with porcelain head and hands on a kid body. Perhaps Kestner hoped to remind mothers of the fine dolls of their own childhoods; today it seems incongruous to find the Gibson girl's elegant, cleanly modeled head, so obviously modern, on such an awkward and badly proportioned body.

Lady Betty Modish, who is far more typical, evidences many of the assumptions under which these dollmakers worked; her proportions are distinctly childlike, with a large head, small body, plump arms and legs, and innocent dolly face. Perhaps the biggest change, however, is that little girls were far more likely to be given a doll designed like a baby or a child than a woman. Lady dolls did not disappear entirely, but they were relegated to a corner of the market place.

Lady Betty Modish and the case in which she is displayed were donated to the Wenham Museum by Mary Weld Pingree in 1956.

Plate 43.

FROM the Pingree trousseau, a selection of turn-of-the-century ladies' sportswear. The rational dress movements of the 19th century had met with little success among the masses or the leaders of fashion, remaining confined to social reformers, enthusiasts, and artistic types. Amelia Bloomer's modest proposal was, as it were, laughed out of court in the 1850s.

However, in the 1890s, the craze for bicycling overwhelmed in a stroke all the traditional arguments against "bifurcated garments" and lightweight corsets. It was simply impossible to ride a bicycle in trailing skirts. For some reason, when women started taking up sports, they deemed mannish stiff collars and tweeds to be the appropriate dress. Despite the fact that many people were scandalized by the sight of a woman pedaling briskly along all by herself, the bicycle became immensely popular in a very short time. Bicycle clubs were organized all over the United States, and they became a wholesome environment for men and women to meet each other in the increasingly liberal atmosphere for courting.

At left, an Edwardian tennis dress consisting of linen skirt and cotton lawn blouse. In dress and many other forms of decoration, white embroidery is highly evocative of this period. The linen skirt is rather narrow and made in two pieces—a conventional front gore and a single back piece in which a large box pleat is made at the back to arrange the fullness. It falls in a single graceful reverse pleat into a short train. The skirt is hemmed with an applied facing secured with several rows of topstitching. The dressmakers had to do this sort of detail inside out, since all they had, apparently, was an old-fashioned chain stitch machine. The closure is at the right side front through a hidden placket set into the seam; the waist is covered with a self belt of linen. The bold embroidered motif, carried out principally with the satin stitch, is repeated at the sides and back. "Mere et Tante" were not highly skilled embroiderers, but all ladies learned this style of work in order to be able to monogram household linens.

The cotton blouse, made in the "pouter pigeon" style so typical of the era, is of machine-embroidered lawn and buttons in front with a covered placket. The collar wraps all the way around to fasten at the back with a single button and worked loop and is detailed with small collar tabs and a lace-edged jabot. In addition to the functional front placket, there is also a back placket that is decorative only, mounted with pin stitches to cover a join in the fabric. The join is asymmetrical, which seems to indicate that the ladies made the blouse from a really tiny scrap which they cleverly pieced under the decorative placket.

The lawn and linen ensemble would have been correct with any of the straw hats shown, four of the many with which the doll was provided by her couturieres. The sisters apparently loved to trim hats. At left on the stands are a pair of cavalier-style hats with dramatic, upturned brims. The cocked brim might be worn at the front or on the side, and was generally ornamented with an elaborate arrangement of trims. One of these hats is trimmed with a breast of feathers, rhinestone buckle, and velvet ribbon; the other with veiling and a spray of flowers. At center front are two "mushrooms" with down-turning brims—left, trimmed with veiling and ostrich, and right, with satin ribbon and large silk roses.

Instructions for the Edwardian waist and five-gore skirt are found in Chapter VIII.

The complicated riding habit at right is a good example of the elaborate style of dress during the Edwardian period even for active sports. It also shows how, as women became more physically active, they sought a men's style of clothing. This approach to dress also found its way into the business wear of the many women who entered the work force at this time. This man-tailored ensemble is essentially a man's riding habit, including the breeches, except that ladies covered them with trailing skirts which had to be carried in the hand when not on horseback. Lady Betty's skirt is hooked to a handy button provided for walking.

The hacking jacket, breeches, and skirt are made of khaki-colored wool serge, with self-covered buttons. The breeches have a leather seat stitched inside. The mannish habit shirt of striped poplin with white pique stock is somewhat compromised by the tucked and gathered front; in this case the fullness was first formed by machine into several narrow vertical tucks before being gathered into a shaped waistband worn outside the skirt. Ladies' shirts designed for sport buttoned in front like the men's shirts that inspired them. The narrow, shaped stock is accessorized with a small gold pin in the shape of a horseshoe.

The outfit is completed by a stiff derby hat, brown leather gloves, and buckled riding boots correctly detailed with butter-colored boot-tops.

Plate 44.

TWO ball gowns from the Pingree collection. At left a dramatic gown of black jet illustrating the consummate skill of the Edwardian dressmaker in a design of great sophistication. It consists of a very heavy layer of metal sequin-embroidered net on an apparently weightless foundation. The ottoman petticoat (see Plate 46) was probably made to support this heavy skirt. The foundation is a typical five-gore bell shape of stiff black taffeta; the hem is finished with a pleated frill. Over this is draped accordion-pleated chiffon with a narrow ruched edging. This is a commonly found "middle layer" in the multiply draped gowns of the period, as it added a great deal of froth with very little bulk or weight. The shell is a semi-circular piece of sequined net that appears to have been commercially made up, perhaps the trimming of a low bodice. Its scalloped edges allow the chiffon edging to peek through at the hem. A robin's egg blue velvet sash is knotted and twisted about the waist and terminates in a pair of long trailing streamers at the back. Black relieved with a bright jewel color was a very fashionable combination of the day.

The bodice shows the characteristic pouter pigeon front. Over a fitted taffeta foundation, chiffon and sequined net are draped in a small balloon. The shoulders of the dress are made of the same knotted and twisted blue ribbon, which forms the straps and runs across the back and breast of the dress under the neckline.

At right, an unusual gown made in 1907 from the Pingree collection, which probably exists only because wealthy ladies at the turn of the century had their clothes made and could get exactly what they wanted regardless of the urgings of the fashion press.

It is a transition gown, with a raised waist and long lines. This lovely dress is made of blue satin and matching chiffon covered with beaded ivory lace.

The skirt foundation is a five-gore skirt finished with a circular flounce and padded hem. Over this is draped a spider-web fine layer of blue chiffon. On the top layer of ivory lace oversewn with bugle beads and small silver sequins, two lines of ruched chiffon emphasize the sweep of the hem. The back has a floating veil let into the center back seams, with four narrow tucks across the hem to help it stand away from the body. The high-waisted bodice is a satin foundation covered with chiffon and lace, gathered in front to give it lightness. The neck is low, plunging nearly to the raised waist at the back, where a small pouf of chiffon gracefully draws all the lines of the drapery together. The neckline is softened by a ruched edge of the chiffon underlayer peeking out from beneath the lace. The short puffed sleeves are simply gathered into elastic cuffs. This dress unfortunately illustrates the travails faced by the conservator of Edwardian clothing, as it has faded almost colorless and the lace has become quite brittle.

Plate 45.

Two suits from the Pingree collection. At left, the "French suit" bears the house label, "Mere et Tante." This elegant ensemble made in 1904 was probably designed for "visiting," an important activity among otherwise unemployed ladies of the day. However, among the outfits of the Pingree collection, this suit of lightweight black melton most suggests the "tailormade," a type of dress that has been the mark to this day of the professional women who began to appear in numbers during this period. The pleated skirt is short enough for comfortable walking; it is trimmed with elaborate soutache and is fully lined. The jacket is embellished with embroidered front facings of ribbon outlined with stiff, narrow black picot braid. It is fully lined with ivory satin-faced cotton and has a small "ticket pocket" inside.

The elaborately detailed blouse with its pouter pigeon front is one of the signature designs of this period. The black and white "stripes" are actually narrow tucks in the black organza. The shell with its tucking is mounted on a fitted white silk lining. It is trimmed at the yoke with ruching, a common period detail, and at the waist with a twisted and knotted velvet ribbon that covers the structural waistband. The waist trim is held in place by a set of tiny hooks and worked loops. The yoke, collar and cuffs are made of heavy ivory lace. The join at the throat is covered with narrow velvet ribbon decorated with French knots in white silk. Three black velvet bobbles dangle down the front.

The black velvet hat with its swaths of organdie, bold ostrich feathers, and bright buckles completes the look.

At right is another elaborate toilette from the Pingree collection made the following year, 1905. It is a more feminine design than the French suit, and certainly a slightly emotional color. The long coat tails are divided all around and outlined with a satin ribbon of slightly lighter shade. Ribbon also defines the jacket waist. Like the jacket of the French suit, this one is trimmed at the front opening with a stiff, knobby picot braid. Collar and cuffs are trimmed with fur, as is the matching muff. The skirt is a rather

plainly cut five-gore style, which is the basic skirt line of the early part of the decade.

The blouse, in a related shade of mauve charmeuse, has the pouter pigeon front. The fullness in front falls from a set of soft tucks taken across the front of the shoulders; the self-fabric cummerbund is ruched into a central pleat. The standing collar and shaped jabot are of stiff white lace.

The purple velvet suit is accessorized by a rather extreme hat peculiar to this period, shaped more or less like a curly tricorn. Hats were very aggressively styled at this time, and eccentric brims are a hallmark of the period, some of them very eccentric indeed. This hat is actually made of stiffened, wired lace, and bound with velvet ruched onto the edge of the brim; it is trimmed with a plume of ostrich.

Plates 46. and 47.

A luscious tea gown made in 1905. It is a fashionable update of a style that originated in the 1880s for women to entertain intimate friends comfortably at home. It required no corset because of its loose cut, undoubtedly an almost inexpressible relief, but was typically rich in fabrication. The use of machine-made lace to form the fabric of an entire gown was a fashion innovation of the late 19th century.

The tea gown consists of a sleeveless, princess-seamed foundation of lavender satin, a layer of accordion-pleated chiffon edged with ruching, and a lace fabric shell. Its low, square neck is buttonholed onto a strip of silk embroidery and secured with ribbon, which trails down the front of the dress. The waist is suggested by gathering at the back and a pair of ribbons laid around like a half belt, but the gown falls freely in front.

Unaccountably for such a fashionable lady, Lady Betty Modish's underthings all reflect the style prevalent at the turn of the century. She has no underwear suitable for any of her clothes made after 1908. However, the underthings she does own are all quite delicious, and very much in keeping with the practice of wealthy ladies, who spent enormous sums on their underwear. With the exception of the silk petticoat, which is the unmistakable work of "Mere et Tante," Lady Betty's underwear is all commercially produced, and exquisitely made, doll clothing from the turn of the century.

The corset (draped over the headboard and shown in detail in **PLATE** 47) is made of embroidered silk jacquard of "butterfly blue," a color that enjoyed a vogue at the turn of the century. The corset shows the fragility of the beautiful colors of this period; it is now faded almost colorless. It is a small copy of a lady's actual corset, trimmed with lace, ruched blue ribbon, and several large elaborate bows. It is complete with a set of small steel "bones," which are secured with decorative hand stitches at the top and bottom. There are eighteen hand-worked buttonholes to lace the front. Twenty-two tiny pieces of fabric are used for the 6½" (16.5 cm) waist, each finished with a lapped seam. This is the so-called "health" corset designed in 1900 by the French corsetiere Madame Gaches-Sarraute. The "straight front" molds the torso into the unmistakable "S shape" of the late Belle Époque. It was originally designed to support without constricting the abdomen, but very shortly after its introduction it was subjected to the sort of exaggeration that seems to be the rule in the fashion world. Fashion illustrations of the period show that a small waist was as desirable in 1905 as at any time in the 19th century. The next innovation in corsetry, accompanying the revolution in the 1908 fashion line, was to discard the entire concept.

One of Lady Betty's two sets of conventional batiste underclothing is draped over the chair and bed. They are exquisite examples of fine Edwardian handsewing, the stitches so fine they are nearly invisible, and trimmed with yards of embroidered flounces, ribbon, and rows of tiny tucks

Lady Betty also possesses a gorgeous silk petticoat that well illustrates the lavish style of the underwear at this time. Although it has no label, it is almost certainly the work of "Mere et Tante." It is made of black and ivory striped silk ottoman. Each seam is individually bound to prevent raveling. The hem flounce is a double wavy row of black lace over white lace, headed with a pink and green embroidered ribbon.

The knitting bag resting on the cane-seat rocking chair is one of the witty details that make the Pingree trousseau such a delight. It is made of warp-print silk (probably a strip of ribbon) and fully lined; the handles were made by wrapping thread in a decorative pattern around two loops of wire; each side is finished with a bunch of small silk fruits with dark lace trim. Lady Betty is provided with a pair of amber knitting needles, a set of four double-point needles (on which a tiny sock is started), and several balls of fine knitting wool.

Plates 48. and 49.

At left, from the Pingree collection, a lovely, intensely detailed gown of the Belle Époque, made by "Mere et Tante" in 1906. That this gown is slightly later than the jet gown is shown by its soft satin foundation and curved padded hem. (The robin's egg blue ball gown is made over a similar foundation.) Over the foundation are draped two layers of white silk netting; the outermost layer is decorated with lines of ruching, which repeat the seaming of the foundation, and swags of pink silk flowers, green leaves, and bunches of blue ribbons draped over the surface of the gown. The center back seam has an inserted panel forming a floating demi-train.

The bodice is very like that of the jet ball gown in cut. The bodice trimming repeats the pattern of the skirt, arranged across the breast of the gown. The shoulder straps are of ribbon trimmed with small posies of silk roses and bunches of blue ribbons. The waist is emphasized by a wide pink satin ribbon formed into a pleated cummerbund; its knotted streamers, decorated with rhinestone buckles, trail down the back.

This velvet evening wrap (shown in detail in Plate 49) is a good example of the richly conceived, loose-fitting coats made to turn out evening ensembles. It is made of soft blue silk velvet and lined with satin striped chiffon overprinted with flowers. The side and back seams are open and filled with godets of gathered lace, which also trims the ¾-length sleeves and the edge of the collar. The broad shawl collar is lavishly beaded, sequined, and tambour-embroidered with silk flowers. The front opening is faced with a pair of trail-

ing scarf draperies, which are trimmed with enamel buckles and gathered into poufs with strings of gold beads. Lady Betty's full-length kid gloves and the posey she will carry at the ball are resting on the seat of the chair.

At center, a gown of about the same period worn by a Simon and Halbig lady is similar both in cut and trimming detail to the white net ball gown. The foundation is a stout silk whose hem is finished with a wide applied band folded into zigzags and worked around the curved lower edge. The top layer of the dress is satin-striped chiffon of lavender and celery green. Like the gowns of the Pingree trousseau, the skirt shell is cut in one piece and shaped where necessary with gathering to the seamed foundation silk. The neckline, short puff sleeves, and hem are all trimmed with lavender flowers laid on in little posies with bunches of green ribbon. It is a tribute to the skill of the designers of this period that so many of their creations, despite their elaborate detail, still present a unified appearance to a contemporary eye.

This lady's fur coat of dyed rabbit is richly trimmed with lace around the dramatic standing collar and is fully lined. The muff is a small treasure. It is shaped, the top being narrower across than the bottom to make it more comfortable to wear; the openings are trimmed with lace to match the coat, as well as with a pair of steel-cut baubles. Its ribbons match the lining of the coat; the muff is fully lined as well.

Plate 50.

The emerald evening gown, made in 1909, is a startling look next to its immediate predecessors. Gowns such as this, with the slit skirt, were introduced by Paul Poiret and other "advanced" designers in 1908 and were much influenced both in line and color by Western conceptions of the "Orient." Leon Bakst, celebrated costume designer for the Ballet Russe, is also associated with this movement. The boned corset was going out, and other changes were imminent as well. The emerald evening dress puts Lady Betty and her dressmakers right on the cutting edge. Originally, this style was meant to be worn with "harem" trousers beneath, but, bicycle skirts aside, the idea of women appearing in public in anything like "pants" raised such furious outrage that they were swiftly abandoned. The slit, however, was not, and women began showing not only a great deal of bare arms and shoulders, but leg as well.

The various layers of the dress simply wrap around and around; they are held in place by their attachment to the sash lining. Complicated, asymmetrical fastenings are typical of this period. The skirt is draped over a form-fitting foundation; excess length forms the folds and pleats, which are tacked invisibly to hold them in place. The use of many rich fabrics in combination is also characteristic. This dress uses gold-embroidered green silk, dyed net, gold lace, and green velvet. Despite its opulence, there is no suggestion of vulgarity in this skillful design.

The lady is wearing a dramatic tiara, a very fashionable finish to her outfit, and her lithographed fan is at hand.

At right is another pre-World War I gown of deceptively simple design and great beauty, made about 1910. This graceful gown with its trailing demi-train is of pink satin, trimmed with bead-embroidered net. The hem is finished with a shaped facing. Although the waist is high, the neckline is quite low; this gown references the Empire period very directly. The asymmetrically arranged bodice is embellished with lace and a bunch of white fabric roses. Like the other beaded gowns, it has suffered some damage from the weight of the beaded trimmings on the fragile netting to which they are attached. This is a chronic problem for conservators of Belle Époque clothing. The dress has sleeves of net, leaving the arms and shoulders tantalizingly almost bare. The erotic appeal of this dress, like the green gown, is rather direct.

Plate 51.

THE "bridge dress," made in 1911, was designed for afternoon social functions, and bears the dated label, "Mere et Tante." The bridge dress is a classic design, explicitly recalling the timeless kimono, with its straight sleeves, slightly raised waist, and narrow skirt drapery.

The neckline is filled in with lace, which also trims the sleeves. When this modest neckline for day wear was first introduced, it caused almost unbelievable outrage. Although women had been baring their shoulders, arms, and necks in the evening for more than 100 years, the "V-neck" was condemned from the pulpit as indecent, and doctors warned that it would "cause pneumonia." As usual, women wore it anyway.

The metallic trim around the neckline is set with small glass beads. The same trim in various widths is used on the sleeves and waistline and to emphasize the drapery of the bodice and overskirt. The overskirt itself is gathered into a low demi-bustle at the back of the knee. The original color was a daring bright rose, now much faded. Along with the change in the silhouette, the second half of the decade indulged itself with much brighter, deeper, and more brilliant colors than the first half.

The bucket-shaped toque accompanying the bridge dress is trimmed with clipped feather and borders of mink. The top of the hat is covered with a rich lace.

Instructions for the bridge dress are found in Chapter IX.

Plate 52.

THE tailormade, a checked suit made in 1915 and worn by a Simon & Halbig lady. This doll's fashionable suit is from the post-corset period. This is the smart but casual style of much of high fashion today. It was exemplified by Coco Chanel, who startled the fashion world by wearing pearls with a sweater to the races. The sporty houndstooth suit in smart black and white is accessorized with a cavalier-style hat with ostrich plume and silk veiling, and coordinated very dressy fur pieces of "ermine" (i.e., dyed rabbit) which reiterate the color scheme. The combination of textures, accessorizing a men's suiting with fur and ostrich, was a new look, but

the Edwardians were adventurous with texture. The skirt displays the narrow silhouette of the First World War, as well as the sensible length. The jacket also shows the new line, shaped to the body but not closely fitted, comfortable and long. The jacket skirt is joined to the bodice with a set of small pleats. The doll wears a pair of long knitted silk gloves and carries a functional black umbrella. The shorter skirt shows her sensible buttoned boots. In addition to its fashion message, this ensemble foreshadows the "utility" clothes necessitated by the grim demands of World War I, which had already started when this doll's ensemble was made.

History, of course, flows in one way only, and we shall never know if, other things being equal, the fashion world might have attempted to give life to a boring season by introducing a "retro" look that brought back the bustle and corset. As it happened, the First World War intervened. While men were uselessly killed and maimed in staggering numbers in the trenches of France, women alleviated the manpower shortage at home and in the rear by entering many areas formerly closed to them.

The uniform worn by women serving in the Motor Corps during the First World War is complete with a pair of breeches to be worn while clambering about on an engine. [Jean L. Druesedow, *In Style: Celebrating Fifty Years of the Costume Institute*, 1987, p.51.] It is impossible to believe that the women who wore this uniform thought themselves ineligible to vote. World War I did not create the social and political changes that appeared in its wake, but it did wreck the structures that had supported the old way of life. Sir Edward Grey, Britain's Foreign Minister, who had spent his entire public career trying to prevent a general European war, said he felt like a man whose life had been wasted. It was Grey who said, "The lamps are going out all over Europe. We shall not see them lit again in our lifetime."

And he was right. When war came to Europe again in 1937, its horrific casualties would make the first engagement pale by comparison. In the meanwhile, there were ten years of frantic overcompensation, followed by a market crash and world-wide depression of unprecedented severity, modern totalitarianism, women's suffrage, Prohibition, and, incidentally, pants.

Among the casualties of the early 20th century were the firms that had made the classic dolls of the pre-War era, some of which survived the War only to be destroyed by the Depression. They were soon competing with firms whose clean and simple designs would make their traditional product look not merely old-fashioned, but irrelevant to modern life.

From our slightly anxious post-modern vantage point, life in the 19th century sometimes seems to have been organized on saner and more honest principles than the world is today. The illusory nature of this idea seems to make it more rather than less attractive. The Victorians too looked back to the time before steam and wondered if life hadn't been better then. Nevertheless, as they considered the cost of progress, from the hurly-burly of their new industrial world, they also created an enduring ideal of childhood. It is that ideal that gives the Victorian doll its timeless appeal.

Projects

THE remaining sections of this book contain detailed instructions for making selected garments pictured in the Gallery. For the most part, I have constructed the dresses exactly the way the originals were made. The particular designs were selected because they are representative of doll clothes of the period. Once you are familiar with the basic silhouette and sewing procedure, you can develop other designs from photographs or from museum pieces by changing the trimming or fabrication, for instance, or substituting a sleeve, or altering a neckline, all of which require only very basic patternmaking skills.

These projects are akin to making a sampler or a quilt in their emphasis on hand work. I recommend turning first to the appendices, Sewing by Hand and Making Things Fit, as a way to get started. It is also useful to review the entire set of instructions before beginning, so you know where you are going and what adjustments you may have to make because of the materials you have available, the size and shape of your doll, or the amount of time you are willing to invest. As we know, there are people who love to do hand work and people who don't. The actual point of this exercise, however, is to have fun. While I have not provided specific recommendations for substituting machine work (except where the original garment could have been assembled by machine), a review of the designs will suggest many points where this is possible.

I think most people who like to make things derive a profound satisfaction from work well done. Our Victorian forebears left us a legacy of needlework that provides a limitless source of inspiration, all the more inspiring since their work was often not a recreational exercise, but a necessary skill for life in their world. I hope the projects that follow will provide not only a creative challenge but a perspective on our shared inheritance.

CHAPTER I

Day Dresses

circa 1837–1845

PATTERN NOS. 1 AND 2

THE dresses presented in this chapter are based on the cotton day dress pictured at right, center. (Plate 1.) It is a characteristic style of the period, probably made in 1837 when the sleeve, after nearly a decade of exuberant display, suddenly collapsed. The fullness of the great gigot sleeve was displaced down onto the arm over the course of the following decade, first in flounces and other decorations on the upper arm, and later in a balloon of material between the elbow and the wrist. The sleeve may also be made plain, without any flouncing or trimming, to suggest the style of the mid-1840s.

The bodice is a typical "half high" style. It is shown with a typical pleated bodice trim, or with a plain corded front more suggestive of the modest 1840s. At the end of this chapter are instructions for making a chemisette of the late 1830s. This is a somewhat challenging white work project, but it completes the 1837 day dress in the traditional way. White fillings for necklines were worn by all grown women through the 1830s, and were gradually abandoned during the 1840s.

⇜MATERIALS⇝

THE fabrics of the 1830s and 1840s are extremely fine. Fashion writing of the time is full of self-congratulatory puffery regarding the high quality of the products of European mills. An irony for the clothing collector or conservator is that the clothes of this time are often in better condition than the more numerous survivals of the late 19th century and early 20th century, since they are made entirely of natural fibers and decorated only with vegetable-based dyes, which are non-destructive to the fabric on which they are imprinted (although, unfortunately, not colorfast).

The typical fabric is thin, with a plain surface and a good deal of body when handled, like taffeta, crisp rather than soft, but not stiff. Thin satins were also popular. Even-weave cottons, blends of cotton and wool and cotton and linen are also found, as well as pure woolens like challis, which is about the maximum softness you should use for the projects in this chapter.

Choose muted or dull colors in preference to bright ones. Busy prints are generally to be avoided, but small, well-organized, monochrome prints are acceptable, especially tiny ones that appear to be a solid color from a distance. Plaids started to become fashionable in the 1840s because of Queen Victoria's love for the Scottish countryside, although the garish modern versions of "old" tartans are to be avoided. Several companies sell "reproduction" versions of the wonderful old calicoes so familiar from this period, but their principal market is serious quilters, and calico is actually a bit stout for the dresses of this period. It is nevertheless a practical and inexpensive choice if the dress is sewn correctly. See Plate 1.1 (page 75), clearly modern but inoffensive on a reproduction doll.

The bodice should be lined with a cotton fabric of slight stiffness. The original day dress in Plate 1 is lined with fine white cotton drill; a modern woven cotton interfacing fabric is an acceptable substitute. You can distress it to dull the whiteness.

You also need an acceptable substitute for the narrow cotton cording with which most seams were reinforced and defined. Cording may be of ecru or off-white No. 5 pearl cotton or natural-colored cotton carpet warp (available from weaving suppliers). Neither looks exactly like the antique material, but if your sewing is accurate the cord will not show. Pearl cotton has the advantage of making a softer, more flexible finished seam; however, carpet warp is easier to use in the sewing, since it gives you a stiffish, clearly defined bump in the seam as a guide for your needle.

The very full skirt of the original dress is gathered closely and stitched to a waistband of even-weave tape. If you have old tape in good condition, you can use it, but new tape is not woven as tightly as the old and is usually a twill weave; it tends to shred as it is being stitched. A better substitute is a double-fold piece of fine white or off-white cotton such as batiste.

DRESS

Challis, cotton broadcloth, batiste, pima cotton, crisp shirting or calico in solids, small patterns, restrained stripes and plaids

Plate 1.1. *Day dress, c.1837, of modern black printed calico with false hem in another fabric. (Pattern No. 1.) A chemisette fills the neckline. (Pattern No. 3.)*

NOTIONS
Thread to match (cotton or silk)

2 yds. (1.8 m) cording (pearl cotton or carpet warp)

5 hooks and eyes

Woven cotton interfacing or lightweight cotton drill (scrap)

Thin, lightweight cotton for folding into waist tape (scrap)

⇒ SUMMARY OF STEPS ⇐
SKIRT
1. Cut and seam skirt.
2. Hem skirt.
3. Set skirt gathers.
4. Assemble and mount waist tape.

BODICE
5. Assemble and mount bodice pleat detail.
6. Close shoulder seams.
7. Close side seams.
8. Measure skirt to bodice and turn center back facings.
9. Bind neck edge and waistline seam.
10. Assemble and mount sleeve decoration.
11. Close sleeve seam.
12. Finish cuff.
13. Cord armhole and set sleeve.

FINISHING
14. Sew skirt to bodice.
15. Tack waist tape in place and sew on hooks and eyes.

GENERAL ⇒ CONSTRUCTION ⇐ NOTES

THE pink cotton day dress is a very good example of the sewing style of this period. At this time, a great deal of sewing was accomplished with the simple running stitch, and this dress was assembled almost entirely in that way. Occasional use was made of the blind stitch. The seams of a dress of this period were generally reinforced with several layers of stitches before the dressmaker considered them "finished," and if the stitching is done evenly and finely, it distributes any strain very efficiently. Most seams are corded, a process requiring three or four passes with the needle for completion.

Shoulderplate dolls come in all shapes and sizes, some quite bizarre if they were made by an amateur, so it is wise to make a muslin before committing yourself.

Despite the amount of sewing detail invested in the clothes of this time, their finished appearance is often rather understated, even plain. The late 1830s and 1840s are a period of determined primness in female dress after the ostentatious 1820s and early 1830s. Woolens and cottons were often printed with colorful, elaborate designs, but the desired effect was of quiet, inconspicuous good taste. Silks, as one would expect, are generally patterned and colored more conservatively. Skirts extended to the floor in the 1840s after having been quite above the ankles ten years earlier. Bonnets were very modest, allowing a lady to see and be seen only directly from the front. Even the neck was covered.

Dress bodices were well constructed and made to fit as snugly as possible. (Doll clothes do not always meet that standard, however.) Bodices, in addition to being stoutly lined, were generally boned to some degree. I have not seen any dolls' bodices provided with bones; however, one example pictured in the plates (see page 11, Plate 4, at right) does have the remnants of a pair of cane stiffeners at the center back opening to support the hooks or eyelets and keep the bodice wrinkle-free across the back when snugly fastened up.

Skirts were generally unlined in the 1840s, since they were supported by many petticoats—stiff, heavy ones underneath and lighter ones on top; six was not unusual. Skirts needed to be light so as not to add unnecessary weight to the mass. Lining was not needed for modesty; those linings and interlinings that do exist are usually there to support and reinforce a silk.

Dresses of this period are finished at the seams with cord. This fashion lasted until the end of the 1850s, when cord began to be used more sparingly. However, well into the bustle period, armholes and facing edges were often decorated and finished with cording. Cords may be covered with self-fabric or a contrasting color and fabric. Velvet, for instance, may be corded with silk taffeta. Most of the cording is simply let into the seams as they are sewn. This makes for a multi-step seaming process, which, although time-consuming, assures that the seam will hold, since it is oversewn several times in the process. Edges may also be finished with a cord facing.

Although the skirts of the period appear perfectly dome-shaped, they were generally shaped slightly at the back waist and worn over a modest bustle like a small cushion on strings to hold the skirt out at the back. Some skirts were also reinforced in the sit-down area between waist and knee with a blind stitched panel. However, most dolls' skirts do not have these details. They are generally cut very simply from a rectangle of fabric, often taking advantage of the selvages to finish the seams and placket.

➤ INSTRUCTIONS ➤

Day Dress, circa 1837

PATTERN NO. 1

SKIRT

1 • CUT AND SEAM SKIRT. There is no skirt pattern, since the typical doll's skirt of the time is made without any shaping. To cut the skirt, measure down the doll's backside *over the petticoat and other underlinen* from waist to floor. Add 1" (2.5 cm) for gathering allowance at the top, and 2" (5 cm) for hemming at the bottom. The skirt should be 6–7 times the waist girth. However, Victorian dressmakers often cheated on this measurement to take advantage of the selvages to finish the seams. Victorian cottons

and silks were about 24–28" (61–71 cm) wide. Two widths is a bit long, but one width is rather short for the girth measurement of a doll this size. Nevertheless, the plates have an example of each pictured. The copies in this chapter were made from a single width of modern 45–48" (114.5–122 cm) fabric, so that there would be one seam falling at the center back of the skirt. If you are cutting from a piece of antique fabric, you may piece on the straight as necessary to get the girth measurement you want. Skirt seams need not be finished.

Stitch the center back seam to the bottom of the placket and press open. Leave about ⅓ of the seam open. If you have cut on the selvage, no other treatment is necessary, but if you have had to leave a raw seam at the center back, take a deep enough seam to allow you to turn it under at the top so the placket is clean. Press.

2 • HEM SKIRT. There are two approaches to hemming. Thie first is to turn up the bottom of the skirt in the conventional way and close with a small hemming or running stitch. The second method is to insert a "false hem." False hems were cut from sturdy, often contrasting, fabric to save the expense of a deep hem in a costly fabric, to reinforce a delicate material, or simply to eke a dress out of a short length. To make a false hem, cut a strip about 2" (5 cm) wide

and long enough to match the skirt's girth. Piece as necessary, pressing the seams open. Close the center back seam of the false hem and stitch the strip to the bottom of the skirt. (Fig. 1.1.) The false hem is otherwise finished like a normal hem. In turning it to the inside, favor the shell. (See Fig. 1.2.)

3 • SET SKIRT GATHERS. Measure again, from the finished bottom of the skirt up the backside of the doll. The skirt should just skim the floor. Add ¾" (2 cm) to that measurement, and trim off any excess at the top of the skirt. (You will have quite a bit if you have added a false hem.) Turn down the top edge ¾" (2 cm), and put in a long (about ¼" or .5 cm) running stitch about ¼" (.5 cm) from the top edge all around the skirt. (Fig. 1.2.)

4 • ASSEMBLE AND MOUNT WAIST TAPE. Gather the skirt. Victorian dressmakers used heavy, even-weave tape for mounting gathers of this type, but modern tapes, even those that look like the old product, are not sturdy enough to take this sort of abuse. Cut a piece of batiste, finissima, or other fine, thin cotton, measuring 1" (2.5 cm) wide by about 10" (25.5 cm) long. Tuck in each short end ½" (1.5 cm) and fold the tape in quarters lengthwise. The open fold where the raw edge tucks under is the bottom edge of the tape. (Fig. 1.3.)

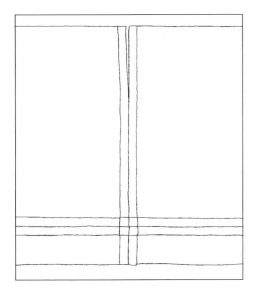

Fig. 1.1. *A skirt with a "false hem," which is joined first to the bottom of the skirt. The center back seam has been sewn to the bottom of the placket.*

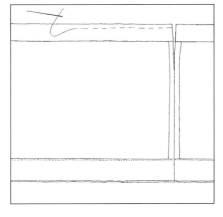

Fig. 1.2. *The finished hem, with the shell side favored in the turning. The hem has been closed with a small running stitch. At the waist edge, the turn-back has been made and the running stitch that will be used to form the gathers is begun.*

Fig. 1.3. *Making a "waist tape" from folded fabric. The ends are turned in first, and then the length folded in fours. The tape should be basted down the center to hold everything in place until it is sewn to the skirt.*

Divide the waist tape and the skirt into quarters to assist in distributing the fullness evenly. Skirts of the 1830s and 1840s are essentially dome-shaped with the fullness more or less evenly spread all around. Draw the skirt up into its gathers. Arrange the gathers so they form a neat row, not a crowd of disorganized folds. (Fig. 1.4.) Working from the right side, take a stitch through the top *of each pleat individually* and go through the folded bottom edge of the tape. (Fig. 1.5.) You are taking the row of close, tiny stitches through four layers of cotton, which should be secure. Notice that the bulk of the pleats is now inside the waistband. When you have finished, try the waistband and skirt around the doll to make sure you like the fit. There should be a short (¼" [.5 cm] or less) overlap at the center back.

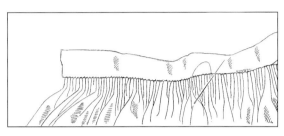

Fig. 1.4. *The skirt, one fourth of which has been gathered.*

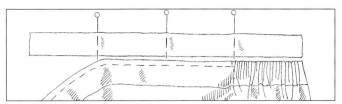

Fig. 1.5. *Stitching the gathers to the waist tape. This is done from the outside, so that the bulk of the pleats is inside the waistband. This ensures that the join to the bodice will be smooth on the outside where it shows.*

BODICE

Before beginning, organize some bias strips of fabric 1" (2.5 cm) wide. Approximately 2 yards of cording is required to complete the bodice of the dress. Not all of the cording is put into the seams the same way, so simply cut your bias fabric and set it aside to be ready as needed.

5 • ASSEMBLE AND MOUNT BODICE PLEAT DETAIL. The bodice detail of the example in Plate 1.1 was simply cut on the straight like the original dress. However, Victorian dressmakers used pattern somewhat differently than we do; if you are making your dress from a tiny windowpane check or a stripe, you might want to cut the bodice detail on the bias or make it in two halves, so the pattern radiates from the center. (See Plate 1.2.)

Form the pleats, using Fig. 1.6 as a guide; press, and baste them down. Using the bodice detail template, cut a pair of pleated forms from the folded and basted material. (Fig. 1.7.)

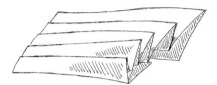

Fig. 1.6. *Folding up the pleated bodice trimming.*

Plate 1.2. *Another day dress, c.1845, showing the plain, intensely modest dress of the 1840s. The dress is of a fine wool challis trimmed with contrast silk cording, and illustrates the typical way striped fabrics were organized during this period.*

The bodice was cut from PATTERN NO. 2, *which has a seam at center front finished with contrast cord*

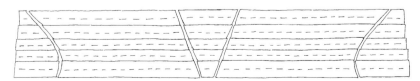

Fig. 1.7. *Placement of the template on the folded fabric to cut the ornament for the breast of the dress.*

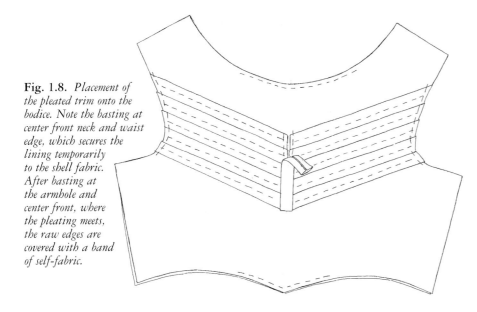

Fig. 1.8. *Placement of the pleated trim onto the bodice. Note the basting at center front neck and waist edge, which secures the lining temporarily to the shell fabric. After basting at the armhole and center front, where the pleating meets, the raw edges are covered with a band of self-fabric.*

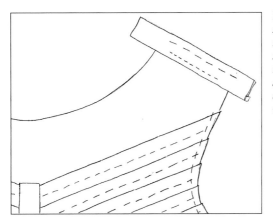

Fig. 1.9. *Beginning the shoulder seam by stitching in the self-covered cord. The stitching does not extend into the neck and armhole seam allowances; this makes the cording easier to trim out when it is completed.*

Baste the bodice to its lining at center front top and bottom and arrange the pleated material on the front of the bodice, using the notches in the armhole as a guide.

Cut the central band ¾" (2 cm) by 2" (5 cm), and fold the edges under about ³⁄₁₆" (.45 cm) all around. The band covers the raw center fronts of the pleat detail. Place it down and stitch with a small blind stitch through all the layers (Fig. 1.8.)

The alternative bodice has a plain contrast corded front seam. The chevron pattern is formed by cutting the woolen fabric on the bias.

6. • **CLOSE SHOULDER SEAMS.** Two strips of bias-covered cord each 2" (5 cm) long are required to close the shoulder seams. Fold the bias strip in half and baste the cord into the folded edge. Trim the bias strip to a ¼" (.5 cm) seam. Lay the strip onto the shoulder seam as illustrated (Fig. 1.9.) and baste in place. Don't stitch into the armhole or neck seam allowances. Trim the bias off at the armhole and neck edge, and then trim the cording out of the seams to reduce bulk.

Join the shoulders, right sides together, stitching edge to edge. Working from the right side of the bodice, turn all the interior seams toward the back and blind stitch along the seam so that they will stay in place. (Fig. 1.10.) Grade the shoulder seams to reduce bulk. (Fig. 1.11.)

Fig. 1.10. *Blind stitching over the shoulder seam to make the seams lie toward the back of the garment.*

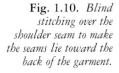

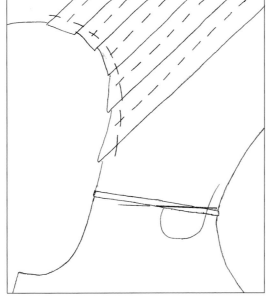

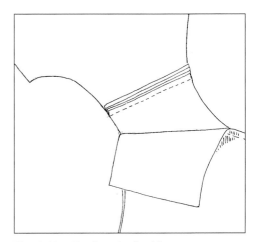

Fig. 1.11. *Grading the shoulder seams to reduce bulk.*

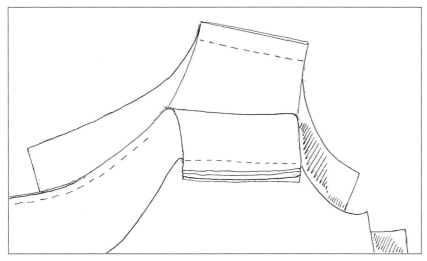

Fig. 1.12. *Stitching the shoulder seams of the lining.*

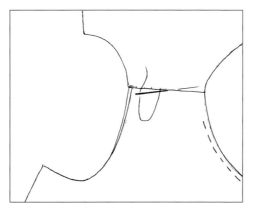

Fig. 1.13. *Blind stitching the lining seams.*

Fig. 1.14. *Stitching the side seams.*

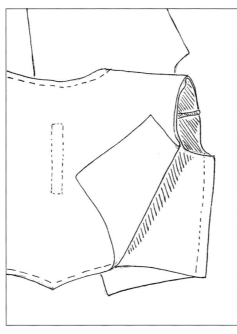

Stitch the shoulder seams of the lining. (Fig. 1.12.) Turn them toward the back and blind stitch the seam, catching the shell seams as you do without penetrating all the way through them. This is one of the characteristic details of the dresses of this time. (Fig. 1.13.) Make sure the lining and the shell are lying together without rippling or buckling.

7 • CLOSE SIDE SEAMS. Close the shell side seams. (Fig. 1.14.) Turn the seams toward the back of the bodice, and topstitch the side seam from the outside, using as small a running stitch as you can handle. The original garment has truly minuscule stitches at every seam that shows on the outside. (Fig. 1.15.) Stitch the lining side seams likewise. You will need to turn the garment out to get access to these seams, since the shoulders are already joined. Topstitch as before, but try to catch the shell seams as you go, so that all the layers are neatly joined together. Again check for buckling.

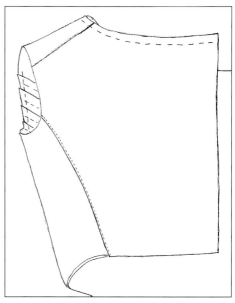

Fig. 1.15. *Topstitching the lining side seams with the running stitch.*

8 • **MEASURE SKIRT TO BODICE AND TURN CENTER BACK FACINGS.** Measure the finished skirt against the bodice at this point to see that they fit together. Because the bulk of the skirt is inside the waist tape, the bodice waist measurement over it will depend to some extent on the type of fabric you chose and how deep you made your little pleats. Put the skirt on the doll and fasten it with a pin. Turn up the bodice waist seam about ¼" (.5 cm) and begin at the center front on each side, laying the bodice over the pleats. At the back, the bodice should just cover the top of the pleats; the point at center front should naturally fall to its own, lower level at the front. You should have about ½–¾" (1.5–2 cm) left over at each center edge at the back. Mark the left and right back where the finished skirt edge falls. The bodice will be net to the skirt.

To finish the left side of the bodice, measure ½" (1.5 cm) from the mark for a turn-back allowance and trim off any excess. To reduce bulk in the turning, trim out ¼" (.5 cm) of the lining. Make a double ¼" (.5 cm) turn-back and stitch it down with a blind stitch. (Fig. 1.16.)

To finish the right side of the bodice, measure ¼" (.5 cm) past the mark for a seam allowance and trim off the excess. Put a line of basting stitches into the edge at ¼" (.5 cm). This is a guide for your stitching. Make a cord facing as illustrated in Fig. 1.17. Cut a bias strip 1" (2.5 cm) wide by 4" (10 cm) long. Fold one edge down ¼" (.5 cm) and baste the cord into the fold. Turn up the other side so the edges meet.

Set the wrong side of the cord facing to the right side of the bodice so the cord itself runs along the basted line. Stitch next to the cord, and pull out the basting. (Fig. 1.18.) Trim off the excess bias fabric, and trim the cord out of the neck and waist seam allowances. Fold the facing inside and close with small a blind stitch. (Fig. 1.19.)

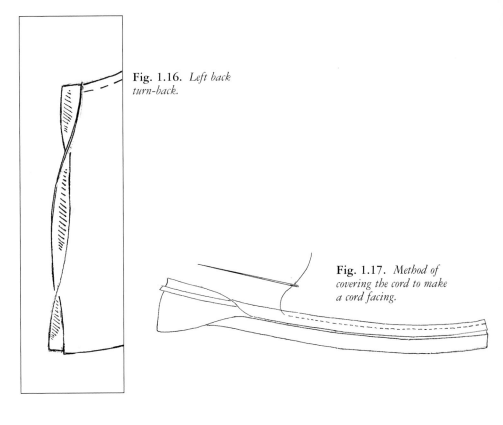

Fig. 1.16. *Left back turn-back.*

Fig. 1.17. *Method of covering the cord to make a cord facing.*

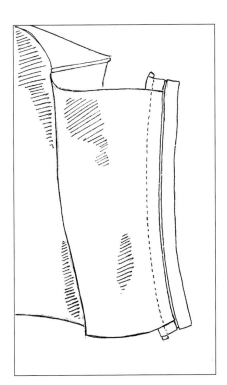

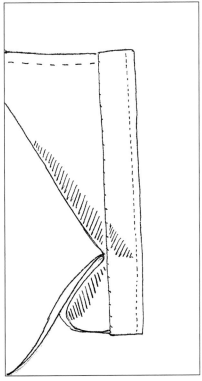

Fig. 1.18. *Attaching the cord facing to the right back. The **wrong side** of the cord facing is joined to the **right side** of the bodice.*

Fig. 1.19. *The cord facing, trimmed at top and bottom and closed inside with a small blind stitch.*

Fig. 1.20. *Joining the cording to the waist seam.*

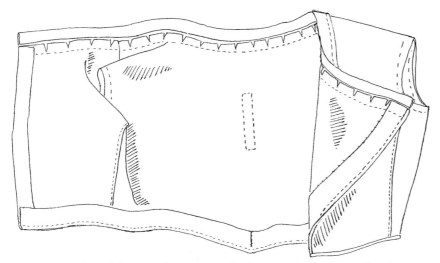

Fig. 1.21. *The cord facing at the waist seam has been turned up and a small tuck taken at center front to take up the excess fabric in the turned bias and to secure it inside the bodice. The raw ends at center back have been tucked in and tacked down. At the neckline, the cord facing has been sewn on. It will be turned down and blind stitched for a clean finish.*

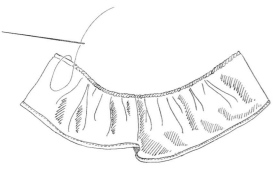

Fig. 1.22. *The sleeve flounce, hemmed at the bottom, and whipped and gathered at the top.*

9• Bind neck edge and waistline seam. The waist edge is finished with a plain piece of bias cording. Make a covered cord 10" (25.5 cm) long and trim the seam allowance down to ¼" (.5 cm). The edges are left raw, since they will be covered by the waist tape when the skirt is joined. To preserve the shape of the point at the center front, ease the cording as you go around. (Fig. 1.20.) Turn the edges in at each center back and tack the bias up into place. Take a small tuck at center front and tack, to take up the extra fabric at the back side of the point. (Fig. 1.21.)

The neckline is finished with cord facing like the right back. Set it around, wrong side to right side, stitch, and turn it in. Blind stitch the edge of the cording to the lining only, not going through the shell at all. See Fig. 1.21.

10• Assemble and mount sleeve decoration. Hem the sleeve flounces ¼" (.5 cm) by taking a double ⅛" (.3 cm) turn at the bottom and closing with a small running stitch. Roll, whip, and gather the top edge. Draw it up to fit the sleeve where it is to be set on. (Fig. 1.22.) The flounce of the original pink dress is about three times the measure around the sleeve at the point where the flounce is joined. The calico copy, however, is only twice the sleeve measure because of the bulk of the calico fabric when it is rolled and gathered at the head of the flounce.

An alternative method of drawing up the sleeve flounce is illustrated in Fig. 1.23. After hemming the flounce, turn the top edge ¼" (.5 cm) and stitch a piece of cording in like a drawstring. The cording should be stitched down firmly as you begin. At the end, draw up the cord and stitch it down again. This may be done with carpet warp or pearl cotton. Distribute the gathering evenly. This method is especially useful with a fabric whose bulk makes it difficult to roll and whip.

Fig. 1.23. *Drawing the flounce up on cord sewn into the header.*

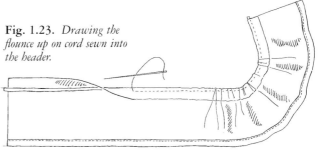

Fig. 1.24. *The sleeve with the lower flounce and the cord header for the top flounce stitched into place.*

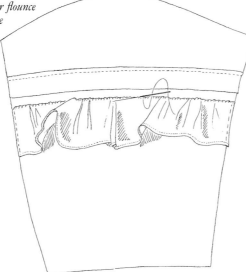

Fig. 1.25. *The sleeve with the top flounce stitched onto its header, and the seam with cord stitched in.*

Fig. 1.26. *After closing the sleeve seam, the sleeve is turned out and the cording blind stitched to reinforce the seam and to make the seams inside lie flat and toward the back.*

The lower flounce goes onto the sleeve at the line indicated on the pattern. Blind stitch the flounce to the sleeve.

The upper flounce has a header of bias cording. (Fig. 1.24.) Stitch it down at the placement line, and then stitch the flounce on top of it. Make two pieces of bias-covered cord 5½" (14 cm) long and baste to each front sleeve seam. (Fig. 1.25.)

11 • CLOSE SLEEVE SEAM. Close the sleeve seam, and blind stitch the cording in the seam, as illustrated, turned toward the back. (Fig. 1.26.)

12 • FINISH CUFF. Measure the end of the sleeve to check the cuff measurement. Add two ¼" (.5 cm) seams. The cuff facing is cut 1" (2.5 cm) wide. Cut two pieces of cording at the cuff measurement and enclose them in the bias to make a pair of cord facings. Baste all the turnings. (Fig. 1.27.)

Working with the sleeve wrong side out, set the cuff facing into the sleeve, wrong side to right side, and stitch it in place. (Fig. 1.28.) The ends should meet at the seamline. Turn the facing inside and blind stitch in place, including the folded ends, which can be butted together and secured to the seam. (Fig. 1.29.)

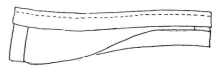

Fig. 1.27. *The cuff cord facing. The cord is cut at the actual finished length needed, and the bias binding wrapped around. The ends are tucked in first, and then the two folds made along the length.*

Fig. 1.28. *Stitching the cord facing in place. The sleeve is turned wrong side out and the facing placed inside. The wrong side of the facing is toward the right side of the sleeve fabric.*

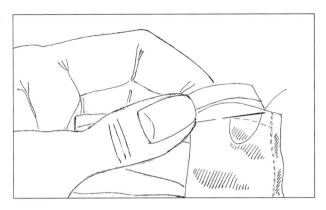

Fig. 1.29. *To finish, the cuff facing will be stitched along the bottom edge with a very fine running stitch. The ends, butted together, are blind stitched to the sleeve seam to close and finish them.*

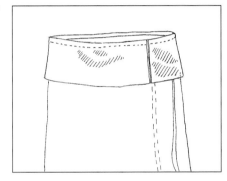

13 • **CORD ARMHOLE AND SET SLEEVE.** In setting the sleeves, I used a slightly different method than a Victorian dressmaker would have used. The authentic method is simply to baste the cording into place and set the sleeve as usual, using the cording as a stitching guide, and turning to finish. This is an operation that I think many people find difficult, however, so I broke the sleeve set down into more, but simpler, steps. (Chapter VII illustrates the conventional procedure at Figs. 7.41–7.43.)

Make two bias-covered cords 6" (15 cm) long to finish the armhole. Before starting to sew, trim the basted cord seam allowance down to ¼" (.5 cm). The cord seam is the exact width of the armhole seam, and you will be able to use the width of the cord to ensure that the armhole is sewn at the right diameter. Beginning at the actual bottom of the armhole (not at the side seam, which is set back) stitch the cording around the armhole in ¼" (.5 cm) seams. Lap and secure at the bottom. Peel the bias fabric open and trim the cording out of the overlapped ends; trim off any excess fabric as well. (Fig. 1.30.) A common problem with setting cord into seams is that it tends to draw up the seam and thereby shorten it. This is to be avoided with special care at the armhole, not only because it will make the sleeve hard to set, but, although most shoulderplate dolls have a relatively bulk-free hanging flange for the arm attachment, the entire shoulder area of the garment may fit awkwardly if the armhole is drawn up too small.

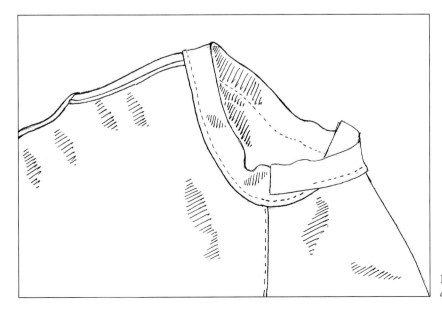

Fig. 1.30. *The armhole with cording stitched in place all around.*

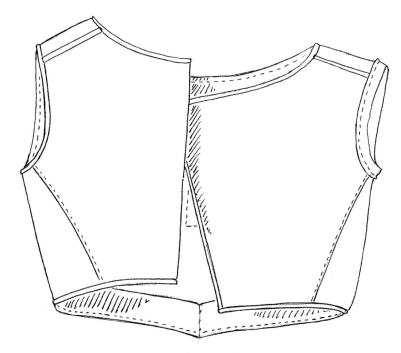

Fig. 1.31. *The corded armholes. On the right, the cording and seam trimmed to about 3/16" (.45 cm); on the left, the seams turned in and blind stitched to hold them.*

Trim the armhole seam to about ³⁄₁₆" (.45 cm) (Fig. 1.31, right side) and turn the corded seam in. Blind stitch in the fold to make the seam stay. (Fig. 1.31, left side.) These armholes are shown folded approximately in half. Note that the shoulder seam and the side seam are set back on the doll's body. However, in placing the sleeve into the armhole, use the actual top and bottom of the armscye, disregarding the seams.

Note the top of the sleeve with a small mark or minuscule notch into the fabric. Place a small gathering stitch around the top of the sleeve and pull it up slightly. Align the sleeve into the armhole. The top of the sleeve goes to the top of the armhole. The sleeve seam goes to the bottom of the armhole. Pull up the gathering in the sleeve as necessary. There is a very small amount of ease in the sleeve, but you should try to distribute it so that it disappears. Ease it in by pushing the sleeve toward your needle as you sew. Blind stitch the sleeve into the armhole from the outside, using the channel between the cording the bodice, and taking a very tiny stitch. (Fig. 1.32.) When you have finished, you will have an extra, slightly visible stitch, but if you have executed the seam carefully, it should not be obtrusive.

Working from the inside, turn the armhole out, and trim the seam to ³⁄₁₆" (.45 cm). Stitch around the armhole again, from the inside, taking all your stitches in the actual seam allowance. In this way, you avoid making any puckers on the face side of the bodice. Overcast the armhole seam to neaten it. (Fig. 1.33.)

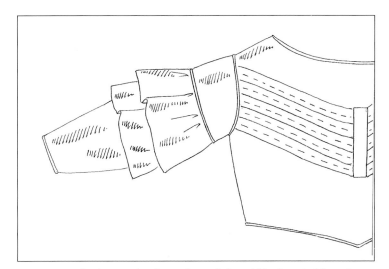

Fig. 1.32. *The sleeve is placed into the armhole and blind stitched from the outside in the channel between the cord and the bodice.*

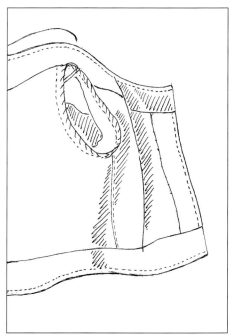

Fig. 1.33. *The inside of the armhole. It has been reinforced with another line of stitches and overcast to neaten and finish it.*

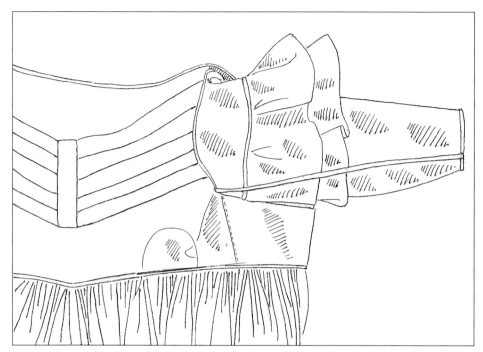

Fig. 1.34. *Joining the skirt to the bodice. The stitches are taken in the channel between the cord and the bodice.*

14 • SEW SKIRT TO BODICE. Sew the skirt to the bodice, stitching in the channel between the bodice cording and the bodice itself.

In some of the bodices of this period, the point at the front was left loose, and you can do that if you wish. On this scale, about 1" (2.5 cm) to the right and left of the center front point would be left unsewn. Make sure if you do this that it hangs correctly. (Fig. 1.34.) It may be the best way to finish the front if the skirt and the bodice don't want to "gel."

15 • TACK WAIST TAPE IN PLACE AND SEW ON HOOKS AND EYES. Tack the waist tape in place with a set of hand bar tacks through the seams and lining only. One goes at center front, one in each side seam, and one in the space between. The tape and the bodice are not exactly the same length except at the very point you measured for attachment of the skirt. Distribute the difference evenly; there should not be so much that it will show once the dress is on the doll, since her torso will fill it up.

Stitch on a set of hooks and eyes as illustrated, setting the eyes a little ahead of the edge, and the hooks a little behind it. This forms the lap. (Fig. 1.35.)

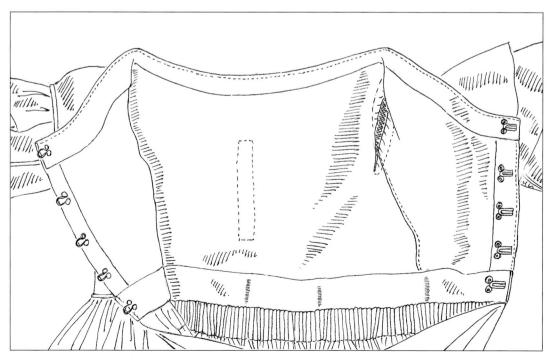

Fig. 1.35. *The finished interior of the bodice, showing the bar tacks securing the waist tape into the bodice and the set of hooks and eyes for closure.*

Chemisette, circa 1840

PATTERN NO. 3

For most of the 19th century, women wore white edgings or fillers of one sort or another at the necklines of their dresses. Although evening clothes were quite bare, at various times it was considered a requirement of modesty to cover the neck and the top of the bosom during the day. At other times, it was merely a fashion indicative of refinement. Collars and chemisettes were of various materials ranging from cambric and batiste to celluloid and paper. These white garments, changed often to keep them clean, also served to protect the often unwashable and expensive dress from body soil and abrasion.

During the 1830s and 1840s, day dresses were often quite low, and it was customary to fill in the neckline with a complete chemisette to the neck. This garment was generally tied with tapes around the body under the arms. The chemisette presented below is based on the one shown in Plate 1.

The original garment is made of a thin but sturdy windowpane thread check cotton, and has a matching cap. The hand-sewing techniques are presented more fully in Appendix A.

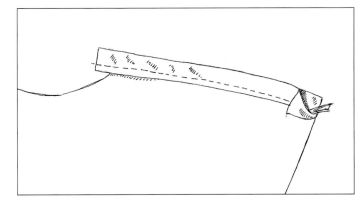

Fig. 1.37.
The shoulder of the chemisette with the bias cord set to the seam. The bias is turned back so the cord may be clipped out of the seam to reduce bulk.

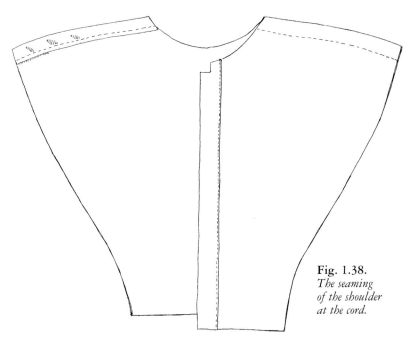

Fig. 1.38.
The seaming of the shoulder at the cord.

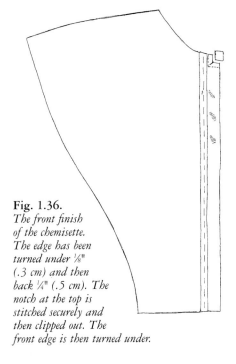

Fig. 1.36.
The front finish of the chemisette. The edge has been turned under ⅛" (.3 cm) and then back ¼" (.5 cm). The notch at the top is stitched securely and then clipped out. The front edge is then turned under.

⊰ MATERIALS ⊱

⅛ yd. (.1 m) semi-sheer, thin, crisp linen or lawn, batiste, organdie or other similar fabric

¼" (.5 cm) or smaller mother-of-pearl button

Cotton thread

¼ yd. (.2 m) No. 5 pearl cotton or cotton carpet warp for cording ½ yd. (.45 m) white ¼" (.5 cm) or narrower tape

⊰ INSTRUCTIONS ⊱

16 • Turn the front edges in ⅛" (.3 cm) and baste down. Fold them back ¼" (.5 cm) and stitch a tiny notch, as illustrated at the center front edge; clip it out. This forms the lap at the center. (Fig. 1.36.)

17 • Cut two pieces of bias self-fabric 1" (2.5 cm) by 3" (7.5 cm), and make two pieces of covered cord.

18 • Baste the cord to each back shoulder seam, beginning and ending on the seam line. Peel the bias fabric back where it has been left unstitched, and clip the cord out of the seam allowances to reduce bulk. (Fig. 1.37.)

19 • Stitch the shoulder seams, placing the stitches as close to the cord (which you should be able to feel in the seam) as you can. Be careful that you do not draw up the stitches too tightly and thereby shorten the shoulder seam. (Fig. 1.38.)

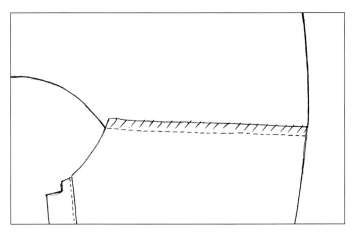

Fig. 1.39. *The shoulder seam, trimmed to about ⅛" (.3 cm) and then neatened with overcasting.*

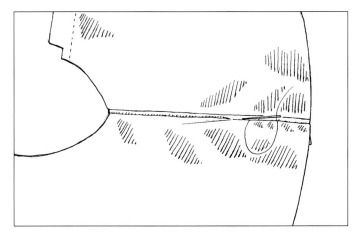

Fig. 1.40. *Blind stitching the corded seam to reinforce it and incline the seam to lie toward the back.*

20. Trim the shoulder seams down to a generous 1/8" (.3 cm) and overcast to neaten them. (Fig. 1.39.) On the right side, blind stitch through the back shoulder seam so that the seam is inclined to the back side. This also reinforces the seam. (Fig. 1.40.)

21. Turn the collar seams under ⅛" (.3 cm) and baste down. (Fig. 1.41.) Fold the collar points together (right sides together) and stitch. (Fig. 1.42.) Turn, press, and close with a tiny running stitch. (Fig. 1.43.)

Fig. 1.41. *The collar, with its edges turned under ⅛" (.3 cm) and basted.*

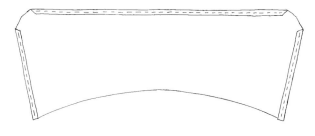

Fig. 1.42. *Stitching the collar points.*

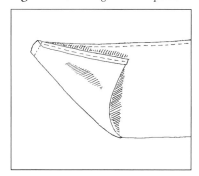

Fig. 1.43. *The finished collar. The turn-back edges have been pressed down and closed with a small running stitch.*

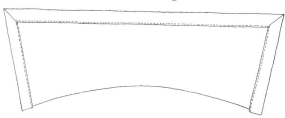

22 • Set the right side of the collar into the wrong side of the neck. (Fig. 1.44.) Stitch around at least twice, close together, and trim out the seam.

NOTE: The *right side* of the collar is stitched to the *wrong side* of the bodice. This is somewhat counter-intuitive, since it turns the neck seam *out* to the right side of the garment.

23 • Finger press the seam in place and overcast to neaten it. (Fig. 1.45, which also shows the placement of the buttonhole.)

24 • Turn the lower front and shoulder edge hems as marked on the pattern, and close with a small running stitch. The casing that carries the tape is formed the same way. Press it, place the tape inside, and close, being careful not to catch the tape. (Fig. 1.46.)

25 • Make one buttonhole, as indicated, and sew on the button. See Fig. 1.45.

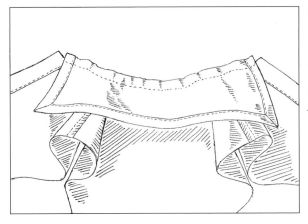

Fig. 1.44. *The finished collar, its right side set to the wrong side of the neckhole edge and stitched in. The finished front edge of the collar is at the corner of the "notch" that was stitched out of the center front of the bodice.*

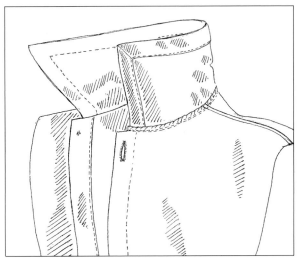

Fig. 1.45. *Neck seam finish. The collar has been stitched twice. The neck seam is then trimmed to about ⅛" (.3 cm) and overcast. Note the position of the buttonhole on the left front.*

Fig. 1.46. *The sides and lower front edges of the chemisette have been hemmed up. The casing is formed like a wide hem at the back, with the tape sewn into it.*

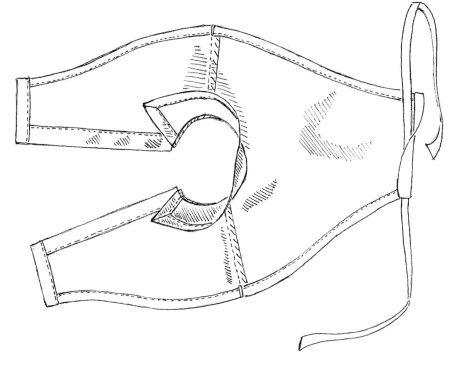

CHAPTER II

Pagoda Sleeve Day Dress

circa 1855

PATTERN NO. 4

THE dress presented in this chapter is based on the pagoda sleeve day dress worn by the seated figure pictured at left. (Plate 13.) During the 1840s, the fullness and decoration of sleeves had gradually worked their way from the upper arm to the forearm. In the early 1850s, this fullness was opened out into the so-called "pagoda" sleeve. Open sleeves of this type were always worn with an undersleeve, or "engageante." During the day, undersleeves were of white cotton; evening styles worn for dinner occasions had undersleeves of lace, usually white but sometimes black. Open sleeves of this general type continued to be fashionable into the early 1860s.

Skirts became ever wider and more elaborate during the 1850s. Their apparent width was made even greater by the use of horizontally applied flounces and swaggings of various widths. Some seasons, single broad flounces were fashionable; at others, ten or twelve narrow flounces might be arranged from hem to waist. Empress Eugénie (not a universally admired role model) is reported to have appeared in 1859 in a white satin ball gown trimmed with 103 flounces of tulle. [Alison Gernsheim, *Victorian and Edwardian Fashion, A Photographic Survey*, 1981, p.43, quoting Max von Boehn, in *Die Mode: Menschen und Moden in neunzehnten Jahrhundert*, 1919.] Plate 10, for instance, shows a skirt with a wide band of tucks; Plate 18 illustrates a skirt with sheer flouncings. Double skirts and separate bodices with long basques became fashionable late in the decade. In 1856, the "artificial" or "cage" crinoline was introduced, remaining fashionable in one form or another until the late 1860s. In the mid-1850s, the crinoline was dome-shaped, causing the skirt to look like an enormous tea cozy.

❧ MATERIALS ❧

In general, choose fabrics with plain surfaces that are stable and thin. Taffeta and other light, crisp silks are good choices. There is a great deal of bulk at the waist in the pleats, which is very difficult to accommodate in heavier fabrics. Thin, even sheer, cottons are also appropriate if the bodice and sleeves are lined. Like the dresses of the 1830s and 1840s, the dresses of the 1850s were supported by several layers of opaque undergarments, and were therefore often made of very thin materials. Bodices were lined stoutly.

Colors were both deeper and brighter in the 1850s than in the previous decade, expressing a more assertive femininity. Flounces may be applied around the dress. Narrow flounces taken whole off an old garment are especially effective; a distinctive pattern of fading left intact lends great verisimilitude to a reproduction garment. If you make up your own flounces, they should be gathered no fuller than 2-to-1. (The easiest way to accomplish this is by drawing up the header with inserted cord.) Light silk fringes were used to decorate the edges of open sleeves and flounces. Old fringes can be carefully cut down to the correct width for trimming a doll's dress. Bows and small posies of flowers were often scattered over the surface of a dress. Plate 18 shows a nice example of lace-edged flounces trimmed with bunches of bright-colored flowers in an asymmetrical arrangement. Nonfunctional buttons were also employed to trim bodices and sleeves. Braid may also be used freely; this is a practical way to trim a reproduction, since braid can be made up very easily. (See Chapter IV at step 7.)

Styles were trimmed flirtatiously. Toward the end of the decade, chemical dyes came into use. See, for instance, the dress pictured in Plate 16. Tartan patterns remained popular; there was also an interest in Asian motifs such as paisley, due to the popularity of Persian shawls and their imitations.

Choose a fabric for your doll that complements her own "style." A highly stylized parian of 1860 wants a much different treatment than a plump and plain china of a decade earlier.

Bodices of this period are always lined. Usually the lining is a functional reinforcement for the shell as well as a finish to the inside. On a full-size garment, the lining provides a base for boning and other interior construction. In the 1850s, linings of doll bodices typically are sewn as one with the shell more or less like the full-size item, with the details simplified. Choose a thin, sturdy fabric like light-weight cotton drill or glazed cotton taken from the inside of an old dress. Ordinary woven cotton sold for interfacing is also acceptable. Linings are typically white.

SHELL

Taffeta, tissue taffeta, or other stable, even-weave silk

Cambric, batiste, organdie

Fine wool challis

NOTIONS

Thread to match (cotton or silk)

2½ yds. (2.25 m) cording (pearl cotton or carpet warp)

5 hooks and eyes or shell buttons

Woven cotton interfacing, glazed cotton, or lightweight cotton drill (scrap)

UNDERSLEEVES

Thin, sheer cottons such as batiste

Scraps of period white-on-white embroideries

Short sections of old lace

TRIMMINGS

Contrast cord (where appropriate)

Braid

Rosettes and ruchings of ribbon

Fringe

Buttons

Small posies of artificial flowers

❧ SUMMARY OF STEPS ❧

BODICE

1. Make darts and close shoulder seams.
2. Close side seams.
3. Bind neck edge and waistline seam.
4. Measure bodice to the doll and turn center back facings.
5. Finish armhole with cording.
6. Make sleeves.
7. Set sleeves.

SKIRT

8. Cut and seam skirt; turn up hem.
9. Make tucks.
10 Set skirt pleats.

FINISHING

11. Sew skirt to bodice. Make back closure.

Plate 2.1. *Pagoda sleeve day dress, c.1855, made from an antique kimono. The fabric is matte black with a woven pattern of taupe and oxblood sprigs. Because it was scattered over with small holes and damages, but basically sound, the skirt shell fabric was fully interlined with black silk organza. The panels of the skirt are all different widths, so I could cut around damages as much as possible; the panels were joined through and through to the interlining at their seams, so the organza supports and strengthens the old fabric. The cording was cut from new silk taffeta. The loose undersleeves were made from strips of antique broderie anglaise, pieced together (under the flounce) to form the necessary length.*

GENERAL ⊱CONSTRUCTION⊰ NOTES

ALTHOUGH there are some very finely dressed, elegant china ladies from this period, a good many of the china heads of the 1850s are rather plain, and they look best when costumed modestly. There are a great many more survivals from the 1850s than from previous eras, and one therefore gets a wider glimpse of ordinary functional sewing styles. China heads were made in enormous numbers and sold through the decade at progressively cheaper prices. A plain sewing style, evidencing a doll dressed at home, is much more typical than an elaborate commercial production in this period.

Compared to the 1840s, dresses of the 1850s have more emphasis on girlish style and less on technical perfection. Tucks and applied trims such as buttons and ribbons were much more freely used. Construction details were abbreviated compared to the full-size garments on which the clothes were based, although the designs were often skillful and quite charming.

In the 1830s, cording was carefully inserted in many seams of a well-made dress, but in the 1850s it was used much less. The pagoda sleeve dress has cording at the armholes and cord facings at neck and waist. Cording may optionally be used to finish the edges of the sleeves as well, depending upon the fabrication. Cotton carpet warp or off-white No. 5 pearl cotton are both acceptable substitutes for old cording. Pearl cotton yields a softer finished seam, but with some fabrics may present some sewing difficulties, since it can be difficult to keep track of in the seam. Carpet warp, which is much stiffer, offers a much more definitive guide for your needle.

Lining the sleeves is optional, and may depend upon your choice of fabric. Sturdy, opaque fabrics like wool challis may be left unlined (as are the sleeves of the dress in Plate 13). Dressier fabrics and sheer fabrics should be lined either separately or in one. The finished sleeve should not be stiff. Both methods are explained below.

⊰INSTRUCTIONS⊱

The front and back bodice should be lined with cotton. Cut the shell and lining from the same pattern and baste the pieces together with small running stitches near the edges. Instead of being separately lined (like the bodice of Chapter I) the shell and lining are sewn as one.

1 • MAKE DARTS AND CLOSE SHOULDER SEAMS. Stitch the front darts and press them toward the side seams. Stitch the shoulder seams and overcast the edges. Press toward the back. (Fig. 2.1.)

2 • CLOSE SIDE SEAMS. Stitch the side seams, overcast, and press toward the back. (Fig. 2.2.)

3 • BIND NECK EDGE AND WAISTLINE SEAM. The neck and waist edges are finished with cord facings. To prepare the neck and waist seam for finishing, put a basting stitch all along both edges at ¼" (.5 cm). This is a guide for the cord facing. To make cord facings, measure the neck and waist seams at the basting and cut a piece of cord for each. The cord in the dress in Plate 2.1 was covered with new silk taffeta because the old dress fabric was somewhat fragile.

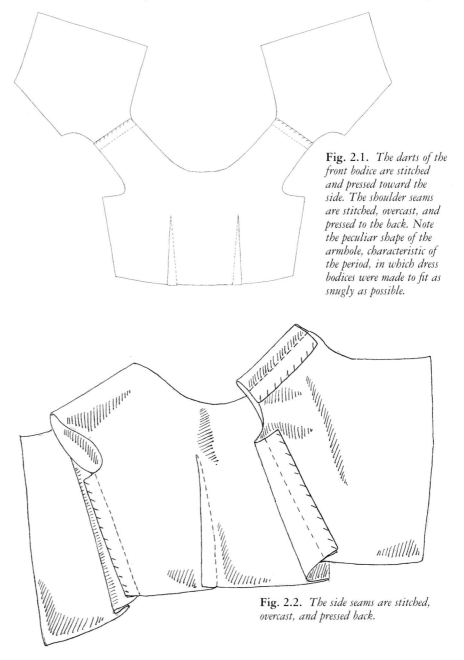

Fig. 2.1. The darts of the front bodice are stitched and pressed toward the side. The shoulder seams are stitched, overcast, and pressed to the back. Note the peculiar shape of the armhole, characteristic of the period, in which dress bodices were made to fit as snugly as possible.

Fig. 2.2. The side seams are stitched, overcast, and pressed back.

Cut two pieces of bias fabric 1" (2.5 cm) wide and slightly longer than the cord. Enclose the cord in the bias fabric, turning down one edge about ¼" (.5 cm) and stitching the cord in with a small running stitch. Fold up the opposite side so the raw edges meet. Baste. (Fig. 2.3.)

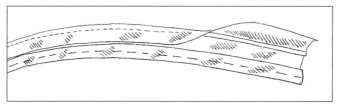

Fig. 2.3. *Making the cording. The top fold, which encloses the actual cord, is folded down about ¼". The bottom is folded up so that the raw edges meet.*

Place the wrong side of the cording against the right side of the neckline. The cord itself runs along the basted line. Stitch the cord facing in place through and through. (Fig. 2.4.) Fold the cord facing inside the bodice, clipping the neck seam allowance if necessary to ease it. Blind stitch the cord facing to the bodice lining to close. (Fig. 2.5.) Leave the last ¼" (.5 cm) or so loose; it will be finished with the center back closure. The waist edge is finished likewise.

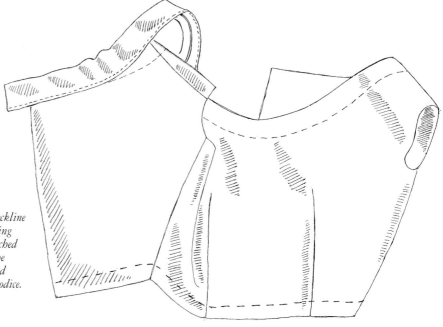

Fig. 2.4. *The seam of the neckline is marked with a line of basting stitches; the cord facing is stitched just inside the basted line. The wrong side of the cord is placed against the right side of the bodice.*

Fig. 2.5. *The inside of the bodice, showing the cord facing turned in and blind stitched.*

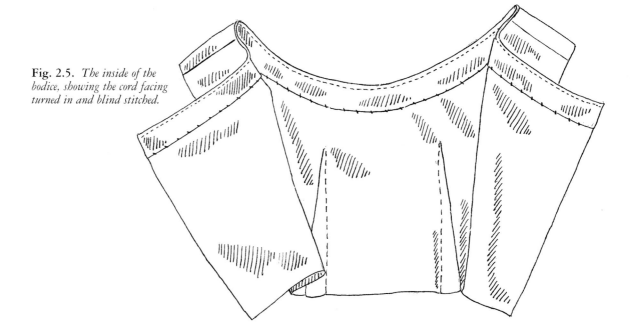

Fig. 2.6. *The center back finishing. The waist edge has been finished with a cord facing like the neck edge. The cording itself is trimmed out at the center back to reduce bulk. The cord facings are tucked under the turn-back at center back. (Note that in Chapter I, the cord facings cover the turn-back. Either finishing style is acceptable.)*

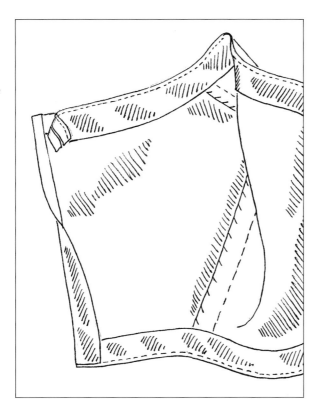

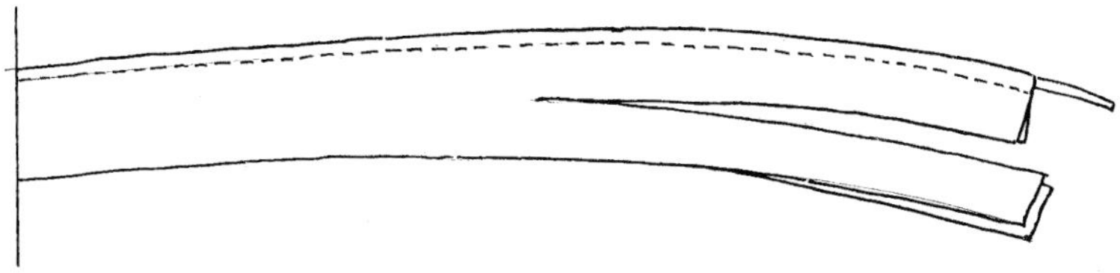

4 • **MEASURE BODICE TO THE DOLL AND TURN CENTER BACK FACINGS.** Try the bodice on the doll at this point, and mark the center back for the closure. The pattern has enough allowed for hooks and eyes; however, the dress may be closed with buttons by adding a lap allowance. The amount of the turn-back will depend on the size of the button; the buttons and buttonholes should be made through a double layer of fabric for security. (See Chapter III at step 11 for a back button closure.)

When you have the measurement, close the back facing with a blind stitch. Clip out excess lining within the fold to reduce bulk. (Fig. 2.6.)

5 • **FINISH ARMHOLE WITH CORDING.** I have used a different method for setting sleeves than most Victorian dressmakers. If you are comfortable with handwork on this scale, you may find it simpler to set the sleeve as usual, putting in a cord around the armhole before setting the sleeve. For others, I offer this slightly more cumbersome but simpler method. (The conventional sleeve set is illustrated in Chapter VII at Figs. 7.41–7.43.)

Make two bias-covered cords 6" (15 cm) long to finish the armholes. Cut two strips of bias fabric 1" (2.5 cm) wide by 6" (15 cm) long to cover the cords. Before starting to sew, trim the seam allowance to ¼" (.5 cm), the width of the armhole seam. (Fig. 2.7.) By using the width of the cording as a guide, you will ensure that the armhole is sewn at the right diameter. Beginning at the actual bottom of the armhole (*not* at the side seam, which is set back) stitch the cording around the armhole at ¼" (.5 cm). (Fig. 2.8.) Lap and secure at the bottom.

Fig. 2.7. *Cord facing.*

Fig. 2.8. *The armhole, edged with cording.*

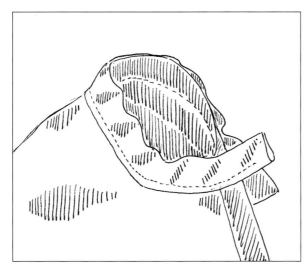

Peel the bias fabric open and trim the cording out of the overlap to reduce bulk; trim off any excess fabric as well. (Fig. 2.9.) A common problem with setting cord into seams is that it tends to draw up the seam and thereby shorten it. This is to be avoided with special care at the armhole, not only because it will make the sleeve hard to set, but may cause the entire shoulder area of the garment to fit awkwardly.

  Trim the armhole seam to about ³⁄₁₆" (.45 cm) and turn the corded seam in. (Fig. 2.10.)

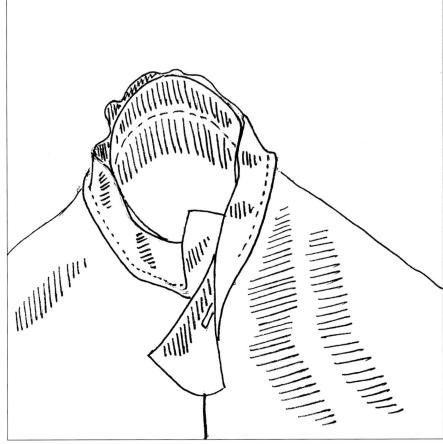

Fig. 2.9. *The lower armhole. The cord itself is trimmed out to reduce bulk where the two ends are lapped.*

Fig. 2.10.
The armhole seam, trimmed to about ³⁄₁₆".

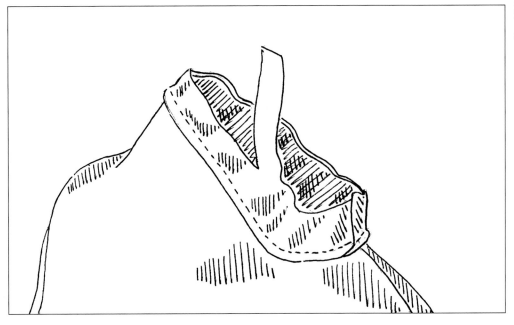

6• MAKE SLEEVES. I took some slight liberties with the shape of the sleeve to get a shape that was easy to sew and to set into the armhole. Cut a pair of sleeves and, optionally, a pair of linings. Three cutting lines are indicated on the pattern diagram; which you use will depend on whether the sleeve is lined separately, lined in one, or unlined.

To make the unlined sleeve, cut at "A" indicated on the pattern. Turn the edges back and hem. The hem can be made wider if it helps your design. For instance, if you trim the sleeve with braid or ruched ribbon, you might want to extend the hem under the trimming to support it.

Fig. 2.11 illustrates the sleeve that is lined "in one." The shell was cut at "A," the lining at "B." This is a good way to deal with a limp or transparent shell fabric. Choose a lining fabric that will not be unsightly when the sleeve falls open in wear. Baste the lining to the sleeve above the hem fold. The hem may be blind stitched through the lining only, to make an invisible hem. Trimming may be added either to the inside, stitched to the hem, or along the edge on the outside.

To make a separate lining, cut shell and lining at "C" on the pattern. Place the sleeve and lining right sides together and stitch at ¼" (.5 cm). (Fig. 2.12.) A bias-covered cord may be placed into the seam if you wish. The cord is basted into place and the seam made on top of it. If you cord the edge, be sure to create a "right" and "left." (Fig. 2.13.)

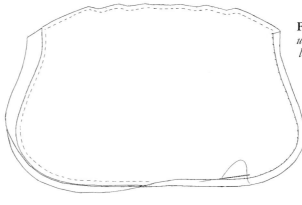

Fig. 2.11. *Hemming the unlined sleeve, or the sleeve lined in one. The illustrated lining is simply omitted for the unlined sleeve.*

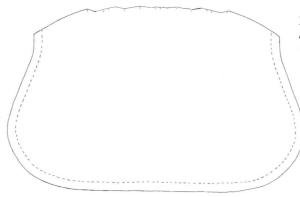

Fig. 2.12. *The shell and the lining are placed right sides together and seamed around. The sleeve is then turned and pressed. The cording described below (at Fig. 2.13) is optional.*

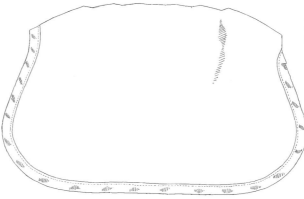

Fig. 2.13. *The sleeve trimmed with cord edging. Cording requires that a left and right be designated. Note that the cording runs into the armhole seam on one side—the front of the sleeve—but is tapered off on the other—the back. The cording is basted to the shell. The sleeve shell is then joined to the lining, using the cording as a guide.*

Fig. 2.14. *The sleeve, with armhole edge made into pleats. If your sleeve is not going to fit comfortably into the armhole, it can be adjusted at the pleats.*

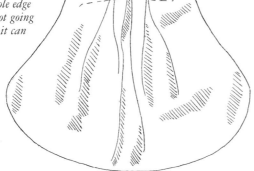

The pagoda sleeve was usually decorated with braid, fringe, ruched ribbon or lace, or some combination.

Pleat the sleeve and baste the pleats in place. (Fig. 2.14.)

7 • SET SLEEVES. To align the sleeve to the armhole, place the center of the sleeve at the shoulder seam. (Fig. 2.15.) Ease the rest of the sleeve in. The open front edge should fall approximately into the deepest part of the front armhole. The front edge of the sleeve should just overlap the back edge. If there is a gap or if the sleeve laps too much, adjust at the pleats. (See below, Fig. 2.17.)

Stitch the sleeve into the armhole by blind stitching behind the cording in the armhole. Inside the bodice, trim the armhole and sleeve seams down to a neat 3/16" (.45 cm) and overcast. If necessary for security, put a running stitch around the armhole from the inside. (Fig. 2.16.) Blind stitch the lapped edges of the sleeves for about 1/2" (1.5 cm). (Fig. 2.17.) The lower end of this seam may be trimmed with a tassel or ribbon rosette.

Fig. 2.15. *Viewed from the back, the sleeve is set into the armhole by aligning the central pleat with the shoulder seam. This should place the open front edge of the sleeve approximately in the deepest corner of the front armhole shape.*

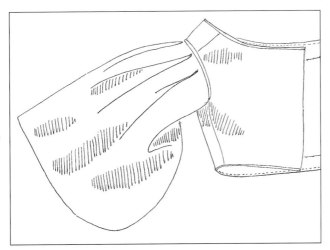

Fig. 2.16. *The inside armhole finish. Trim the armhole seam neatly and overcast. Another seam may be put in from the inside if the sleeve seems insecure.*

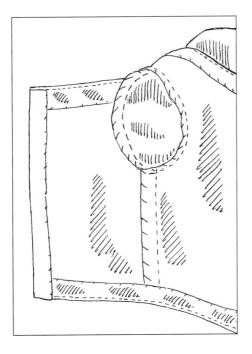

Fig. 2.17. *The sleeve set, viewed from the front. The front sleeve edge is lapped very slightly over the back edge and blind stitched.*

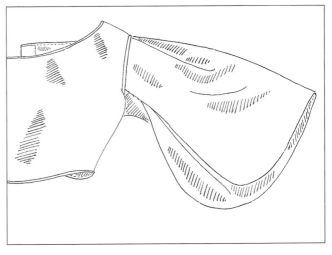

8 • CUT AND SEAM SKIRT; TURN UP HEM. Skirts were very wide in the 1850s, although dolls' dresses often do not express this accurately. If you have the fabric, by all means, use it; however, you may need to skimp a bit, like many Victorian mothers. The skirt may be 5 to 8 times the waist girth; width can also be made up from pieced sections. The skirt should be cut on the straight and crosswise grain of the fabric, and pieced on the straight.

To find the skirt length, measure from the doll's natural waist down her back to the floor over her petticoats. Add about 1½" (4 cm) for a hem and about 1" (2.5 cm) for a waist turn-back. To allow for tucks, figure twice the finished width of each tuck. (For instance, to make three ½" (1.5 cm) tucks, allow 3" or 7.5 cm) If you are cutting from a piece of fabric with a clean selvage, you may use it to finish the opening at the center back. If you have an odd-shaped piece of old fabric, you may also piece the length of the skirt if you are able to hide the joins under tucks, flounces, or other trimmings; however, this requires meticulous planning.

Stitch the center back seam to the bottom of the placket opening. Press the seam open. If you have used selvage edges to finish the seams, you need do nothing else. However, if you have a raw center back seam, double the placket edges back so the opening edge is clean. (Fig. 2.18.)

Turn the hem up conventionally, closing with a small, neat hem stitch. If you are planning to make tucks, be very careful to make an even hem parallel to the folded bottom edge of the skirt, since the hem stitches provide the point of reference for the tucks.

9 • MAKE TUCKS. Because the skirt is a simple rectangle without shaping, tucks are relatively easy to make. The stitches securing the hem should be precisely parallel to the turned-up lower edge of the skirt. Tucks are ineffective if they are not neat. Working from the right side, establish the first tuck. Measure up from the line of hem stitches twice the finished tuck width and then fold the rest of the fabric under the hem. The folded lower edge of the finished tuck will fall at or just above the hem stitches. You can put a neat line of pencil or tailor's chalk along the tuck stitching line, on the underside. (Fig. 2.19.)

When you are satisfied with your markings, make the tuck with a small running stitch. In some kinds of fine handwork, this sort of seam would be made between two threads of the weave of the fabric. Although that degree of precision is not necessary here, if your skirt was cut correctly, its hem and parallel tucks should be more or less on the crosswise straight; your line of running stitches should not be wandering widely back and forth across the weave. Turn the tuck down and press. Repeat for as many tucks as you have planned. (Fig. 2.20; Fig. 2.21.)

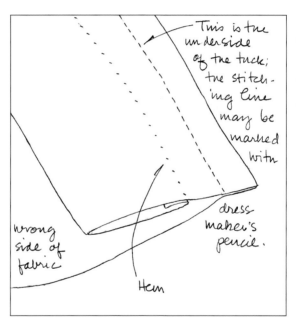

Fig. 2.19. *The first tuck is pressed down; it just clears the hemstitched edge. Above the first tuck, the allowance for the second tuck and the tuck itself with the skirt folded under for stitching.*

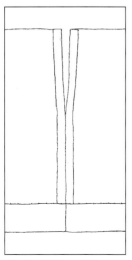

Fig. 2.18. *Hem and center back closure with turn-back placket.*

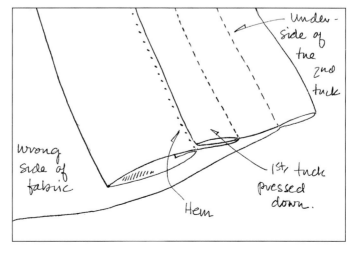

Fig. 2.20. *Tucking the hem of the skirt. Above the hem, the allowance for the first tuck and the tuck itself. The rest of the skirt is folded under as the tuck is sewn.*

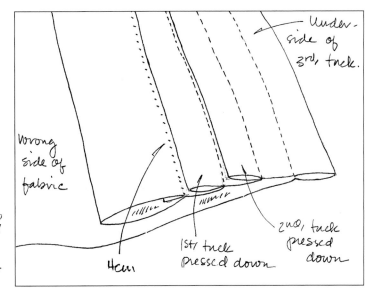

Fig. 2.21.
The first two tucks pressed down and the third arranged for sewing.

10 • SET SKIRT PLEATS. The fullness of the skirt is arranged into double pleats around the waist. Fold the top edge under at the correct length and press it. The raw excess remains as is inside the waist edge. Although most dolls' skirts were cut as simple rectangles, full size skirts of the period often have a deeper turn-back at the waist in front in order to shape the skirt slightly.

Once the length is established, distribute the fullness more or less as illustrated. Divide the skirt and bodice waist evenly into quarters to allocate the fabric. (Ignore the bodice side seam in doing this.) Usually there is a double inverted box pleat at center front and center back. The pleats change direction at the side, forming a double box pleat. The under pleats are offset slightly from the upper pleats to distribute the bulk as smoothly as possible. (Fig. 2.22.) Baste the pleats in place. (Fig. 2.23.)

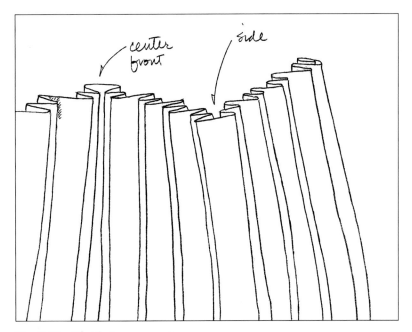

Fig. 2.22. *The pleat arrangement.*

Fig. 2.23. *The skirt. The excess fabric has been trimmed off at the waist edge, and the double pleats are made. The double "box" pleat is placed at the side. A double pleat at the side is used to change the direction of the pleats' opening.*

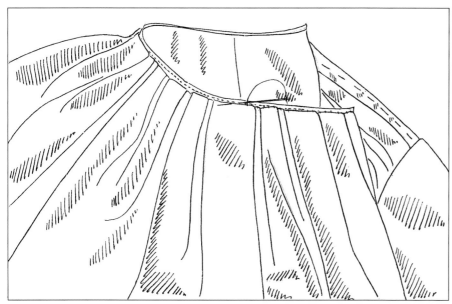

11 • SEW SKIRT TO BODICE. The wrong side of the skirt waist is placed against the wrong side of the bodice waist. Join the two with a close whip stitch taken through the folded upper edge of the pleats and the back side of the bodice cord facing. (Fig. 2.24.) When the dress is opened out, the cording covers the stitches. (Fig. 2.25.)

Fig. 2.24. *Setting the skirt to the bodice. The top of the pleats are whipped to the underside of the cord facing at the waist. The skirt and bodice are aligned wrong sides together.*

Fig. 2.25. *The bodice and skirt joined. When the bodice is turned out again, the cording covers the stitches.*

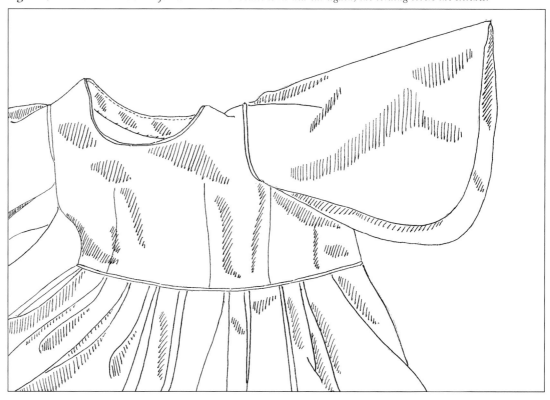

MAKE CLOSURE. On the right, the hooks are set slightly behind the edge of the opening; on the left, the eyes are advanced slightly. This forms the narrow lap for the closure. (Fig. 2.26.)

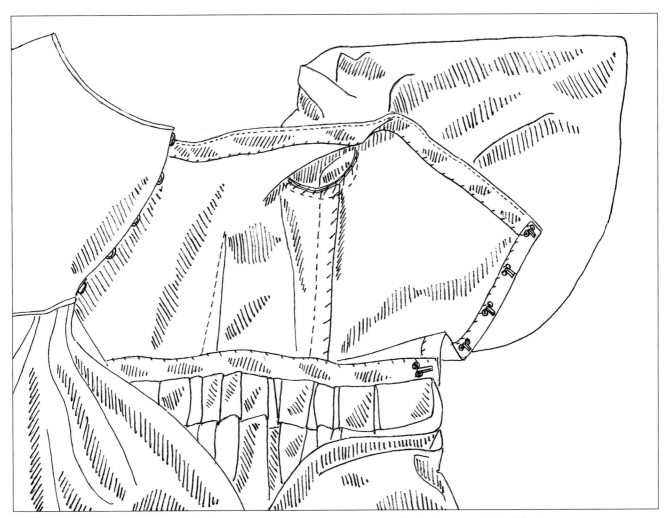

Fig. 2.26. *A view of the inside of the bodice and arrangement of the hooks and eyes. The hooks are set slightly behind the back opening, the eyes advanced slightly, to form a narrow lap.*

Fig. 2.27.
The first strip of embroidery, joined at one edge. The narrow seam is overcast to neaten it.

Fig. 2.28.
The strip is slightly gathered and tied off in the seam.

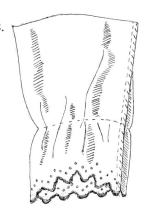

Fig. 2.29.
The second strip of embroidery is placed inside. Its lowermost edge should cover the gathering stitch of the first strip. The two strips are joined with another gathering stitch which is drawn up and tied off.

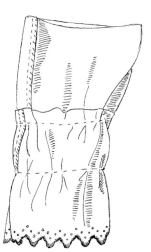

Fig. 2.30.
The sleeve, turned out. The top edge is formed into flat pleats to fit into the armhole of the dress.

Fig. 2.31.
The raw edge is finished with a narrow bias strip, set inside, turned, and closed with a blind stitch. The front of the sleeve is decorated with a bow like a flat rosette.

Fig. 2.32. *The undersleeve, set into the armhole and tacked in place.*

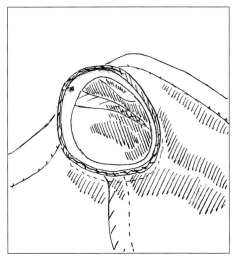

UNDERSLEEVES

12 • To make the loose undersleeves shown in Plate 2.1, you need a short length of embroidered edging. This style can also be made from sturdy lace; a completely sheer or very flimsy lace will be difficult to work with. In an evening style, black lace may be used. The illustrated sleeve was made with edging 4" (10 cm) wide. Two strips were joined to make the required length of the undersleeve inseam. The measurements provided below are based on the pictured example, but this sleeve is quite easy to alter to accommodate the material you have.

Cut four pieces of edging 2 ¾" (7 cm) wide x 6" (15 cm) long. Seam the edge and overcast to neaten it, as illustrated, forming a tube. (Fig. 2.27.) Put a fine gathering stitch into the sleeve about halfway to the elbow. The finished edge is the cuff. Pull the gathering up slightly and tie it off at the seam. The gathering should just fluff the sleeve up a bit. (Fig. 2.28.)

Seam and overcast a second tube, and place it inside the first. The embroidered edge of the upper tube should cover the gathering of the lower tube. Put a second line of gathering into the top edge of the lower tube and through the upper tube, joining them together. Draw up the gathering as you did the first, and tie it off. (Fig. 2.29.) Turn the sleeve right side out.

Measure the armhole of the dress and determine its total finished circumference, i.e., measure the actual armhole, not the pattern. Form a set of pleats in the front of the sleeve (directly opposite the seam) to the determined circumference. (Fig. 2.30.) Bind the top edge with a narrow bias binding. The front of the sleeve may be decorated with a small bow. (Fig. 2.31.) Actual undersleeves of the period are often made plain at the top with a narrow, turned hem. The bound and pleated arrangement makes a much easier insertion into the tiny armhole.

Set the undersleeve into the dress, tacking at the shoulder and side seams to secure the undersleeve in place. The seam of the undersleeve is aligned to the shoulder seam of the dress. (Fig. 2.32.) The bow should fall naturally into the open front of the dress sleeve.

CHAPTER III

Yoke Bodice Day Dress

circa 1855

PATTERN NO. 5

THE dress presented in this chapter is based upon the day dress worn by the standing figure pictured above. (Plate 13.) Also, Plate 5, Plate 9 (right), and Plate 11 (center rear) illustrate similar styles. It is usually a juvenile style, the hem falling at mid- to lower calf. Women who worked in mills and other factories often wore the so-called "infant" bodice with short skirt and short sleeves for comfort, ease of movement, and safety around the machines. A large number of mid-19th century china dolls whose bodies are modeled like mature women are dressed as adolescents. This may indicate that the desired doll would have been a representation of a child and none was available. During the 1850s and 1860s, the trend toward dolls modeled as children was established. In the 1880s, toddler types displaced lady dolls definitively. Lady dolls have never been as popular since. The yoke bodice dress is not inappropriate for a lady, however; where you place the hem is up to you.

This style is useful for a doll who is oddly shaped. Many china dolls who still have their original bodies suffer from this problem, since the heads were frequently sold alone, to be attached to a homemade body. While the dolls themselves are often quite fetching, their strange proportions can offer a challenge to the dressmaker. (The more mature style offered in Chapter IV also addresses this problem.) The yoke bodice can accommodate a peculiar figure without much alteration, since it is cut more loosely than a fitted shoulder; the only place the bodice actually meets the doll's form is at the waist. The loose bodice is also very simply altered for waist length.

MATERIALS

THE most commonly used material for this dress is a printed, even-weave cotton such as calico. Lighter weight materials are also acceptable, but choose a fabric that has good body and is opaque. This type of dress would be a sturdy, washable gown worn at home or at work.

Many authentic-looking printed calicoes are available from vendors who cater to quilters. The typical trim would be contrast appliqué strips and cordings, which can be made in a related cotton print or coordinating solid. Colors were generally strong, even bold, with imaginative use of contrast fabrics for individualistic and creative finishing. The dress in Plate 13 is a fine example of this style. The Wenham Museum owns a fabric doll by Izannah Walker who wears a dress of this type; it is made all in one printed fabric except for the left sleeve, which is of a similar but not identical printed cotton. She was apparently dressed from the scrap bag. This is an option if you have a small amount of authentic fabric.

The dress pictured in Plate 3.1 was made from a print fabric and trimmed with a coordinated stripe (around the skirt, sleeves, and waistband) and a solid (for the cording). Many variations on this theme are possible, bearing in mind that the Victorian sense of color sense was somewhat different than our own. Old quilts can provide clues for working with printed cottons.

The dresses of the 1850s show a lesser use of cording than the 1840s, but, although the seams of the bodice itself were seldom corded, it was used as a decorative detail around the neck and shoulders; the waistband is generally corded as well. Cording can be made from cotton carpet warp or No. 5 pearl cotton. Pearl cotton makes a softer finished seam, but may be more difficult to sew with. Carpet warp is stiffer, and provides a more definitive guide for your needle.

SHELL
Cottons such as calico

LINING
Thin cotton such as old muslin or modern batiste

TRIMMINGS
Coordinating printed or solid fabrics

NOTIONS
Thread to match (cotton)
2 yds. (1.8 m) cording (pearl cotton or carpet warp)
4 shell buttons

SUMMARY OF STEPS
BODICE
1. Trim yoke with cording.
2. Gather bodice.
3. Join bodice to yoke.
4. Insert bodice linings.
5. Insert yoke facing.
6. Finish armholes with cording.
7. Make sleeves.
8. Set sleeves.

SKIRT
9. Assemble skirt.
10. Make waistband and join skirt.

FINISHING
11. Sew skirt to bodice. Make back closure.

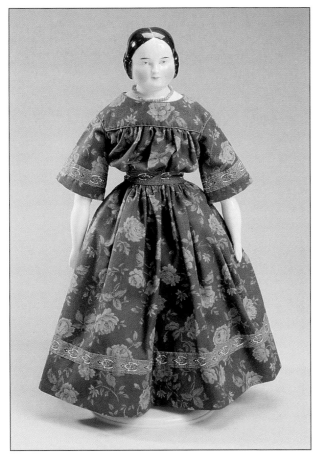

Plate. 3.1. *The yoke bodice day dress, a commonly found 1850s doll costume, although it was typically made at calf length to indicate that the doll was an adolescent. It is easy to fit and may be made from ordinary "washing materials," as they used to be known. The pictured example was made from several reproduction calicoes designed for quilters. The brown and red rose-printed dress is trimmed with appliqué borders cut from a coordinating striped fabric. The cording is a matching solid red. The bodice is half lined and closed with buttons at the center back.*

GENERAL CONSTRUCTION NOTES

Like the wrapper presented in Chapter IV, the very popular yoke bodice dress usually shows the practical handwork of a busy mother. Dresses of this period are often well cut but very quickly put together with minimum fuss over seam finishings and other details.

Unlike the dress bodices of Chapters 1 and 2, only the yoke is fully lined in this day dress. It is useful to have a thin, neutral fabric such as batiste or old muslin for use as bodice linings. Many old dresses have self-facings, but modern calicoes are slightly heavy for this application, although they will work.

The half lining provided for the bodice is a nice feature that I found in a dress some of whose details, however, made me wonder if it was an authentic mid-19th century piece. The doll herself, an attractive lady made of wood, had been repaired and repainted. I offer the bodice lining with this disclaimer: it is entirely optional.

The dress explained below has contrast appliqué trimmings. It can also be trimmed with tucks in the hem of skirt and sleeves, although making tucks on a curved hem (necessary for the sleeve) can be a challenge.

INSTRUCTIONS

1 • TRIM YOKE WITH CORDING. The yoke is trimmed with cord along the front lower edge, and along the neck and back lower edge.

To make the cording, cut two pieces of cord, one 6" (15 cm) long (for the front) and the other 16" (40.5 cm) (for the back and around the neck). Cut two pieces of fabric on the true bias 1 x 6" (2.5 x 15 cm) and 1 x 16" (2.5 x 40.5 cm), respectively. Fold the cord into the bias strips and secure with a neat running stitch. Trim the seam to ¼" (.5 cm) along its length. (Fig. 3.1.)

The cording trimming the front is simply laid in place along the seam edge and stitched down. The back cording must be worked around the angles at the center back. Clip the bias fabric to make the turn, being careful not to clip into the stitches securing the cord. (Fig. 3.2.)

2 • GATHER BODICE. Turn the center back facings and secure with a small hem stitch. (Fig. 3.3.) Both front and back bodice sections are gathered along the yoke and waist edges. Put a line of neat gathering stitches into both seams as indicated on the pattern.

Fig. 3.1. *Construction of bias-covered cord.*

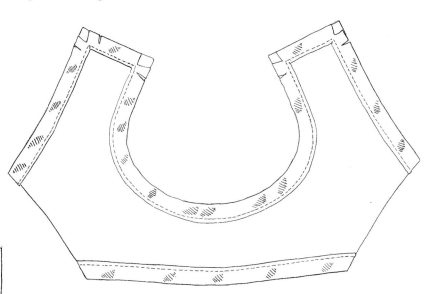

Fig. 3.2. *The yoke with cording stitched around the neckline, center back, and bodice seam edges.*

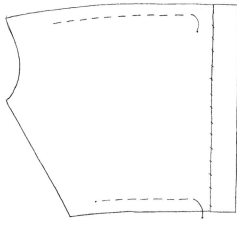

Fig. 3.3. *The center back turn-backs and the placement of the gathering stitches along the yoke and waist edges. The front is gathered in the same manner.*

3 • JOIN BODICE TO YOKE. Draw up the gathering in the yoke seam of the front bodice and stitch the bodice to the yoke through all the layers. (Fig. 3.4.) Turn the seam up toward the yoke. (Fig. 3.5.)

Do likewise with the back bodice pieces, noting that the yoke center back seam projects past the finished bodice center back facings. (Fig. 3.6.) The yoke seams may be reinforced with a blind stitch through the seam next to the cording if it seems necessary.

Stitch the side seams. If you are planning to insert the half bodice lining, press the seams open. If you are omitting it, overcast the side seams and press them toward the back.

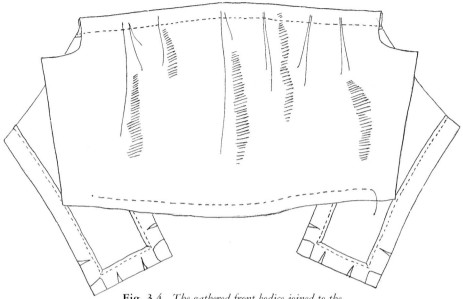

Fig. 3.4. *The gathered front bodice joined to the yoke. The cording provides a guide for stitching.*

Fig. 3.5. *The front bodice, with seam turned up toward the yoke and reinforced with a blind stitch.*

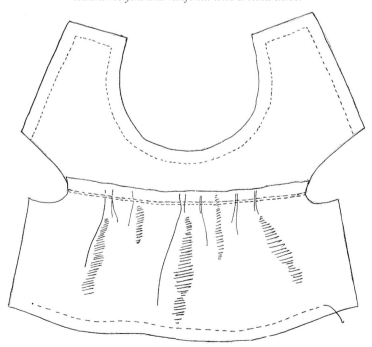

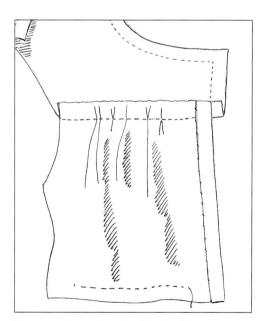

Fig. 3.6. *The gathered back bodice. The center back is finished with a double turn-back and hemmed. The bodice is then joined to the yoke. The seams are turned up toward the yoke. Note the offset at center back; it will be finished by the yoke lining.*

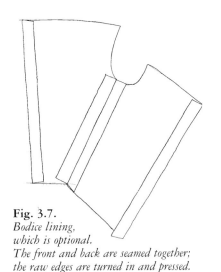

Fig. 3.7.
Bodice lining,
which is optional.
The front and back are seamed together;
the raw edges are turned in and pressed.

4 • INSERT BODICE LININGS (OPTIONAL). Stitch the bodice facing side seams and press them open. Turn the raw front and back edges under ¼" (.5 cm) and press. (Fig. 3.7.)

To insert into the bodice, align the underarm seams and armhole shapes of bodice shell and linings, and baste along the top (yoke) edge. The raw top edge of the linings should conform to the existing bodice seam to the yoke. For the time being, leave the lower edge loose. (Fig. 3.8.)

5 • INSERT YOKE FACING. The following instructions explain how to finish the neckline with a yoke facing stitched to the neck edge and turned inside. The neck edge may also be finished with a cord facing if you prefer. The yoke, in that case, would be finished in one with the shell; the center back, instead of being corded (as follows) would be finished by simply turning the yoke facing and shell edges together.

Press the center back seams of the yoke under at ¼" (.5 cm). Set the yoke facing neck seam to the yoke and stitch along the neck edge only, stopping at the center back opening. The cording provides a guide for your needle. (Fig. 3.9.)

Clip the neck edge to ease the seam, and turn the yoke facing in. Press lightly to make a smooth neck edge. You may reinforce the neck seam with a blind stitch next to the cording if necessary.

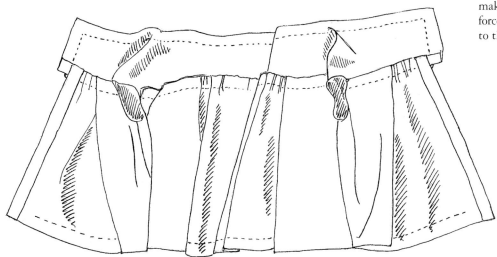

Fig. 3.8. *Setting in the bodice lining. Align each lining piece at the armhole and baste along the yoke edge. The waist edge is left free for the time being.*

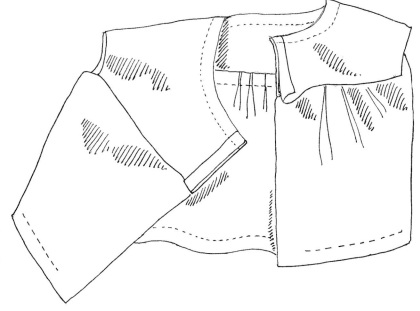

Fig. 3.9. *Yoke facing. Right sides together, stitch the facing to the shell around the neckline, using the cording as a guide. The center back edges are folded back. The neck seams are clipped to ease the turning.*

Tuck the center back edges together and pin. Working your way all around the lower edge of the yoke, tuck the seam under, pinning as you go, to provide a clean finish all around the yoke. The upper edges of the bodice linings (if you have used them) will be enclosed by this operation as well. Be sure as you work your way past the armhole that the yoke shell and facing are net to each other. This will ensure that the sleeve is not difficult to finish. Close the yoke facing seams with a blind stitch from the inside all the way around. (Fig. 3.10.)

6 • FINISH ARMHOLES WITH CORDING. Make two more bias covered cords each 6" (15 cm) long to finish the armholes. Before starting to sew, trim the folded bias down to ¼" (.5 cm), the width of the armhole seam. You should be able to use the width of the cording to ensure that the armhole is sewn at the right diameter. Beginning at the back of the bottom of the armhole, which, in this style, actually falls at the side seam, stitch the cording around the armhole at ¼" (.5 cm). (Fig. 3.11.) Lap and secure at the bottom. Peel the bias fabric open and trim the cording out of the overlap to reduce bulk; trim off any excess fabric as well. (Fig. 3.12.) A common problem with setting cord into seams is that it tends to draw up the seam and thereby shorten it. This is to be avoided with special care at the armhole, not only because it will make the sleeve hard to set, but the entire shoulder area of the garment may fit awkwardly if the armhole is drawn up too small.

Trim the armhole seam down to about ³⁄₁₆" (.45 cm) and turn the corded seam in. Blind stitch in the channel next to the cording to make the seam stay put.

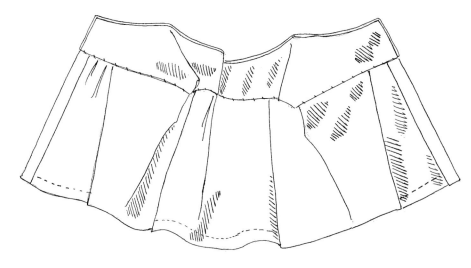

Fig. 3.10. *The yoke facing turned in. The center back and yoke seams are turned in and closed with a blind stitch. This also covers and finishes the yoke edge of the bodice lining.*

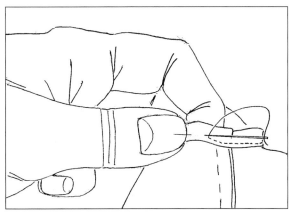

Fig. 3.11. *The armhole, with cording.*

Fig. 3.12. *Opening the cording to trim out excess cord.*

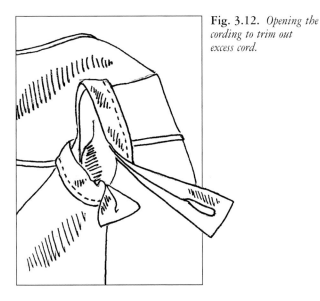

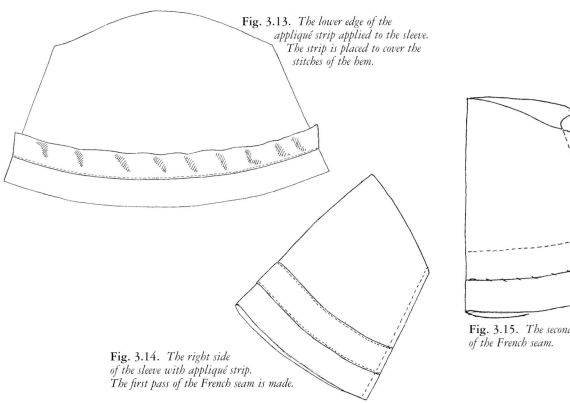

Fig. 3.13. *The lower edge of the appliqué strip applied to the sleeve. The strip is placed to cover the stitches of the hem.*

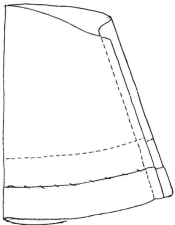

Fig. 3.15. *The second pass of the French seam.*

Fig. 3.14. *The right side of the sleeve with appliqué strip. The first pass of the French seam is made.*

7 • MAKE SLEEVES. In assessing the pattern's fit to your doll, you should have determined whether these half sleeves are an appropriate length. Authentic dresses from the period do not necessarily cover the junction of china to cloth or leather on dolls of this type, but you should not neglect to check this out before starting to sew. The sleeve inseam is ¼" (.5 cm) and is joined with a French seam requiring two passes. If you need more than ¼" (.5 cm) for a French seam (and you may, since the seam contains the edges of the contrast strip of trimming within it), you may add a small amount to each sleeve seam. Add as little as possible; if you find as you sew that you don't need it, trim it away. Additionally, the sleeve must be lengthened if you are planning to add tucks.

Finish the lower edge of the sleeves with a double turn-back and small hemstitch. Or, cut the sleeve to the correct length and finish the lower edge with a bias binding in the contrast color you have chosen. (See Plate 13.)

Apply appliqué trim, if any. There are two approaches to the trimming. One is to cut from a contrast fabric with all-over pattern (or plain fabric). Trim of this type may be cut on the bias, which will make it very simple to apply either to the skirt or sleeve. The very shallow curve of the sleeve hem will not present any difficulty. However, if you are picking out a stripe, as was done with the dress illustrated in this chapter, you will be cutting your contrast on the straight. The skirt hem is easily accommodated, since it too is cut on the straight. However, a stripe must be eased rather carefully onto the sleeve hem to avoid puckering and pulling. On the pictured example (Plate 3.1), the lower edge of the contrast stripe was placed to cover the hem stitching.

Prepare the strip by folding back its long edges and pressing firmly to make a clean edge for stitching. Determine the placement on the sleeve, and begin by stitching the lower edge of the strip with a very small running stitch placed very close to the fold. The lower edge is the longer edge and must be dealt with first. (Fig. 3.13.) When you are done, the strip will be slightly rippled along the upper length, and should protrude a bit over the edges at the side seam. Trim off as much as possible at the seam, to reduce the amount you must deal with. Pin out the upper edge of the strip, distributing the fullness as evenly as possible. Stitch with a small running stitch into the edge of the strip, easing the excess toward the needle as you go. The sleeve will naturally drape itself over your hand as you sew, and this too will help, since the upper side (the strip) will present you with a slightly longer edge than the under side (the sleeve). As you work, use your thumb to push the strip slightly toward the needle. When you are finished, press out any remaining bubbles.

Sew the sleeve seam with a French seam. (Fig. 3.14.) The first pass is made with wrong sides together. Stitch with a small running stitch, trim off any ravelled bits, and turn the sleeve. Make the second pass, taking care to enclose the raw edges completely. (Fig. 3.15.)

8 • **SET SLEEVES.** Fold the armhole in half to determine its "natural" fall. The sleeve seam goes to the bottom of the armhole. The head of the sleeve is distributed evenly around the armhole. If you find you have excess length in the sleeve, ease it in. The notch on the pattern indicates the approximate top of the armhole.

Set the sleeve with a blind stitch in the channel behind the cording of the armhole. (Fig. 3.16.) When the seam is completed, turn the armhole out, trim the seam to about ³⁄₁₆" (.45 cm), and overcast to neaten it. You may reinforce the sleeve set with a small running stitch around the inside. (Fig. 3.17.)

9 • **ASSEMBLE SKIRT.** The skirt is cut from measurements taken from your doll over her petticoats and other undergarments. For width, allow about 6 times the finished waist girth. Selvages may be used to finish the center back seam. The skirt may be pieced on the straight as necessary. For length, determine where you want the hem to fall by measuring down the back of your doll from her natural waist. As previously discussed, the hem may finish anywhere from mid-calf to the floor. If you are using a piece of old fabric and need to economize, length is one way to do it. You may also use a false hem that is pieced, if necessary. (See Chapter I for false hems.) Skirts may be pieced on the straight for width. They may also be pieced for length, provided the seams are hidden under lines of trim or tucking. To the length measurement, add a ¼" (.5 cm) seam allowance at the top and a hem allowance at the bottom; 2" (5 cm) provides for a comfortable hem. You must also add length for any tucks. (Tucks are covered in Chapter II.)

Turn the hem and close with a small hem stitch. Press. Apply contrast trim, if any, now.

If you have used the selvages of the fabric to form the center back facings, turn them back about ¼" (.5 cm) and press at the top only. If you have raw back edges, make a double turn-back to present a clean finish at the placket and press. (Fig. 3.18.)

Put two parallel lines of gathering into the waist seam of the skirt. The backs and front should be gathered separately to allow more control over the fullness in setting the waistband.

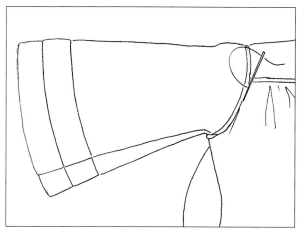

Fig. 3.16. *The sleeve, blind stitched into the armhole.*

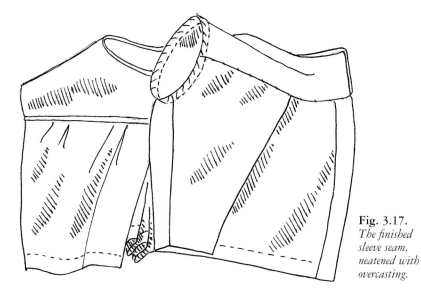

Fig. 3.17. *The finished sleeve seam, neatened with overcasting.*

Fig. 3.18. *Interior and exterior view of the skirt back, showing placement of the hem, the appliqué strip of trim, and the turn-back at center back to form the placket for the closure.*

Fig. 3.19. *The waistband. The edges are trimmed with bias-covered cord.*

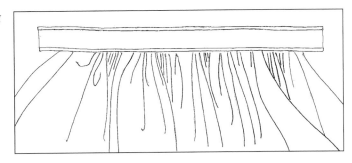

Fig. 3.20. *Setting the skirt to the waistband. It is blind stitched from the outside through the waistband into the gathering.*

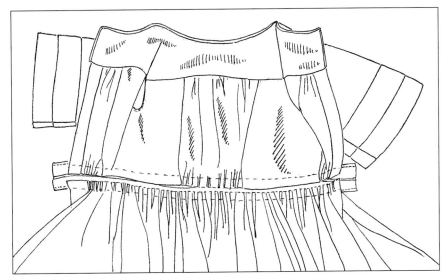

Fig. 3.21. *The arrangement of the inside of the dress. Bodice and skirt are joined to the waistband, which may be left raw. The ends will be tucked under to finish. The bodice lining is arranged over the gathered bodice waist and tacked down with a running stitch.*

Fig. 3.22. *The finished dress with back closure.*

10 • MAKE WAISTBAND AND JOIN SKIRT. The illustrated dress has a waistband cut from the same contrast strip used to trim the sleeves and skirt. Cut the waistband by measuring your doll over her petticoats; add 1" (2.5 cm) for two turn-backs (at center back), ½" (1.5 cm) to lap over, and about ¼" (.5 cm) for ease (to accommodate the bulk of the gathers and cording). The width of the pictured waistband is ½" (1.5 cm), determined by picking a stripe that looked proportionate on the doll (who is 17½" or 44.5 cm tall). Two ¼" (.5 cm) seams were added, for a total width 1" (2.5 cm). The waistband should be cut on the straight.

Make two pieces of bias-covered cord, and stitch them to the edges of the waistband. (Fig. 3.19.) Turn the seams under and press.

Gather up the skirt and set to the waistband, distributing the fullness evenly to the edges of the turn-backs. In gathering the skirt, arrange the gathers into a neat line; don't allow them to get bunched up. The gathering should look like a set of tiny pleats. Blind stitch the skirt to the waistband, placing the stitches into the edge of the waistband behind the cording. (Fig. 3.20.)

11 • SEW SKIRT TO BODICE. Make back closure. Place first the skirt and then the bodice on the doll and pin them closed. Mark the waistband with a pin where the bodice side seams fall correctly. After removing them from the doll, draw up the bodice gathers and set the bodice to the waistband with a blind stitch behind the cording. Catch the bodice lining (if any) down to the waistband, allowing the lining to fall naturally into place.

Tuck in the center back edges of the waistband and secure with blind stitches inside. (Fig. 3.21.) Most dresses of this type are left raw at the waist. If you wish to cover the inside of the waistband, however, cut another waistband shape and blind stitch it over the work inside.

The dress is closed at center back with a set of buttons and buttonholes. (Fig. 3.22.) See Appendix A for how to work a buttonhole.

CHAPTER IV

Wrapper

circa 1860

PATTERN NOS. 6 AND 7

THE dress presented in this chapter is based on the wrapper shown above. (Plate 17.) This stylish but comfortable dress would have been worn at home. It is an important transitional style. The skirt is quite full but is gored and has a shaped hem. The design hints at the highly structured styles of the late 1860s through the 1890s.

The wrapper has the distinctive mid-19th century coat sleeve, which springs like a question mark from the armhole. Unlike the modern coat sleeve, the sleeves of the 1850s and 1860s were made in two nearly equal pieces and were nearly flat. Fullness in the head of the sleeve was concentrated into a pleat under the arm, probably the last place a modern dressmaker would put it. [☛ The modern coat sleeve is generally drafted with a wide top sleeve and narrow undersleeve; when finished the sleeve is usually very carefully pressed to form a curved cylinder. The fullness of the modern sleeve is concentrated around the head, so that the sleeve hangs naturally, like the arm.] Pattern No. 7 is a basic, two-piece coat sleeve, the fundamental sleeve for ladies' day wear in the third quarter of the 19th century. (Pattern No. 7 is also used for bodices in Chapters V, VI, and VII.)

111

⤝MATERIALS⤞

SMOOTH-SURFACED, even-weave fabrics such as calico and wool challis are appropriate for the wrapper. The 1850s and 1860s saw a return to favor of smart printed cottons. Cotton was especially appropriate for wrappers and home dresses, since it was a "washing material" that would stand hard wear. Typical trims are plain, sturdy cotton braids of various types, or tape. Machine-made lace was becoming less expensive in the mid-1850s, and dolls' dresses often have a prim frill at the throat and wrists. Closures are generally ordinary pearl buttons and functional buttonholes. Favorite colors for dolls' dresses were blue, red, brown, and white. Intricate prints in deep colors were popular. The wrapper made of cotton may also be trimmed with contrast strips of fabric. (See Chapter III.)

Cording was used at this time to trim neckline and shoulder details; waistbands were often corded as well. Cotton carpet warp or No. 5 pearl cotton may be used to make dolls' scale cording. Pearl cotton makes a softer finished seam, but may be difficult to sew with. Carpet warp will make a stiffer finished seam, but because of its stiffness is easier to insert into seams and provides a more definitive guide for your needle.

WRAPPER
Printed calico or other plain surface cotton

Wool challis, plain or with small pattern

NOTIONS
Thread to match (cotton or silk)

1½ yds. (1.35 m) cording (pearl cotton or carpet warp)

Buttons, 8 pearl or shell buttons

Hooks as necessary

TRIMMINGS
Braid

Cotton tape, either plain or with contrast embroidery

Narrow lace

Coordinating fabric for applied bands of trim for the wrapper

⤝SUMMARY OF STEPS⤞
BODICE
1. Turn front facings; stitch shoulder seams.
2. Finish neck edge.
3. Close side seams.
4. Assemble sleeves.
5. Set sleeves.

SKIRT
6. Make waistband.
7. Assemble skirt.
8. Sew skirt to waistband.

FINISHING
9. Sew skirt to bodice; make front closure.

GENERAL ⤝CONSTRUCTION⤞ NOTES

IN general, as the "china doll period" progressed, the dolls became more affordable to more people. A great many dolls from the mid-19th century survive and their clothes exhibit a wide variety of sewing styles. China dolls are often oddly shaped, since the heads were frequently bought to be put on a homemade body. A very large number of china dolls wear sturdy, home-made outfits that well illustrate the sewing skills of mid-Victorian homemakers. The sewing does not necessarily evidence sophisticated dressmaker techniques. The clothes of mid-century china dolls often have a plain, no-frills charm, an almost primitive quality, which is enduringly appealing. The wrapper illustrated in this chapter falls at the end of this period.

Home dresses like the wrapper are typically unlined or partially lined. Dolls' clothes often have raw work left inside while the outside presents an attractive finished appearance. Less cording was used in finishing dresses. The wrapper in Plate 17 is a good example: it is a very well-cut garment, put together in a sturdy, slightly rough sewing style.

⤝INSTRUCTIONS⤞

☞ Both the original wrapper and the copy are lapped left over right to close the bodice. This is an idiosyncrasy of this garment. If you wish to make a conventional closure, you need only reverse some of the directions.

1 • TURN FRONT FACINGS; STITCH SHOULDER SEAMS. After cutting the bodice parts, put a fine gathering stitch into the waist edges of the bodice as marked on the pattern. This will distribute the fullness properly onto the waistband.

Turn the front edges back with a double fold and secure them with a small hem stitch. (Fig. 4.1.) Stitch the shoulder seams with a neat running stitch; ¼" (.5 cm) is allowed for seaming. Overcast the edges to neaten them, and press toward the back. (Fig. 4.2.)

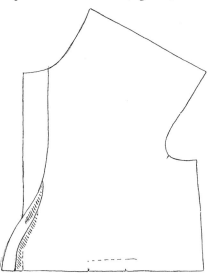

Fig. 4.1. *The bodice, with turned-back center front.*

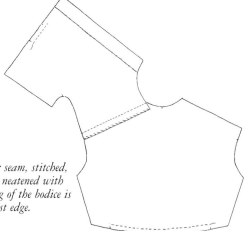

Fig. 4.2. *The shoulder seam, stitched, pressed to the back, and neatened with overcasting. The shaping of the bodice is with gathers at the waist edge.*

2 **•** **FINISH NECK EDGE.** The neck hole is finished with a cord facing. To prepare the neck seam for finishing, put a basting stitch around the neckline at ¼" (.5 cm). This is a guide for the cord facing. To make a cord facing, measure around the neck edge at the basting line and cut a piece of cord at that length. Cut a piece of bias fabric 1" (2.5 cm) wide and slightly longer than the cord. The wrapper is made with self-fabric cording; a dressier garment of challis might be trimmed with self-colored silk taffeta. Enclose the cord in the bias fabric, tucking the short ends in and turning down one edge about ¼" (.5 cm). Stitch the cord into the fold with a small running stitch. Fold up the opposite edge so the two raw edges meet. Baste. (Fig. 4.3.)

Place the raw side of the cording against the right side of the neck edge. The cord itself runs along the basted line. (Fig. 4.4.) Stitch the cord facing in place through and through. Turn the cord facing inside the neck. Clip the neck seam if necessary to ease it. Blind stitch the facing to close. If the bodice is lined, the blind stitch may go through the lining only, invisible from the outside. (Fig. 4.5.)

The neck edge may be trimmed with a frill of lace. Cut the lace about twice the finished neck circumference. Stitch to the back side of the cording all around, drawing the lace into loose pleats as you go. Note that at the front edge, the lace is drawn around the corner at center front. The lace more or less surrounds the top button when the bodice is buttoned up. This is done by fulling the lace around the corner and drawing the turned-back leading edge of lace down against the front of the dress. (The lace is drawn around the *buttonhole* side.) (Fig. 4.6.)

☛ If you have a lightweight, flexible trim such as the tape decorating the original garment in Plate 17, you can put it around the neck and front of the dress. That should be done now, before the bodice is fully assembled.

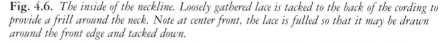

Fig. 4.3. *Cord facing. The cord is cut to measure around the neck seam and covered with fabric.*

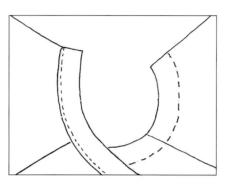

Fig. 4.4. *The neck seam. The basted line at 1/4" (.5 cm) is a guide for the cording. The wrong side of the cording is set to the right side of the bodice and turned in. The bodice neck may be clipped as necessary to ease the cording seam.*

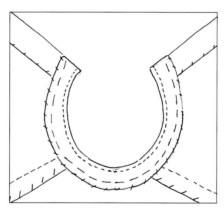

Fig. 4.5. *The finished inside of the neck. The cord facing is blind stitched to close.*

Fig. 4.6. *The inside of the neckline. Loosely gathered lace is tacked to the back of the cording to provide a frill around the neck. Note at center front, the lace is fulled so that it may be drawn around the front edge and tacked down.*

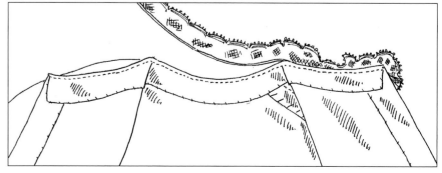

3 • **CLOSE SIDE SEAMS.** Close the side seams with a neat running stitch, overcast, and press to the back. (Fig. 4.7.)

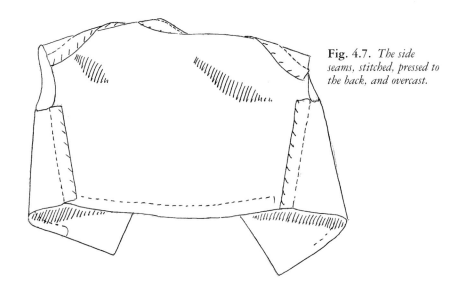

Fig. 4.7. *The side seams, stitched, pressed to the back, and overcast.*

4 • **ASSEMBLE SLEEVES.** Right sides together, stitch the inseam and outseam of the sleeve. Overcast, and turn the seams toward the undersleeve. Turn up the hem and stitch with a small hem stitch. This should also secure the seams in place. (Fig. 4.8.) Or, you may hem with a cord facing. (See the sleeve hems explained in Chapter I.) This is especially effective if you are using a contrast cording of some type. Turn the sleeve out and steam, but don't crush the sleeve; the coat sleeves are nearly flat. Make sure the seams are fully turned so the resulting shape is a smooth curve. The hem may be trimmed with a frill of lace sewn to the turned hem or stitched behind the cording.

☛ If you are trimming the cuff of the sleeve like the original dress in Plate 17, you should do that before the sleeve is fully assembled. The easiest way to handle tape or braid cuff trim is to stitch the inseam of the sleeve, overcast as usual, and then spread the sleeve flat. Turn the seam toward the undersleeve. Stitch on the tape or braid, running the ends into the outseam, which will fall toward the back of the garment; the join will be inconspicuous there. Finish the sleeve as usual.

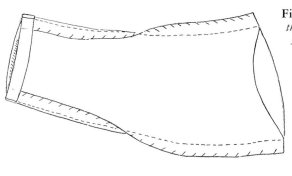

Fig. 4.8. *The construction of the coat sleeve. The seams are sewn and overcast. They should both be inclined to the underside of the sleeve and tacked down as the sleeve is hemmed. The hem may optionally be finished with cord facing instead of a hem.*

5 • **SET SLEEVES.** Make two bias-covered cords each 6" (15 cm) long to finish the armholes. Before starting to sew, trim the seam on the folded bias down to ¼" (.5 cm), the width of the armhole seam. (Fig. 4.9.) You will be able to use the width of the cording to ensure that the armhole is sewn at the right diameter. Beginning at the bottom of the armhole, stitch the cording around the armhole at ¼" (.5 cm). (Fig. 4.10.) Lap and secure at the bottom. Peel the bias fabric open and trim the cording out of the overlap to reduce bulk; trim off any excess fabric as well. (Fig. 4.11.) A common problem with setting cord into seams is that it tends to draw up the seam and thereby shorten it. This is to be avoided with special care at the armhole, not only because it will make the sleeve hard to set, but the entire shoulder area of the garment may fit awkwardly if the armhole is drawn up too small. Trim the armhole seam to about ³⁄₁₆" (.45 cm) and turn the corded seam in.

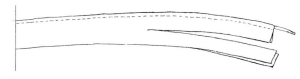

Fig. 4.9. *The arrangement of the cording.*

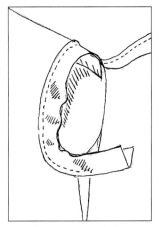

Fig. 4.10. *The armhole seam, finished with cording.*

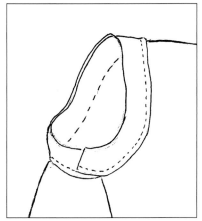

Fig. 4.11. *The finished armhole seam. The cord is trimmed from the ends of the cord and they are neatly lapped.*

The seams of the sleeve are aligned with notches on the armhole. The outseam aligns with the notch behind the shoulder; the inseam goes to the notch deep in the front armhole. (Fig. 4.12.) There is a small amount of excess in the sleeve: form it into a small, forward-opening pleat at the bottom of the armhole. (Fig. 4.13.) Working from the right side, blind stitch the sleeve in place, putting the stitches in the channel behind the cording.

Turn the bodice out and reinforce the sleeve with a running stitch around the inside. Trim the seam and overcast to neaten it. (Fig. 4.14.)

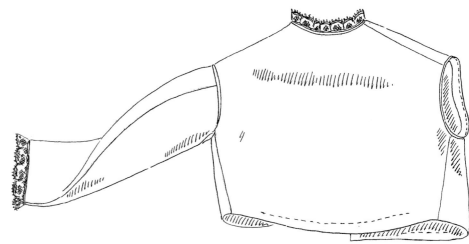

Fig. 4.12. *The sleeve set. The sleeve outseam is aligned with the notch on the back shoulder. The inseam is aligned with the notch in front.*

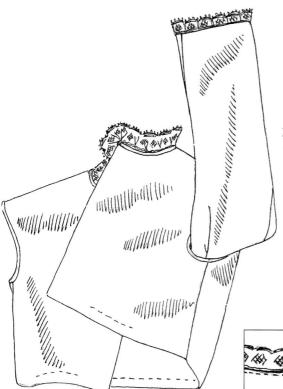

Fig. 4.13. *The sleeve set. Fullness in the sleeve has been made into a small pleat under the arm.*

Fig. 4.14. *The finished armhole. The seam is trimmed and overcast.*

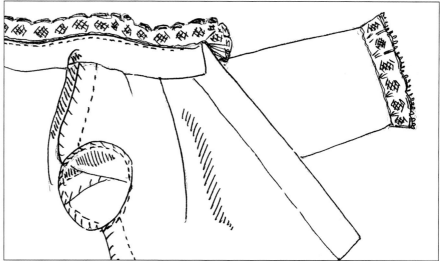

6 • MAKE WAISTBAND. Before cutting the waistband, measure the doll's waist over her petticoats; add 1" (2.5 cm) for two turn-back allowances and about ¼" (.5 cm) to accommodate the bulk of the gathering. Make two pieces of bias-covered cord and stitch them to the edges of the waistband. Turn the seams under and press lightly. (Fig. 4.15.)

Fig. 4.15. *The waistband, finished with cording.*

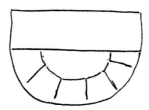

Fig. 4.16. *Construction of the pocket. The seams are turned in and pressed. If you have chosen a lightweight trimming (like the thin cotton tape of the original dress) you can trim the pocket; a pocket is better left plain than stiffened with heavy trimming, however.*

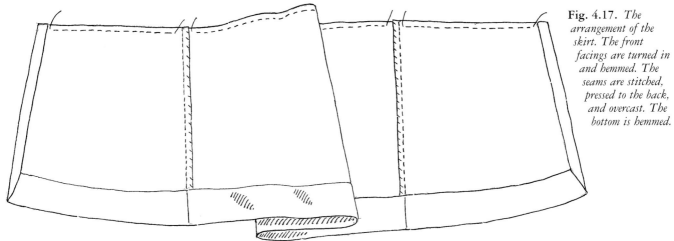

Fig. 4.17. *The arrangement of the skirt. The front facings are turned in and hemmed. The seams are stitched, pressed to the back, and overcast. The bottom is hemmed.*

7 • ASSEMBLE SKIRT. Patch pockets may be put onto the skirt as indicated on the pattern. Cut two pockets, turn the edges under and baste. (Fig. 4.16.) Press. If you are trimming with a narrow flexible braid or tape, you may outline the shape of the pocket with trim. Refer to Plate 17. The pocket is then blind stitched along its outer curve to the skirt, as indicated on the pattern.

Turn the front edges of the skirt under with a double fold as noted on the pattern. Join the side seams, overcast, and press them toward the back. Turn up the hem and close with a small hem stitch. (Fig. 4.17.)

☛ A line of braid may be set along the hem as a trim. The braid illustrated in Plate 4.1 was made from cotton carpet warp. When completed, it was slightly stiff and was much too heavy for use on the sleeves, bodice, or pocket. However, it is a commonly found trimming of the time. (See Plate 13 and Plate 8; both dresses are trimmed with handmade braid.) To make the braid, six strands of carpet warp were braided up in the conventional way; care was taken that the braid be flat, i.e., all the strands laid parallel to each other rather than forming a rope-like cord. If your braid is recalcitrant, pin it out on your ironing board and use steam to set it. Sew the braid in place, using a small blind stitch through the center of the braid. At the front of the skirt, the braid is lapped around and sewn off. (Fig. 4.18.)

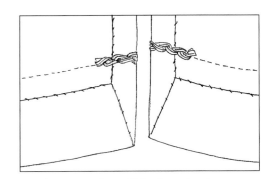

Fig. 4.18. *Finishing off the skirt trimming. This example was trimmed with braided cotton carpet warp.*

Plate 4.1. *An unlined cotton wrapper made of a modern reproduction calico. The dress is trimmed with self-fabric cording, braided cotton carpet warp, and lace, and closed with pearl buttons.*

8 • SEW SKIRT TO WAISTBAND. Put two parallel rows of gathering stitches into the waist edge of the skirt and draw it up. Set the skirt to the waistband, distributing the fullness evenly. Be sure to arrange the gathers, which are quite close, in a neat row. Blind stitch the skirt to the waistband, placing the stitches in the channel between the turned edge of the waistband and the cording. (Fig. 4.19.) Reinforce from the inside with a second row of stitches if necessary.

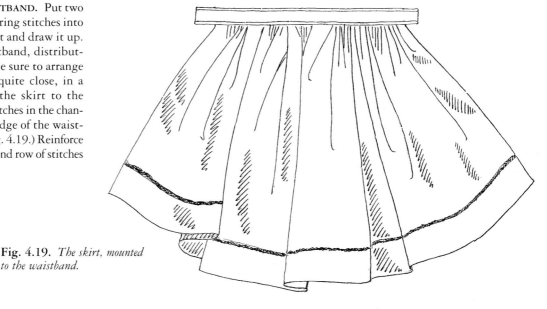

Fig. 4.19. *The skirt, mounted to the waistband.*

9 • **SEW SKIRT TO BODICE; MAKE FRONT CLOSURE.** Put the skirt and bodice on the doll and pin them closed. The skirt side seams should fall more or less at the doll's side. Arrange the bodice fullness, noting from the pattern where the bodice side seam should fall, approximately. On this semi-fitted bodice, the bodice side seams are set back slightly on the body. Blind stitch the bodice to the waistband in the same manner as the skirt, reinforcing as necessary with a second line of stitches inside. (Fig. 4.20.)

Tuck the front edges of the waistband inside to finish. Most of the examples of this type of dress I have examined were left raw around the waist. If you follow this method, make a double tuck at the front to finish the opening cleanly and blind stitch. If you want to make a clean finish inside the waistband, the work can be covered with a strip of fabric. It is simply blind stitched in place inside.

Mark the front for buttonholes. The original dress has functional buttonholes only from the neck to the waistband. Below the waistband are two buttons sewn to the overlapped edge only; below them are several more sewn through and through, as though the skirt were buttoned. (Fig. 4.21.) Real buttons and buttonholes are the typical closure for a cotton dress. A woolen or silk dress might have decorative buttonholes with hooks and loops set underneath.

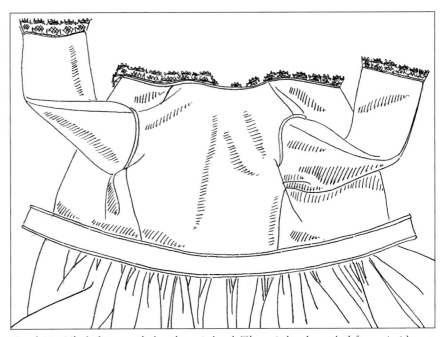

Fig. 4.20. *The bodice, attached to the waistband. The waistband may be left raw inside.*

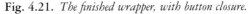

Fig. 4.21. *The finished wrapper, with button closure.*

CHAPTER V

Walking Costume

circa 1865

PATTERN NOS. 7, 8, AND 9

THE ensemble presented in this chapter is based upon the walking costume shown at right. (Plate 21.)

In the early 1860s, the line of ladies' clothes changed definitively. The crinoline, which had gradually been assuming a more elliptical shape that threw the bulk of the skirt to the back, became triangular rather than dome-shaped. Skirts were cut with carefully shaped gores to cover the geometric shape smoothly. At the same time, bodice styles eschewed the frills of the 1850s, and dresses presented a slightly severe and very structured appearance for a short time before reverting to a draped style with the advent of the true bustle or "tournure."

Plate 5.1. *Walking "costume," c.1865. This copy of the original dress shown in Plate 21 is a crisp plum, light blue, and black even-weave silk from an old kimono. The loosely woven cotton kimono lining has been used to line the costume. This dress is made entirely from antique materials, including the buttons, lace, and small, faceted jet beads.*

⇒ MATERIALS ⇐

DURING the 1860s, "costume" was the name given to an ensemble of distinctly separate pieces made up in the same fabric. The green satin-striped silk costume in Plate 21 is very well cut and strikingly illustrates the smart military motifs that were fashionable during this period. The trimming of lace and faceted beads not only accents the cuffs and hem, but forms a pair of feminine shoulder boards.

The walking costume requires a thin, crisp fabric, to accommodate the pleats in the skirt neatly and still maintain its shape. Silks such as taffeta are appropriate, as well as woolens with a smooth, tight weave, and stout, woven-pattern cotton fabrics such as pique or faille for summer styles. Most silks and woolens should be fully lined. Whether to line the skirt is a design judgment. If the fabric is crisp, choose a lightweight, loosely woven lining that will add richness to the hand when the lining and shell are joined together. For a softer shell fabric, choose a thin, crisp lining that will help support it. A petticoat made from the skirt pattern in thin, crisp cotton is also appropriate and may be necessary for support. The original garment is supported by a miniature wire crinoline. An unlined cotton or woolen skirt will need a petticoat. Although summer jackets, often designed to be worn open over a coordinating bodice, were frequently unlined, it may be wise for neatness' sake to line a cotton jacket with a light fabric such as batiste.

Trimmings were smart rather than frilly at this period. Silk and woolen costumes may be trimmed with braid or ruched and pleated ribbon as well as the illustrated beaded lace. The original jacket is trimmed with a double-edged lace, which can be duplicated with a more conventional lace by lapping the straight edges very slightly and stitching them together with the line

of beads. The metallic braid pictured in Plate 30 is associated with a slightly later period, but can be used in a pinch by non-purists. For some reason, it is one of the period trimmings most frequently available from antiques dealers (at least at this writing). Cottons may be trimmed with tape or decorative cord.

There are still old beads to be had inexpensively, and they trim a garment very elegantly, providing not only color and richness, but textural interest as well. In addition to jet, that late Victorian favorite, faceted iridescent metallics like bronze and gun-metal were popular, as well as pearlescents and clear glass.

SHELL
Crisp silks such as taffeta or light-weight satin

Old jacquard, satin-striped or other woven-pattern silks

Thin, stable woolens such as broadcloth or challis (should be lined)

Woven-pattern cotton fabrics such as pique or faille

LINING
Thin cottons such as old muslin or batiste

Stiff woven interfacing or similar fabric to finish skirt hem

TRIMMINGS
Lace

Tape

Ruched or pleated ribbon

Old faceted beads

NOTIONS
Thread to match

10 hooks (skirt and jacket, 5 each)

5 metal loops (skirt)

5 shank buttons (jacket)

⇒ SUMMARY OF STEPS ⇐
SKIRT
1. Baste lining to shell.
2. Join center back section to left side back gore; finish placket.
3. Make hem.
4. Turn down waist edge and gather up back gore into pleats.
5. Set waistband.
6. Make closure.

BODICE
7. Baste lining to shell.
8. Make dart and front turn-back.
9. Join back sections.
10. Join shoulders and finish neck edge.
11. Join side seams.
12. Finish hem.
13. Make and set sleeves.
14. Make closure.

GENERAL
✠CONSTRUCTION✠
NOTES

THE green ensemble pictured in Plate 21 was assembled very roughly. Doll clothes are frequently found in this style, fashionably cut and stylishly trimmed but assembled with little fuss over the finishing details. One of the giveaways of reproduction clothing is that it is "too neat," but, bearing that in mind, you may still opt to finish your costume a bit more neatly than this particular example. I have compromised, finishing the inside of the jacket with overcasting but not the skirt, as the petticoat hides the inside of the skirt anyway.

If you have a stout silk similar to the original satin-striped taffeta, you may not need to line. However, the lining is very simple if it is needed; it is basted to each piece and sewn as one with the shell. Depending upon your fabric, you may opt to line the body of the jacket, but not the sleeves.

The coat sleeve of the period is drafted in two nearly equal parts for the top and undersleeve. Fullness at the head of the sleeve is accommodated by easing around the top; however, the undersleeve is formed into a small pleat at the bottom of the armhole to handle fullness there. The characteristic shape of the sleeve is full but flat; this is very noticeable in photographs of men in Civil War uniform, in which the coat appears to a modern observer to be too tightly fitted to the body while the sleeve is wide, flat, and baggy.

You may note in passing the slightly odd shape of the gores. The hem edges of the side gores meet at a down-sloping angle, since skirts through the bustle period were often made with trains, even for day wear, and are therefore substantially longer at the back than the front. (Compare, for example, pattern No. 8, the Edwardian five-gore skirt, shaped somewhat similarly, but cut at a comfortable walking length.) To protect the trailing hem from excessive wear and help hold it out, skirts with trains were often provided with dust ruffles.

By the 1860s, many women owned sewing machines. The green walking costume, as it happens, is entirely sewn by hand; however, examples of machine-sewn clothing from the period are common. Any seam that your machine can handle may therefore be closed by machine. The sleeve set and neckline finish, because of their size and shape, are best done by hand.

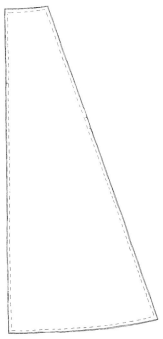

Fig. 5.1. *Skirt lining and shell, joined with basting around the edges.*

✠INSTRUCTIONS✠
Skirt
PATTERN NO. 8.

1 • BASTE LINING TO SHELL. The lining, if any, is cut exactly like the shell and basted together in the seams. (Fig. 5.1.)

☛ The placket is allowed on the left side only, and trimmed off on the right. (Don't worry if you do this backwards, i.e., set the placket onto the right instead of the left; the completed placket is completely hidden by the pleats and jacket tails.)

2 • JOIN CENTER BACK SECTION TO LEFT SIDE BACK GORE; FINISH PLACKET. Stitch from the hem into the placket about ¼" (.5 cm). (Fig. 5.2.) Press the seam open. Tuck the edges of the placket under and secure with a small hem or blind stitch. (Fig. 5.3.)

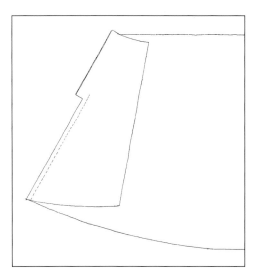

Fig. 5.2. *The left side back gore stitched to the center back gore from the hem to the bottom of the placket.*

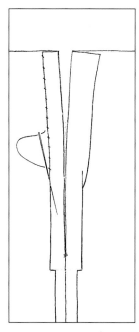

Fig. 5.3. *Closing the inside of the placket. The edges are tucked in and stitched down with a small hem or blind stitch.*

3 • MAKE HEM. The hem is made with an applied bias strip. Make a strip of bias from a stiff interfacing fabric 2" (5 cm) wide by 75" (190 cm) long, piecing as necessary. Turn down one long edge ¼" (.5 cm) and press. Set the raw edge to the skirt hem, right sides together, and stitch by machine at ¼" (.5 cm), stretching the bias very slightly as you sew, to ensure there will be no ripples in the hem. (Fig. 5.4.) Turn the bias inside the skirt, favoring the shell, and close with a small, neat hem or blind stitch. (Fig. 5.5.)

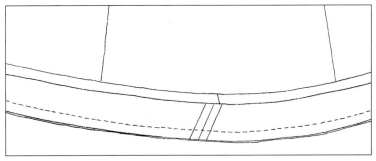

Fig. 5.4. *The applied bias hem. The top edge is pressed down. Right sides together, the lower edge is stitched to the bottom of the skirt.*

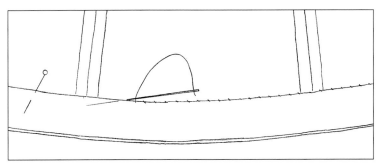

Fig. 5.5. *The hem, turned up into the skirt. The shell is favored in the turning. The hem is closed with a hem or blind stitch. If you have lined the skirt, the hem stitching may be done through the lining only, invisible from the outside.*

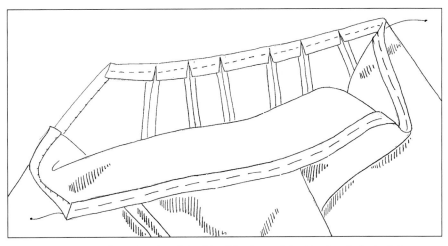

Fig. 5.6. *Preparing the waist edge of the skirt. The front of the skirt (at the back of the drawing) is merely turned down and basted. The back of the skirt (in the foreground) is turned down and basted with a long gathering stitch. This will be drawn up to form the pleats across the derriere.*

4 • TURN DOWN WAIST EDGE AND GATHER UP BACK GORE INTO PLEATS. Join the gores of the skirt from the hem to within ⅜" (1 cm) of the top, using the notches as a guide, and press the seams open. You will note at this point the proportions of the drapery. The front of the skirt describes a near half-circle; it will fall nearly straight in front with a gentle flare around the sides, while the back requires deep pleating to arrange its spreading fullness. Measure your doll from the waist to the floor over her petticoat at the front to determine the finished skirt length. Measure loosely: some of the length will be "used up" in draping over her form and petticoats. Turn and baste the waist edge down, beginning at the measure you have established at the center front, and proceeding evenly around. The back gore should be basted with a separate thread, since the basting thread will be used to draw up the actual pleats across the back. The basting stitches at the back should be long, about ½" (1.5 cm) in and out, to create a set of deep, even pleats when they are drawn up. Leave a short tail and knot the thread. (Fig. 5.6.)

5 • Set waistband. Check the doll's waist measurement over her petticoats. In cutting the waistband, allow about ¼–⅜" (.5–1 cm) for fitting ease, to accommodate the bulk of the pleats inside the band, and a short (less than ¼" or .5 cm) overlap. Cut the waistband and turn the edges under ¼" (.5 cm) all around. Fold lengthwise and baste. (Fig. 5.7.) The waistband is divided into approximate quarters, plus the short overlap for the closure. The pattern diagram is marked to help you get oriented. Basically, the back gore must be tightly pleated into the back quarter; the front gore is set nearly plain into the front quarter; and the sides are made into three or four soft pleats in the side quarters that open toward the front.

Once the fullness is organized, begin at the back by catching the top fold of each pleat with a single stitch and whipping it to the waistband. There is a great deal of fullness across the back, and the pleats will probably touch each other as they lay side by side. The pleat itself is inside the skirt; it helps provide the characteristic shape by holding the skirt out from the small of the back. (Fig. 5.8.)

I generally do this type of stitching from the outside of the waistband because it is easier, but it makes a neater join if you work from the inside. The waistband is in any case hidden completely by the jacket.

Once across the back gore, whip the side pleats down flat to the band. The center front should have a small amount of ease to make it drape gracefully, but should fall nearly straight. The last quarter is the set of pleats at the left side front. (See Fig. 5.9.)

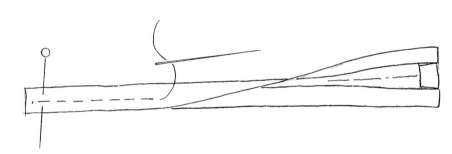

Fig. 5.7. *Making the waistband. The narrow ends are tucked in first; then the long edges. The band is folded in half and basted.*

Fig. 5.8. *Setting the waistband to the skirt. A single stitch is taken through each pleat across the back. The center front is eased on slightly. The fullness at the sides is taken up with pleats that open toward the front.*

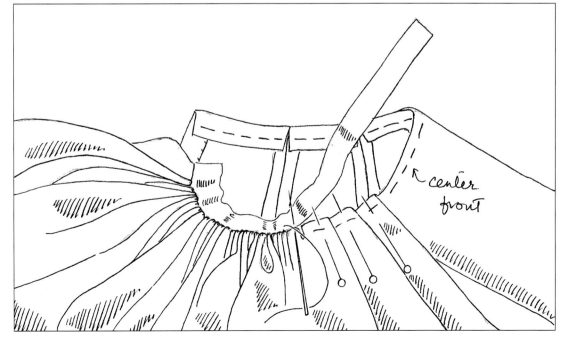

center front

6 • **MAKE CLOSURE.** The skirt is closed with a narrow lap and a set of hooks and eyes. The eyes extend just past the placket edge on the front; the hooks are set back slightly on the underside of the back placket. When they are closed, the back laps the front very slightly, and appears to be one of the side pleats. (Fig. 5.9.) The placket should disappear completely.

Bodice

BODICE: PATTERN NO. 9.
SLEEVES: PATTERN NO. 7.

7 • **BASTE LINING TO SHELL.** The shell and lining are cut from the same patterns. However, to minimize bulk in the bodice, trim the lining out of the hem and turn-back allowances. Baste along the edges. The basting will be pulled out as each area is finished. (Fig. 5.10.)

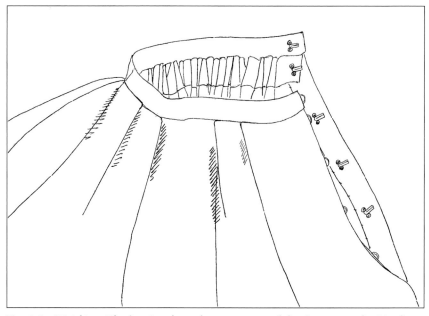

Fig. 5.9. *Finishing. The drawing shows the arrangement of the pleats across the side of the skirt as well as the hooks and eyes used to close. The lap at side back is very narrow.*

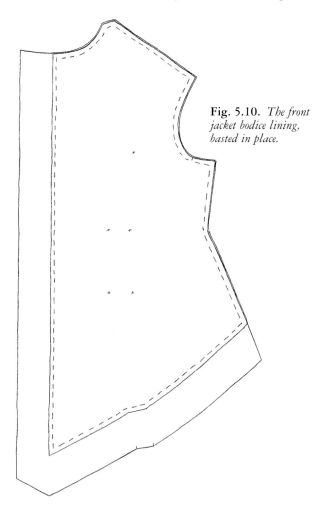

Fig. 5.10. *The front jacket bodice lining, basted in place.*

8 • MAKE DART AND FRONT TURN-BACK. Stitch the dart by machine. Because of its curved shape, one side of the dart is slightly longer than the other (i.e., the seam nearest the center of the bodice is longer than the seam nearest the side of the bodice). It is easiest to sew this type of seam with the longer side down, against the throat plate of your machine, where the feed dogs will draw it up slightly as you sew. (Fig. 5.11.) Press the dart toward the side seam, taking care not to flatten the curved shape of the garment. If you don't have a small tailor's ham, drape the bodice over the edge of a sleeve board instead of laying it flat on the board surface.

Turn the front edges back and close with a small, neat hem or blind stitch.

9 • JOIN BACK SECTIONS. Join the side back sections to the center back. Joining opposing curves sometimes presents difficulties. This operation is best approached in sections; in this garment the back seams actually change direction at the waist. Pin at the top and bottom of the section and guide your machine to that point by pulling very gently as the fabric is drawn under the needle. When you reach the end of the first section (at the waist), move the pin to the bottom of the next section. It is actually not very useful to attempt to baste or pin the whole seam at once, since the curving shape gets in the way. If you have great difficulty, you may want to give it a try by hand. If you are unsure your hand seam will hold, it can be pressed and then invisibly reinforced with a blind stitch from the outside. It may also help to make a small clip into the seam at the waist; however, if you do this, be extremely careful not to shred the seam in the handling.

Cut a shallow notch in the seams at the waist, overcast to neaten, and press toward the center. (Fig. 5.12.)

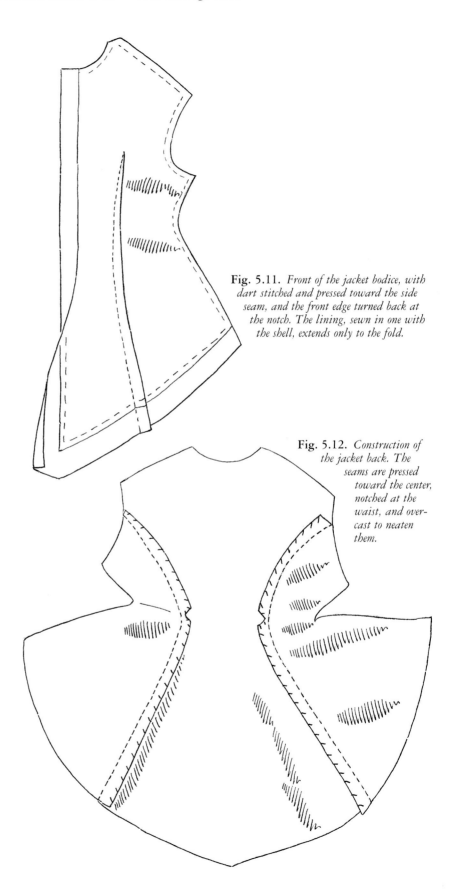

Fig. 5.11. *Front of the jacket bodice, with dart stitched and pressed toward the side seam, and the front edge turned back at the notch. The lining, sewn in one with the shell, extends only to the fold.*

Fig. 5.12. *Construction of the jacket back. The seams are pressed toward the center, notched at the waist, and overcast to neaten them.*

10• JOIN SHOULDERS AND FINISH NECK EDGE. Stitch the shoulder seams by machine at ¼" (.5 cm), press the seams toward the back, and overcast. (Fig. 5.13.)

The original garment was finished at the neck by clipping the seam, turning it in, and covering the raw cuts with a piece of the black lace trim folded in half over the edge and stitched in place. The white ruffle was then added on top. If you have an appropriate piece of lace, you may certainly use this method.

The lace I had available was not only inappropriate, but I had very little of it, and I therefore finished the neck edge in a more conventional manner with a bias facing. To finish the neck with bias fabric, cut a piece of self-fabric 1" (2.5 cm) wide by 7" (18 cm) long on the true bias. Set to the neck edge and stitch at ¼" (.5 cm), preferably by hand. (Fig. 5.14.) Turn the bias strip in, favoring the shell as you do so. Clip the neck seam as necessary to make it lie smoothly. Tuck in the raw edges of the bias and close with a small blind stitch. (Fig. 5.15.)

The white lace ruffle is whipped along the inside neck edge; note that the lace is drawn around the center front edge to surround the top buttonhole. (Fig. 5.16.)

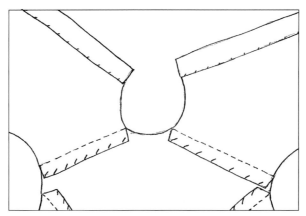

Fig. 5.13. The shoulder seams, stitched, pressed toward the back, and overcast to finish.

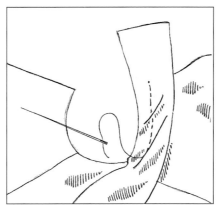

Fig. 5.14. Finishing the neck edge. The bias strip is stitched at ¼" (.5 cm).

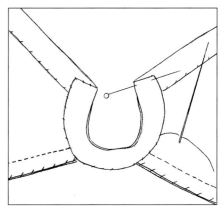

Fig. 5.15. The bias neck facing, turned under and stitched in place. Note that the shell is favored in the turning.

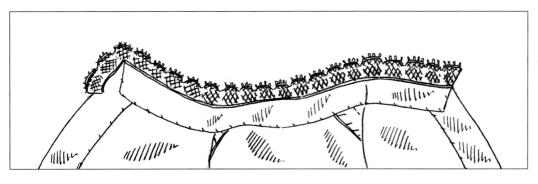

Fig. 5.16. The neck edge, with a whipped-on trimming of lace. Note at center front, the lace is worked around the front edge of the closure; it will surround the top button when the bodice is fastened up.

11 • JOIN SIDE SEAMS. Stitch the side seams at ¼" (.5 cm), clip at the waist, and press open. Take care not to crush the shape of the bodice. Overcast each seam edge. (Fig. 5.17.)

12 • FINISH HEM. Turn the hem up at the line established by the edge of the lining. Although the original, unlined bodice is finished by turning the hem out and covering it with the lace trim, in order to make a clean finish, I hemmed the copy conventionally by turning the hem in. The hem in this way encloses the raw edge of the lining.

At the side seams, there is an actual break in the shape of the jacket tails that requires the hem to be opened on the inside. The lowest point of the opening in the hem should be reinforced with a couple of back stitches to prevent the seam from parting. The center back point is mitered. Close with a neat hem or blind stitch. (Fig. 5.18.)

The hem trimming can now be applied. In addition to decorating the bodice, the trimming emphasizes the smart shape of the hem. The original jacket bodice has a line of double-edged lace secured with a row of beads stitched through its center. The copy has a more conventional lace, secured with beads stitched through the top edge. Lay the lace lightly around the hem. The shaped edge of the lace should cover the hem edge slightly. Since the jacket flares at the lower edge, there will be a small amount of easing required to secure the lace at the top. Stitch through the top edge, easing in any excess as you go. If you are using beads, pick one up on your needle with each stitch. The beads should be arranged in a slightly irregular line, and the stitches may be slightly loose, so the trimming does not look nailed in place. (Fig. 5.19.) Old beaded trims are frequently working loose on the garments they decorate, since beads tear the threads. (See Plate 22 for another example of beaded lace trim, an applied yoke detail.)

Alternative trimmings are metallic or silk braid laid on in a conservative pattern, embroidered tape or ribbon, or ruched or pleated ribbon edgings. The trimmings should complement the neat, strong lines of the costume. This is in contrast to the previous period's frilly, feminine style.

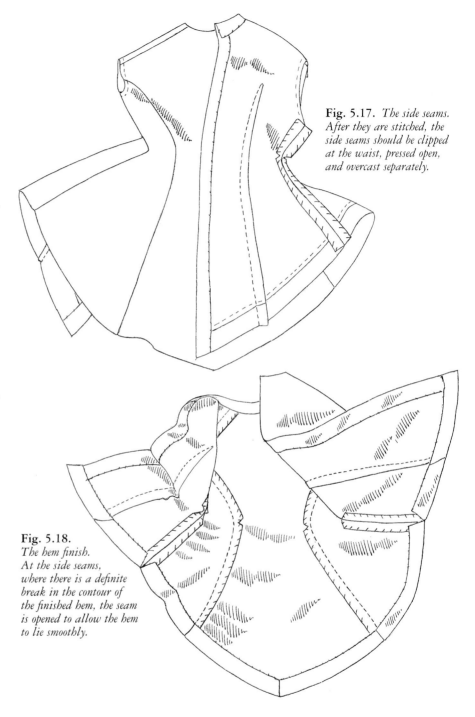

Fig. 5.17. *The side seams. After they are stitched, the side seams should be clipped at the waist, pressed open, and overcast separately.*

Fig. 5.18. *The hem finish. At the side seams, where there is a definite break in the contour of the finished hem, the seam is opened to allow the hem to lie smoothly.*

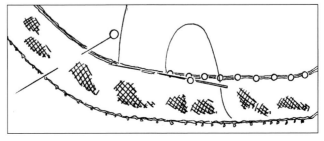

Fig. 5.19. *The hem trimming. The lace should be laid lightly around the hem so there is no strain or buckling anywhere. The lace is tacked down along the top edge only. The beads are picked up with the needle as you go along.*

13 • MAKE AND SET SLEEVES. Stitch the sleeve seams, overcast each separately, and baste the seams open to keep them neat while the sleeve is being worked. Turn the cuff and close with a hem or blind stitch. (Fig. 5.20.) A lightly gathered frill of lace can now be added to the inside edge of the cuff. Turn, and lightly steam the sleeve.

The original jacket has a line of lace laid around each cuff. The copy is trimmed likewise; however, the lace on the sleeve is arranged opposite to that around the hem. The straight edge of the lace is placed at the bottom, with the beads running along the edge of the cuff; the shaped edge of the lace is turned up.

Set the sleeve into the armhole, placing the outseam between the shoulder seam and the side back seam. The inseam should fall near the deepest part of the front of the armscye. (Fig. 5.21.) Fullness in the top of the sleeve should be eased in; fullness under the arm is tucked into a small, forward opening pleat at the bottom of the armhole.

The seam may be reinforced from the outside with a blind stitch around the armhole, if necessary. Turn both seams toward the body as you sew. (Fig. 5.22, at left.) Turn the armhole out, trim to about ³⁄₁₆" (.45 cm), and overcast to neaten it. (Fig. 5.22, at right.)

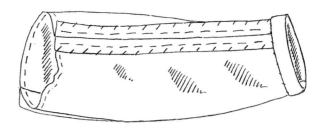

Fig. 5.20. *The sleeve. The seams are stitched, opened, and basted down so they remain neat as the sleeve is worked. The sleeve shown in Plate 5.1 is finished with a conventional hem. Before turning, the hem may also be trimmed with a ruffle of lace whipped to the edge on the inside. (See Fig. 5.23 below for placement of additional lace trim onto the outside of the sleeve.)*

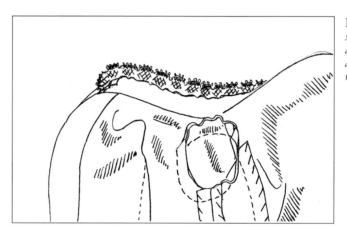

Fig. 5.21. *The sleeve set. The sleeve is aligned to the armhole and stitched in with a running stitch.*

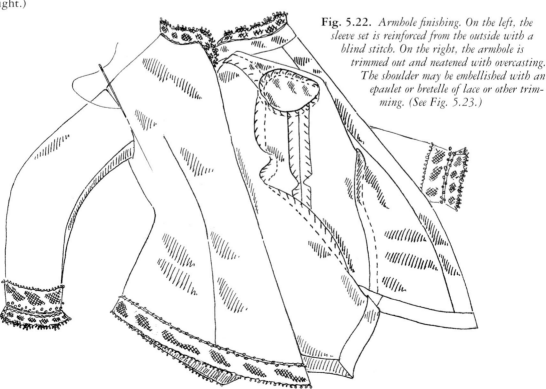

Fig. 5.22. *Armhole finishing. On the left, the sleeve set is reinforced from the outside with a blind stitch. On the right, the armhole is trimmed out and neatened with overcasting. The shoulder may be embellished with an epaulet or bretelle of lace or other trimming. (See Fig. 5.23.)*

14 • MAKE CLOSURE. The original jacket bodice is closed with a set of hooks and worked loops. The copy, however, is closed with hooks and eyelets. Although none of the particular pieces I chose from this period had this type of closure, it is a neat way of securing a bodice. Stitch the hooks in place first; the functional closure should be dealt with before the decoration. The buttons are then arranged on top. The buttons and hooks do not have to correspond. You should have enough hooks close enough together to make a smooth, gapless closure to the waist. The basques fall open from waist to hem. The buttons are simply an embellishment; this is a useful way to cope with too few old buttons to close a bodice correctly. Corresponding to the hooks, make a set of worked eyelets. You may have to force the hooks open slightly to slip them into the eyelets. (Fig. 5.23.)

Fig. 5.23. *Finishing and closure. The jacket is closed with hooks and eyelets. The buttons are decorative only. The last fastening is at the waist, so the jacket falls open over the skirt.*

CHAPTER VI

Promenade Dress

circa 1873

PATTERN NOS. 7, 10, AND 11

The two-piece dress presented in this chapter is based on the promenade dress shown at left. (Plate 28.) The dress is a typical two-fabric arrangement of the period. The copy shown in Plate 6.1 uses the fabrics in a slightly different way from the original gown; many variations are possible. This style developed from the triangular crinoline with its flowing expanses of fabric. In the late 1860s, the excess fabric began to be arranged in hanging draperies supported by a bustle. Small "bustle pads" had been worn early in the 19th century, until the artificial crinoline rendered them pointless. When the bustle returned in the late 1860s, it was with a vengeance. For the next fifteen years, the drapery of the skirt dominated women's fashions. A longer, slimmer line emerged in the late 1870s; after a brief revival in the mid-1880s, the bustle disappeared forever.

The doll's version explained here suggests the fashionable early 1870s bustle very successfully and requires only an appropriate petticoat to support it. The original gown is a homemade effort. Although it presents the classic early 1870s silhouette, the dressmaker was clearly improvising. I have therefore taken a few liberties with her design, which are detailed below.

＊MATERIALS＊

Like the period immediately following (see Chapter VII), the early 1870s were characterized by elaborate ensembles of contrasting fabrics. The original promenade dress is made principally of a very fine, crisp taffeta of French blue; the contrast fabric is a lighter weight taffeta in a tiny ivory and black windowpane check. The ribbon draped over the bustle is a light silk grosgrain in matching French blue. The undersleeves were also cut from the ribbon.

Although fine woolens were also employed at the time, this particular style is best organized so as to cut the actual skirt from a light fabric such as silk taffeta, light slubbed silk, or similar material that will sustain the back drapery without drooping. Heavier, softer fabrics like woolens or velveteens may be used for the bodice. The apron will also work in lightweight challis. Plate 33 and Plate 36 illustrate dresses of the same general period; their fabrications are appropriate for the project shown in this chapter.

Fabric combinations may be silks of different colors, or different hues of the same color, or different fabrics in coordinating colors and/or patterns.

The bustle drapery is decorated and enhanced with a wide ribbon bow. Ribbon is the typical material for this embellishment, even on full-size dresses of the period, which often employed long streamers of wide, rich ribbons artistically arranged to trail over the bustle and down the train. However, "ribbon" can be improvised from taffeta or other lightweight silk if you have no matching or coordinating old ribbon. Modern, synthetic ribbon is to be avoided.

Only the body of the original gown is lined. The silk is backed with cotton batiste sewn in one with the shell. Most fabrics will have to be lined to achieve the structured appearance of the bodice; a full-size garment would likely have been boned.

The copy presented in this chapter is nearly identical in trimming and construction to the original garment. This style of dress is the beginning of the "upholstery" approach to fashionable ladies' wear, and the ensemble may be trimmed with bows added on the sleeves, apron drapery, the back neck, the top of the front closure. Fringe was coming back into style; see Plate 34 at left for an example of a dress trimmed with fringe and velvet ribbon. The bodice may be trimmed with lace in the style of the walking suit explained in Chapter V; the trimming style of the dress explained in Chapter VII is also appropriate for this ensemble.

During this period cording was gradually going out of general use in finishing seams. The only use made of cording in the original dress is at the neckline. Cotton carpet warp or No. 5 pearl cotton may be used as a substitute for real cording. Pearl cotton makes a softer finished seam but provides a less definitive guide for your needle than carpet warp and thus may be slightly more difficult to handle.

SHELL
Silk jacquard, taffeta, lightweight satin
Slubbed silk, such as duppioni
Challis, lightweight worsted (bodice)
Velveteen (bodice)

LINING
Glazed cotton
Batiste

TRIMMINGS
Contrast fabric
⅔ yard wide ribbon (bustle)
Narrow silk or velvet ribbon (optional)
Lace (neckline)
Shank buttons

NOTIONS
Thread to match
Seven hooks (1 for skirt, 2 for apron [optional], 4 for bodice)
⅓ yard cotton carpet warp or pearl cotton

＊SUMMARY OF STEPS＊
SKIRT
1. Make placket.
2. Join sections.
3. Finish hem.
4. Apply waistband and closure.
5. Assemble "apron" and apply to waistband; arrange bustle drapery.

BODICE
6. Turn front edge; make darts.
7. Join back sections.
8. Join shoulder seams; finish neck edge; apply trimming.
9. Bind lower edge.
10. Make and set sleeves.
11. Make front closure.

Plate 6.1. *A promenade gown of the early 1870s. The skirt and apron are made of black silk taffeta with a white windowpane check. The back drapery detail, attached to the skirts of the apron, is made of a piece of old black ribbon. The bodice is made of old black slubbed silk, and has two-piece coat sleeves and short basques cut in one with the body. The bodice is trimmed with old buttons and lace.*

GENERAL ⟶CONSTRUCTION⟵ NOTES

THE original skirt is cut in a somewhat old-fashioned way, with skirt sections that are almost without shaping. The skirt shape is established principally with the arrangement of the pleats. Nevertheless, the finished garment is very effective in suggesting the style of the early 1870s. Most skirts of this time would have been cut with gores.

The sleeves of the bodice are very tight-fitting and slightly short. This is actually the characteristic form of the early to mid-1880s sleeve. In this case, the dressmaker seems not to have had enough fabric to complete the "look" she wanted, since she resorted to piecing the top sleeves (under the pleated cuff trimming), while cutting the undersleeves from the ribbon used for the bustle trimming. Additionally, I am supposing that the arms of the doll have swollen slightly, as is often the case with kid bodies stuffed with sawdust. This is what causes the gusseted legs of this type of doll to draw up the way they do. Rather than copying the original very tight

sleeves, I took the liberty of using the basic coat sleeve used for the other 1860s and 1870s styles. In addition to being more typical, these looser coat sleeves are easier in all respects to deal with, not only in cutting and assembling but in getting the doll in and out of. If you want to achieve the tight look of the original garment, instructions on altering the sleeve are given in Appendix B.

The hems of the bodice and apron are finished with a bias binding. This is not terribly difficult, but it is a slightly fussy operation. You may add a hem allowance if you prefer, and turn it up like the bodice in Chapter V.

The original bodice has a somewhat irregular neck. It is difficult to determine what the dressmaker actually had in mind, but I have taken the liberty of interpreting it as a modest V-neck. There is a good deal of detail applied around the neckline in layers; this should be planned so that no bulky fabrics have to be employed around the neck. The neck was finished inside with cord facing, also slightly old-fashioned by the 1870s. I have used this method on the copy, but a plain, bias fabric facing may also be used.

⟶INSTRUCTIONS⟵ *Skirt*

PATTERN NO. 10

1 • MAKE PLACKET. The original skirt has a very simple placket made by turning back the edges of a slash into the center of the back breadth of fabric. An equally acceptable closure can be made, however, using the instructions for the skirt placket contained in Chapter VII.

To make the placket, cut into the skirt as marked on the pattern, about 6" (15 cm), in the center of the skirt back. Turn the edges of the slash in about 1/8" (.3 cm) at the top, tapering to nothing at the bottom of the cut, and baste. Turn the edges back again in the same fashion, and close with a small hem stitch or running stitch. There will probably be some puckering at the bottom of the slash; a small amount is unimportant. (Fig. 6.2.)

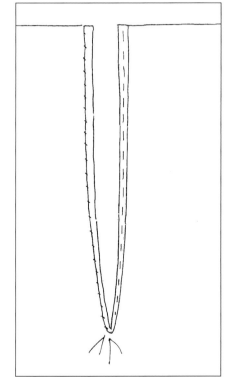

Fig. 6.2. *The construction of the placket. The edges of the slash are turned twice, from 1/8" (.3 cm) at the top to nothing at the bottom of the cut.*

Fig. 6.1 illustrates the shape of the petticoat required to support the bustle skirt correctly. It can be made from the skirt pattern. Choose a thin, crisp even-weave cotton fabric. The flounces can be made from broderie anglaise or strips of fabric. The front may be decorated with several tucks over the flounce.

Fig. 6.1.
This flounced petticoat supports the skirt's bustle shape.

Insert a placket into the center of the back breadth. This can be done as in step 1 below, or preferably with the placket explained in Chapter VII (step 1). Join the back and front and turn the hem. The actual hem can be an applied facing or a conventional turn-up. (Allowance for a turned hem must be added to the pattern.) The flounces are then applied to the surface of the petticoat. The hem flounce is a single long strip. The flounces finishing the back breadth reach from seam to seam or from the side seam to the edge of the placket, as the case may be. The flounces should be cut twice the length of the skirt section they are intended to be joined to. Petticoat flounces typically were rolled, whipped, and gathered; however, if you are simply making a support for the skirt, rather than a close reproduction, the heads of the flounces can be gathered on cord. Gathering on cord is explained in Chapter I. After gathering the flounces, whip them to the skirt.

To apply the waistband, gather the top edge of the petticoat. The back breadth should be gathered into about 1½" (4 cm) on either side of the back opening. A small amount of fullness should be allowed in about 2" (5 cm) across the front, so the petticoat drapes gracefully, and is not drawn tight against the doll's figure. The rest of the fullness is distributed over the hips. The waistband may be closed with ties or a button.

Turned slashes of this type, which were often used to make openings in lingerie, are reinforced with buttonhole stitches around the bottom. Work your way around, about ³⁄₁₆" (.45 cm) each side from the bottom of the slash. (Fig. 6.3.) Make a short bar across the slash with a couple of stitches, and cover the bar with buttonhole stitches, in the manner of a worked loop. (Fig. 6.4.)

2 • JOIN SECTIONS. Join the front and back sections with a ¼" (.5 cm) seam. The original skirt's seams are unfinished. If your fabric is unlikely to ravel much, you can leave the seams alone. Otherwise, press the seams open and finish with overcasting.

3 • FINISH HEM. The original skirt has an applied hem made of a length of grosgrain ribbon. It was lapped over the hem allowance and closed with a small running stitch. (Fig. 6.5.)

If you have no ribbon (and I don't use my precious antique ribbon for finishing hems), a strip of fabric may be substituted. The hem may also be turned in the conventional way if a hem allowance is added to the pattern.

4 • APPLY WAISTBAND AND CLOSURE. Measure your doll's waist over her petticoats; allow about ¼" (.5 cm) fitting ease and ¼" (.5 cm) for a lap closure. Cut a waistband. Turn the edges in ¼" (.5 cm) and baste. (Fig. 6.6.) The distribution of the fullness, as follows, will determine the shape of the skirt.

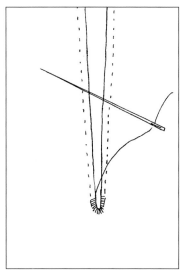

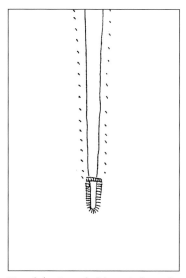

Fig. 6.3. *The bottom of the turned slash is reinforced with a buttonhole stitch.*

Fig. 6.4. *A worked bar reinforces the buttonholed placket.*

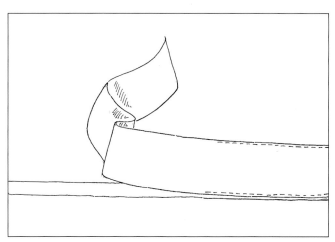

Fig. 6.5. *The hem, made from applied ribbon.*

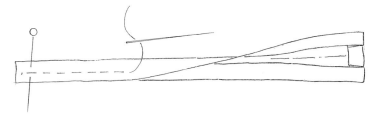

Fig. 6.6. *Construction of the waistband.*

Refer to Fig. 6.1, which illustrates the correct silhouette. The entire back breadth of the skirt should be made into flat pleats that will fall over the doll's derriere, about one quarter of the total waist girth on the waistband arranged on either side of the back opening. The front of the skirt, another approximate quarter, should have about ½" (1.5 cm) of fullness eased into it so that the skirt drapes fluidly over the petticoats. The remainder of the fullness must be made into deep gathers, about ½" (1.5 cm) in and out, and worked into the remaining two quarters (one on each side, over the hips); as much of this as possible should be inclined toward the back of the hips. (Fig. 6.7.)

Whip the skirt to the waistband, picking up one gather with your needle at a time. (Fig. 6.8.)

Make a closure with hook and worked loop at the back. See Fig. 6.14.

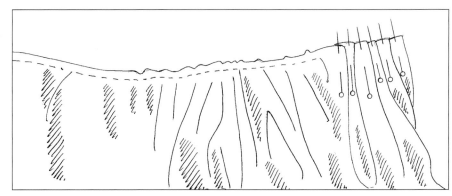

Fig. 6.7. *The back breadth of the skirt is pleated into about 1½" (4 cm) on either side of the placket. The sides are drawn up with gathers.*

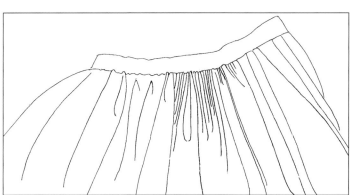

Fig. 6.8. *The arrangement of the fullness whipped onto the waistband. The fullness at the sides is picked up one gather at a time.*

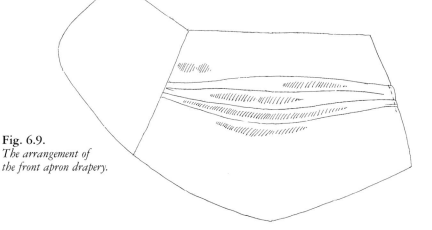

Fig. 6.9. *The arrangement of the front apron drapery.*

Fig. 6.10. *Binding the apron edge.*

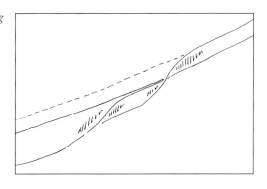

5 • ASSEMBLE "APRON" AND APPLY TO WAISTBAND; ARRANGE BUSTLE DRAPERY. Tuck up the pleats indicated on the front apron pattern, and baste. (Fig. 6.9.) The pleats open upward. Stitch the apron front to the apron sides, easing the pleats together to take up the fullness in the front seam. Press both seams toward the back, taking care not to crush the drapery. If your fabric is ravelly, overcast the seams to keep them neat.

Finish the lower edge with contrast bias binding. Cut the binding 1" (2.5 cm) wide by 26" (66 cm) long on the bias. Set the right side of the bias to the wrong side of the apron hem and stitch at ¼" (.5 cm), stretching the bias very slightly to ensure that it will turn without ripples. (If it is stretched too tight, it will buckle the edge of the apron.) Turn the bias out, tuck in the raw edge, and blind stitch to close. (Fig. 6.10.)

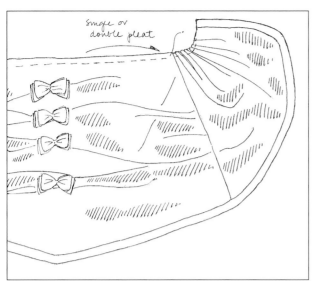

single or double pleat

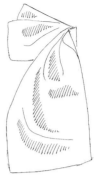

Fig. 6.11. *The arrangement of the apron waist fullness. The back breadth is gathered. The front will be pleated between the center and the side seam. The apron side seam should fall in its approximate "natural" position, somewhat forward of the skirt side seam.*

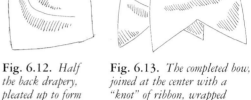

Fig. 6.12. *Half the back drapery, pleated up to form a soft bow.*

Fig. 6.13. *The completed bow, joined at the center with a "knot" of ribbon, wrapped around, and steamed into shape.*

The apron front is decorated with a line of little ribbon bows. The original garment is actually trimmed with short strips of raw fabric gathered in the center and stitched to the apron. I used doubled bits of black and white ribbon. Although a more elaborate bow is certainly acceptable, I made mine like the original, putting a gathering stitch through the center of the bow and drawing it up. The center front of the apron is then either drawn up slightly with gathers down the center front or puckered with little pleats. The bows are stitched over the line of gathers or pleats. (Fig. 6.11.)

The apron waist is arranged, essentially, opposite to the skirt. The back is gathered, and the side front taken up with a couple of deep pleats. The back sections are gathered up slightly looser than the skirt; the apron side seam should fall in its approximate natural place at the doll's side; this will bring it slightly forward of the seam on the skirt. The remaining fullness should be arranged across the front. A small amount is allowed in the center, so the apron will not be pulled back tightly against the skirt, but most of the fullness taken up with a pair of pleats at the side front. The fabric is arranged in naturally-falling soft folds.

The back drapery may be assembled at this point, but it may be well not to fix it to the skirt until the bodice is completed and you can judge the effect on the whole gown. The original dress uses a length of blue grosgrain ribbon. The two ends are simply stitched to the edges of the apron in back,

and the ribbon tied in a loose, attractive bow. The effectiveness of this treatment depends upon whether you have an acceptable ribbon, which must have good draping qualities. At this period, this type of trimming typically was made with ribbon. Plate 34, right, shows a dress of slightly later date with a similar arrangement. If you do not have any ribbon that will work, you can improvise with thin taffeta, seamed into a tube and pressed flat. If it is a good quality silk, you can ravel the ends out for ¼–½" (.5–1.5 cm) rather than hemming.

The ribbon decorating the copy was too wide and too short to tie into a bow. It is therefore arranged into a bow-like drape, which is fastened to the apron with a set of

hooks and worked loops. Fig. 6.12 illustrates half the arrangement. Because the ribbon was so wide, it was first folded loosely in thirds lengthwise; it was then formed into a loop and secured with a few stitches. There is a short "tail" underneath for joining to the apron. The two halves were assembled together with a "knot," a short piece of plain silk ribbon wrapped around the center and blind stitched at the back. (Fig. 6.13.) The bow was lightly steamed to set the draped shape. Ultimately, the left side of the bow was stitched to the apron. The right side was provided with a set of worked loops. The apron drapery has a set of hooks stitched to the binding underneath. (Fig. 14.)

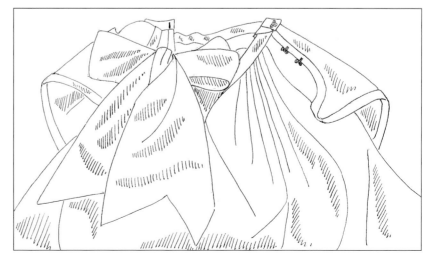

Fig. 6.14. *The arrangement of the back drapery with the back closure.*

Bodice

PATTERN NOS. 11, 7

THE body sections of the bodice (and, optionally, the sleeves) should be lined before beginning to sew. Cut shell and lining from the same pattern, and join each piece around the edges with a small basting stitch. Much of the basting need not be pulled out, since it will be buried in the seams as you sew.

6 • **TURN FRONT EDGE; MAKE DARTS.** The lining may be trimmed out of the front turn-back if it creates too much bulk. Turn the front edges back at the notch and close with a small hem stitch or blind stitch. Stitch the darts and press toward the side seams carefully, so as not to crush the curved shape of the bodice. (Fig. 6.15.)

7 • **JOIN BACK SECTIONS.** Join the back sections from the neck edge to the top of the vent. Press open and overcast the seams. (Fig. 6.16.)

8 • **JOIN SHOULDER SEAMS; FINISH NECK EDGE; APPLY TRIMMING.** Join the shoulder seams, press open, and overcast to finish them. (Fig. 6.17.)

The neck has several layers of trimming that are applied one at a time. First, the neck edge itself must be finished. This can be done either with a cord facing, like the original garment, or with a plain bias facing. The latter procedure is explained in Chapter V.

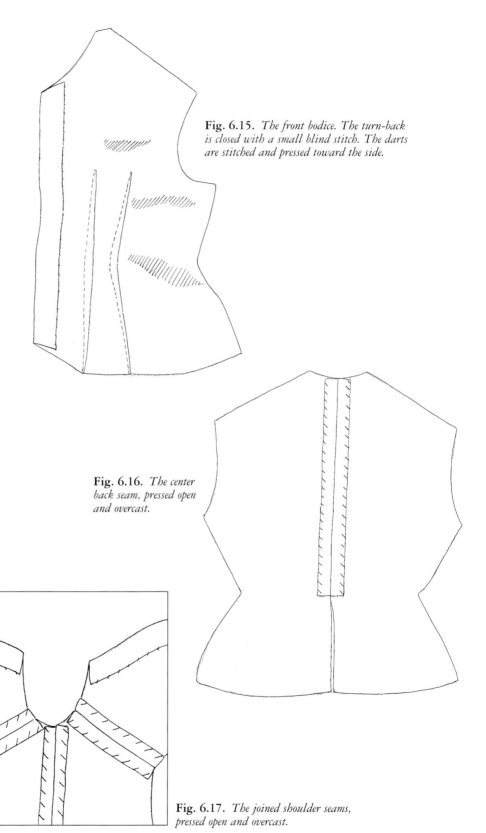

Fig. 6.15. *The front bodice. The turn-back is closed with a small blind stitch. The darts are stitched and pressed toward the side.*

Fig. 6.16. *The center back seam, pressed open and overcast.*

Fig. 6.17. *The joined shoulder seams, pressed open and overcast.*

Fig. 6.18. *The construction of the cord facing.*

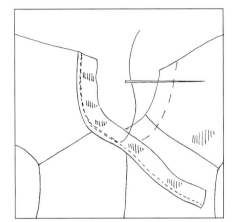

Fig. 6.19. *The cord facing, set to the outside of the neck edge.*

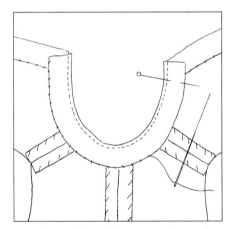

Fig. 6.20. *The cord facing, turned in and blind stitched to close.*

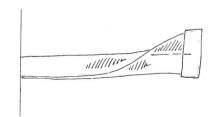

Fig. 6.21. *The construction of the neck frill.*

To prepare the neck edge for a cord facing, put a line of basting stitches around the neck edge at ¼" (.5 cm). This is a guide for your stitching. Measure the basted line, and cut a piece of cotton carpet warp (or pearl cotton) to that length. This is covered with a piece of silk, cut 1" (2.5 cm) wide by the measure of the cord plus 1/2" (1.5 cm) for two seams. Stitch the cord into the bias fabric with a ¼" (.5 cm) fold, tucking in the ends. Fold up the other edge until the raw edges meet. Baste. (Fig. 6.18.)

The cord facing is laid wrong side down against the right side of the neck edge. The cord follows the line of the stitches. Stitch the cord facing to the neck edge with a neat running stitch. (Fig. 6.19.)

Turn the cord facing in, clipping the neck seam as necessary to ease it. Close with blind stitch or hem stitch. (Fig. 6.20.) Pull out the basting.

The pleated neck frill is applied next. This is made from a strip of silk cut 13" (33 cm) long by 1½" (4 cm) wide, cut on the straight or the bias, whichever uses the fabric to better effect. Tuck in the short ends about ⅜" (1 cm) (to make sure they will be caught), and fold the strip in half lengthwise. (Fig. 6.21.) Make the strip into a set of little pleats around the neck, laying the raw edges of the frill onto the shoulders about ¼" (.5 cm) from the corded neckline. Baste. (Fig. 6.22.)

Cut another strip 6½" (16.5 cm) long by ⅞" (2.2 cm) wide (more or less), on the bias. This may be a matching or contrasting silk. Turn all the edges in ¼" (.5 cm) and baste. The finished piece should be ¼–⅜" (.5–1 cm) wide. Work the bias strip around the edge of the frill, covering the raw edge, and blind stitch it down, securing it all around. (Fig. 6.23.) The center back of the neck, at the base of an applied panel such as this one, was a favorite spot for the placement of bows.

The neckline is finished with a frill of lace stitched to the inside edge of the cording. This is the usual neck edge finish. Allow fullness of about 2:1 or less, i.e., cut the lace no more than twice the neck circumference; typically it is a bit less. The lace is drawn into small pleats as it is whipped to the neck edge. (Fig. 6.24.)

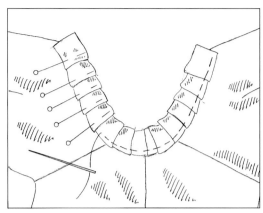

Fig. 6.22. *The neck frill, pleated and basted into place. The raw edge of the frill is about ¼" (.5 cm) from the cording.*

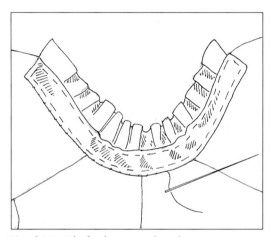

Fig. 6.23. *The finishing strip, basted over the raw edge of the frill and blind stitched to close.*

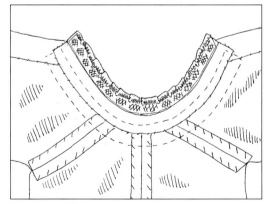

Fig. 6.24. *The lace edging, set to the edge of the cord facing and whipped in place.*

Fig. 6.25. *The bodice side seams, stitched, clipped at the waist, pressed open, and overcast to finish.*

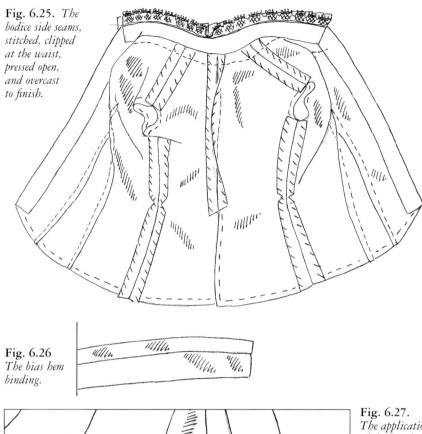

Fig. 6.26 *The bias hem binding.*

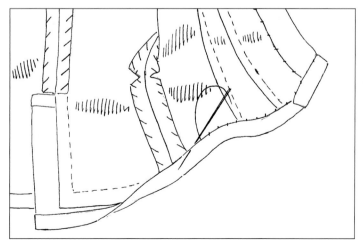

Fig. 6.27. *The application of the bias hem binding, along the line of basting stitches. The corners are mitered as you go around.*

Fig. 6.28. *Turning and closing the bias hem binding with blind stitch or hem stitch.*

9 • **BIND LOWER EDGE.** Close the side seams, and clip out a shallow notch at the waist. This allows the seams to lie flat without pulling on the shell. Press the seams open and overcast. (Fig. 6.25.)

The lower edge of the jacket bodice is bound with contrast bias fabric in the original garment. The copy is bound with self-fabric. Binding an edge that has angles, such as this jacket's at the front opening and back, and at the edges of the vent, can be a messy operation. You can achieve the same look, however, by doing the binding "backwards," i.e., blind stitching it to the outside first, turning the bias inside, and turning the raw inner edge in last.

First, place a basting stitch all around the jacket hem at ¼" (.5 cm) from the edge as a stitching guide. Cut two pieces of bias 12" (30.5 cm) long by 1" (2.5 cm) wide, and press down one long edge of each ¼" (.5 cm). (Fig. 6.26.) Pin the bias around the jacket hem, placing the fold next to the basted line, and mitering the corners as you go around. Stitch with a neat blind stitch. (Fig. 6.27.) Turn the bias inside, tuck in the raw edges, and close with a small hem stitch or blind stitch. Finish the angles as neatly as possible as you go around—they are inside and will not show. (Fig. 6.28.)

The top of the vent in back is trimmed with a pair of buttons (see Fig. 6.34 below.)

Fig. 6.29.
Construction of the sleeve. The seams are stitched, overcast, and basted open. The hem is turned.

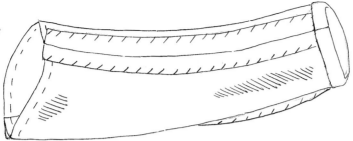

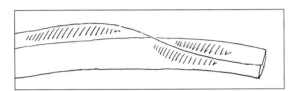

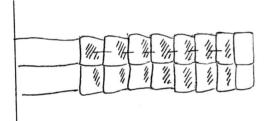

Fig. 6.30. *Arrangement of the pleated sleeve frill. The "bottom" raw edge is tucked right up into the fold. The "top" edge is left raw, but will be caught down in the sewing.*

Fig. 6.31. *The sleeve frill, formed into knife pleats and basted down.*

Fig. 6.32. *The sleeve frill. The frill is left raw underneath to begin. The other end is tucked under and stitched over it to hide the raw edge.*

10 • MAKE AND SET SLEEVES. As explained above, the copy shown in Plate 6.1 uses a sleeve that is cut substantially fuller than the original, as a comparison with Plate 28 will show. If you are dressing an antique doll, whose old kid body may be somewhat fragile, the ease of getting her in and out of her clothes may be a consideration. However, instructions for altering the sleeve are provided in Appendix B should you wish to make a sleeve more like the narrow original. The construction method is the same.

Stitch the sleeve parts together, overcast the seams and baste them open. Turn the hem and close with a neat hem stitch. (Fig. 6.29.)

The pleated sleeve frill is assembled slightly differently from the neck frill, because it is loose at both the top and bottom edges. Cut a piece of contrast silk 10" (25.5 cm) long by 1¼" (3 cm) wide on the straight or the bias, whichever uses the fabric to better advantage. Turn one long edge ½" (1.5 cm) and press. Turn the other edge over the first. Be sure that the first raw edge is tucked securely against the fold of the second. (Fig. 6.30.) Form the strip into a set of little knife pleats; baste. (Fig. 6.31.) Lay the strip around the sleeve at an angle. The bottom of the frill nearly touches the cuff in front; it is about ½" (1.5 cm) from the edge of the cuff in back. The frill is most neatly arranged so that the under lap is placed first on the undersleeve. The end of the under lap is left raw. The other end of the frill is tucked under, to resemble one of the pleats, as it is lapped over. (Fig. 6.32.) Blind stitch the frill in place, putting a stitch into the fold of each pleat to secure it. (Fig. 6.33.)

Fig. 6.33. *Stitching the sleeve frill. The little blind stitches are taken through the edge of the pleats to catch them down into a neat line about ⅛" (.3 cm) below the top edge. This should secure the raw edge that was left when the frill was folded. When the basting is pulled out, both top and bottom edges should frill out slightly.*

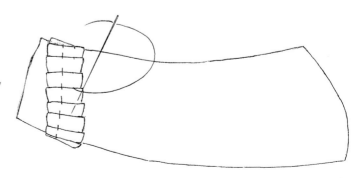

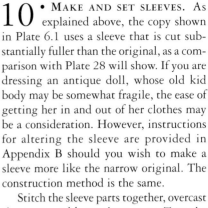

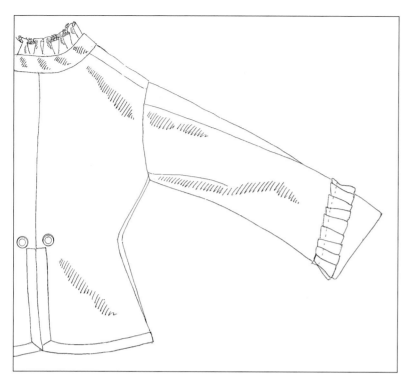

To set the sleeve, place the outseam about ⅜" (1 cm) below the shoulder seam. The inseam falls into the deepest part of the armhole in front. Fullness around the top of the sleeve should be eased. (Fig. 6.34.) Underarm fullness, however, is formed into a small pleat to take it up. This is characteristic of this style of sleeve. (Fig. 6.35.) Stitch around with a small running stitch. If you feel you need to, the armhole seam may be reinforced with a neat blind stitch from the outside. On the inside, trim the armhole seam to about ³⁄₁₆" (.45 cm) and overcast. (Fig. 6.36.)

Fig. 6.34. *The alignment of the sleeve into the armhole.*

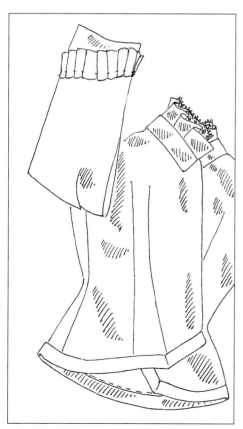

Fig. 6.35. *The armhole, with pleat in the undersleeve.*

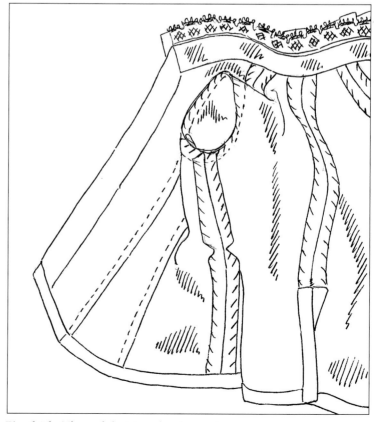

Fig. 6.36. *The armhole, trimmed and overcast.*

11• **MAKE FRONT CLOSURE.** The front is closed with a set of hooks and worked loops covered by buttons. Place the hooks first; be sure they provide a smooth, gapless closure. The functional closure should be dealt with first; the decorative buttons are added later. The hooks are closed with a set of worked loops. The pleated frill is tacked down at the front edges to open it away from the center front like revers. The original garment had a pretty watch and fob to trim the breast. In place of that, I made a small bow from a scrap of lace and secured it with a single, old button worn like a brooch. (Fig. 6.37.)

Fig. 6.37. *The completed jacket, with front closure and trim.*

CHAPTER VII

Princess Polonaise

circa 1877

THE two-piece dress presented in this chapter is based on the princess polonaise shown at left. (Plate 36.)

The dress cut "en princesse," after Princess Alexandra of Wales, was first introduced in the late 1860s. It refers to a dress made without a waist seam. The cut was first used to make a dress with close-fitting bodice flaring into the typically angular but wide skirt of the late crinoline period.

The polonaise of the late 1870s was well suited to the princess cut, and it is this style dress that we usually associate with the term "princess." At this time, long narrow lines were coming into fashion. The "polonaise," first introduced to ladies' wear in the 1770s, was originally a bodice with attached skirt draperies that fastened at the front; the skirt was drawn back to expose the "petticoat" (actually an underskirt) and arranged in hanging folds at the back, secured by tapes underneath. The term "polonaise" passed in and out of fashion describing various garments; in the early 19th century, it referred to a short "Polish" cloak. When taped skirt draperies came back into fashion with the bustle around 1870, the polonaise once again resembled in some respects the original design of the 1770s with its back drapery drawn up with interior tapes. The arrangement of drapery on skirts of the late 1870s took a somewhat drooping form.

━━MATERIALS━━

THE characteristic arrangement of fabrics of this time was ensembles of contrasts, ranging from the understated and simple to the ostentatious and complex. Plate 36 shows a plain and patterned silk in related colors. Plate 7.1 illustrates another approach, two silk fabrics in different shades of the same color and different surface textures. Combinations of wool and silk or velvet and silk are also appropriate. The degree and type of contrast (colors, textures, fabrics) allows scope for much creative manipulation of the basic design.

The fabrics should drape fluidly, even though they are layered several times. This is especially important with regard to whatever is chosen for the main fabric of the polonaise itself. To ensure that the polonaise not be too stiff, it is lined in one with the shell to the hip only. Choose a fabric with body (i.e., one that does not depend upon a lining for draping body); if the fabric is too limp the drapery will simply collapse.

The lining fabric should be chosen with care, to enhance the entire construction. The skirt actually is constructed on a foundation of cotton or other lining fabric. The original dress uses glazed brown cotton. The visible part of the skirt is a set of frills stitched to the surface at the bottom. Glazed cotton is not easy to find; calico matching the shell fabric in color may do for a reproduction, since it is invisible in the finished garment.

The "collar" detail is stitched to the surface of the bodice after the neckline is finished. The original garment, made of lightweight silk, has a self bow to complete the bodice trim; the copy uses a bow of grosgrain ribbon, also used in place of buttons down the back. Bows of ribbon or silk ravelled out at the ends may be used to trim the sleeves, back opening, and the little pleats drawing up the drapery of the polonaise.

The interesting ball buttons with which the original polonaise is trimmed are made of a ball base covered with very fine brown crochet. This is a good project on which to use old buttons that are slightly large, since they are decorative only and run down the back.

The pocket detail was one of those frivolous fashion statements that was considered ridiculous by many contemporary

Plate 7.1. *An afternoon dress in two shades of French blue silk in the princess style, consisting of skirt and long polonaise. The lighter color fabric, a star-pattern silk jacquard, is a good reproduction of an old pattern. The contrast color is a silk "faille," which resembles the grosgrain texture silks so popular at this time. The dress is trimmed with a piece of old grosgrain ribbon in a third shade of blue.*

critics. Even very dressy gowns had them, rendered in patches of velvet and silk. It is optional. The original dress has a tiny doll's handkerchief displayed in the pocket; the copy uses a small old round doily, which works very well, since it is basically all trimming and folds with very little bulk into the pocket. This type of exquisite old frippery can often be obtained at very little expense from antiques and collectibles dealers.

Cording was going out of style at this time. The original brown polonaise is trimmed with cording only at the armhole but it may be omitted. Cotton carpet warp or No. 5 pearl cotton may be used to substitute for cord. Pearl cotton makes a softer seam, but may be more difficult to sew with, as it provides a less definitive guide for your needle.

SHELL
Silk jacquard, taffeta, lightweight satin
Wool challis, broadcloth,
lightweight serge or worsted
Silk faille

LINING
Glazed cotton
Calico
Batiste (for heavier shell fabrics)
Lightweight cotton or silk
twill (for lighter fabrics)
Medium weight interfacing
(scrap, to line pocket)

TRIMMINGS
Contrast fabric
Ribbon
Lace (neckline, sleeves, hem ruffle)
Ball-type buttons

NOTIONS
Thread to match
Five hooks (4 for bodice, 1 for skirt)
½ yd. (.45 m) cotton carpet warp or
pearl cotton (optional)

⊁ SUMMARY OF STEPS ⊱

SKIRT

1. Make placket.
2. Join sections.
3. Finish hem.
4. Add bands of trim.
5. Make waistband and closure; establish skirt drape.

POLONAISE

6. Make placket.
7. Join back sections.
8. Join front sections.
9. Join shoulders.
10. Finish and trim neck edge.
11. Join side seams and finish hem.
12. Apply pocket (if any).
13. Make and set sleeves.
14. Make closure; organize drapery.

GENERAL ⊁ CONSTRUCTION ⊱ NOTES

IN organizing the two-piece ensemble, the skirt should be made first, measurements being taken over the petticoat (if any). The polonaise is then fitted and draped over the skirt. The original garment on which the polonaise and skirt is based was sewn entirely by hand, but the long seams of the ensemble may be executed by machine. I found when I attempted to do the bands of skirt trimming by machine that the lines of machine stitching made the garment drape rather stiffly. As the seams securing the trim are not structural seams, they are easy enough to do by hand.

The basic structure of the skirt is a foundation of cotton with a bound hem. A flounce is mounted onto the surface. The flounce is surmounted by two bands of trim all the way around. Additional bands trim the back, where the drapery lifts the hem of the polonaise, exposing more of the skirt.

The polonaise is lined to the hip with lightweight cotton. The lining pieces are basted to each shell piece as appropriate, and the basting ripped out as you go along.

⊁ INSTRUCTIONS ⊱
Skirt

PATTERN NO. 12

1 • **MAKE PLACKET.** The placket is made in a slash cut into the center back of the skirt. After cutting the slash, as marked on the pattern, turn back both edges ⅛" (.3 cm) at the top tapering to nothing at the bottom of the cut, and baste them down. (Fig. 7.1.) Turn one edge in a further ⅛" (.3 cm) and close with a small hem stitch. Turn the other edge in ¼" (.5 cm) and stitch. (Fig. 7.2.) Lap the wider turn-back over the narrower one, forming a small pleat at the bottom of the slash. Secure at the bottom with a neat bar tack. (Fig. 7.3.) Since no allowance is made for one side of the placket being slightly narrower than the other, it finishes slightly off-center, but it does not show when the dress is worn.

2 • **JOIN SECTIONS.** Join the sections of the skirt, using the notches as a guide. Press all the seams toward the back and overcast to neaten them. (Fig. 7.4.)

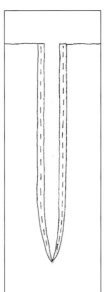
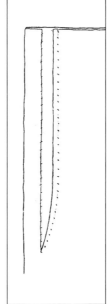

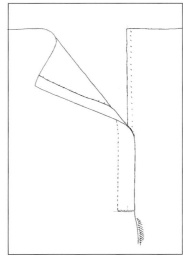

Fig. 7.3. *The overlap is drawn over the underside of the placket, forming a small pleat at the bottom. The bottom of the placket is secured with a small hand bar tack.*

Fig. 7.1. *First step in forming the placket. Both edges of the slash are basted back ⅛" (.3 cm), tapering to nothing at the bottom of the cut.*

Fig. 7.2. *One side of the slash is hemmed down ⅛" (.3 cm); the other is turned in ¼" (.5 cm) to form the overlap.*

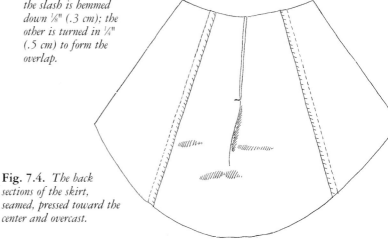

Fig. 7.4. *The back sections of the skirt, seamed, pressed toward the center and overcast.*

3 • FINISH HEM. The skirt is finished with an applied hem, which is turned out to the right side of the garment. Make a bias strip 36" (91.5 cm) long by 1½" (4 cm) wide, piecing as necessary. Press one long edge down ¼" (.5 cm). Set the right side of the bias to the wrong side of the skirt and stitch at ¼" (.5 cm). (Fig. 7.5.) Turn the bias out, favoring the right side—in this case, the bias itself, which is covering the skirt foundation at the bottom. Press and close with a neat blind stitch. (Fig. 7.6.)

4 • ADD BANDS OF TRIM. The first trim to be added is a flounce. Cut a piece of bias fabric 36" (91.5 cm) long by 3" (7.5 cm), piecing as necessary. Finish one long edge in the same manner as the skirt hem, cutting the contrast bias 36" (91.5 cm) long by 1¼" (3 cm), turning the bias out and blind stitching to close. Put a gathering stitch into the other long edge, and arrange the flounce onto the skirt. There is not much excess allowed; the flounce is merely to trim the lower edge and provide a light drapery. It is not intended to make a ruffly "statement." There should be almost no fullness across the front—the flounce should not interrupt the hem of the polonaise. Most of the fullness should be concentrated at the back to provide the suggestion of a train. Baste the flounce in place close to the top edge. (Fig. 7.7.)

Make two strips of bias 1½" (4 cm) wide by 32" (81.5 cm) and 30" (76 cm) long respectively, piecing as necessary. These will trim the top of the flounce all the way around the skirt, one over the other. Lay the longer band in place first, right sides together, aligning the raw edges of flounce and band. Trim off the excess length, if any, and tuck in the short raw edge where the band laps itself. Stitch at ¼" (.5 cm), turn the band up, and baste in place. (Fig. 7.8.) These rows of applied bands should be laid lightly in place. They are not pressed flat or pulled tight.

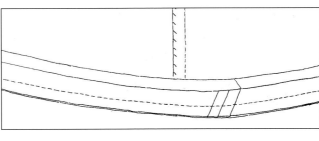

Fig. 7.5. *The applied hem. The top edge is pressed down before the bias strip is set to the skirt bottom. The bias is stitched to the skirt by hand or machine.*

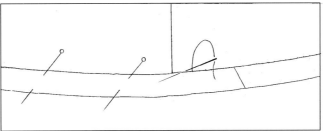

Fig. 7.6. *The hem, turned up, and closed with a blind stitch.*

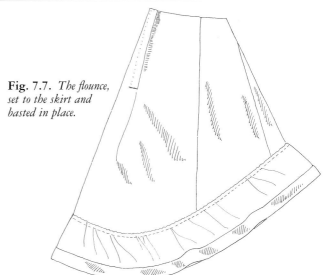

Fig. 7.7. *The flounce, set to the skirt and basted in place.*

Fig. 7.8. *The first band. The seam setting it to the skirt covers the flounce basting.*

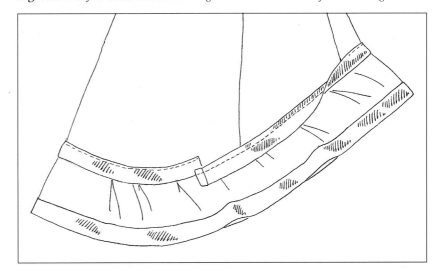

The second band is applied in the same fashion. However, this is the last band of trimming across the front. After stitching the band on and turning it up, tuck the top edge under ¼" (.5 cm) across the front and side sections of the skirt, as illustrated. A small clip must be made in the top edge of the band at the seam of the back gore of the skirt to do this. Blind stitch across the front sections to finish the band. (Fig. 7.9.) Baste across the back.

The original skirt was trimmed across the back breadth with three bias bands. Two were adequate for the copy. The bands need only to cover the cotton skirt foundation as far as the polonaise is draped up. Cut the bias bands 13" (33 cm) long by 1½" (4 cm) wide. Lay the first one across the back section of the skirt, cutting off the excess length and tucking in the raw edges at the side seam. (Fig. 7.10.) The second is applied on top of the first. The final band has a finished top edge. This can be steamed (not pressed) down before the band is joined to the skirt. (Fig. 7.11.)

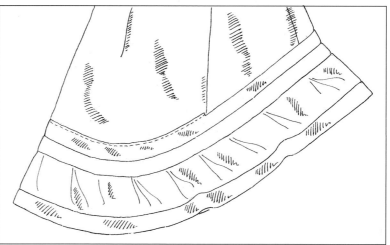

Fig. 7.9. *The second band. The band is turned under along the front sections of the skirt, to the back gore of the skirt.*

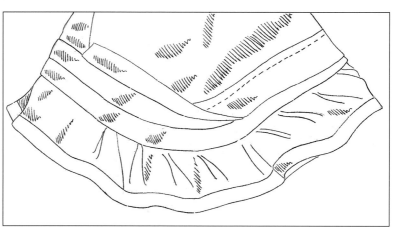

Fig. 7.10. *The third band, covering the back portion of the skirt only.*

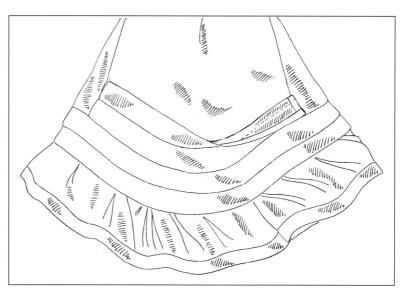

Fig. 7.11. *The fourth band. The top edge is turned under and blind stitched to finish.*

5 • MAKE WAISTBAND AND CLOSURE; ESTABLISH SKIRT DRAPE. Measure the doll over her petticoats for a waistband. Add two ¼" (.5 cm) seams plus about ½" (1.5 cm) for fitting ease and to lap at the back; cut the waitband 1" (2.5 cm) wide. Tuck in the seams, fold lengthwise, and baste. (Fig. 7.12.) Measure the doll down the center front to establish the finished length of the skirt, turn the waist edge down evenly, and baste.

Arrange the fullness of the skirt waist on the band. In front, the skirt should fall nearly straight, with no ease. The fullness of the skirt back should be pleated into about 1" (2.5 cm) on either side of the placket. The remaining fullness is formed into soft pleats over the hips of the doll. All the pleats open toward the back.

Whip the skirt to the band. The closure is with a hook and worked loop. To provide the correct drape, run a line of basting across the back of the skirt at about the level of the doll's knees, and draw it up so that the entire fullness of the back section is held behind the doll. You may want to wrap your drawn-up thread around a pin rather than sewing it off at this point, until you can view the polonaise and skirt together and judge the success of the arrangement. (Fig. 7.13.)

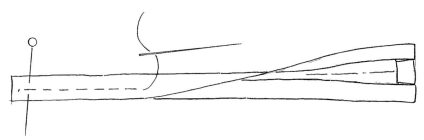

Fig. 7.12. *Construction of the waistband.*

Fig. 7.13. *The arrangement of the pleats on the waistband, the back closure, and the arrangement of the skirt drapery behind the knees.*

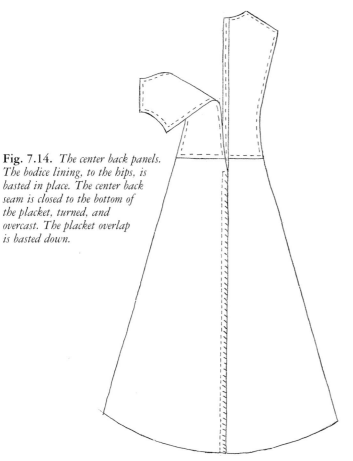

Fig. 7.14. *The center back panels. The bodice lining, to the hips, is basted in place. The center back seam is closed to the bottom of the placket, turned, and overcast. The placket overlap is basted down.*

Polonaise

PATTERN NO. 13 AND NO. 7

Before beginning to sew, join each shell piece to its appropriate lining piece by basting all around the lining.

6 • MAKE PLACKET. Stitch the center back seam to the notch. Press the seams to the left side of the opening, and overcast to neaten them. (Fig. 7.14.)

No allowance is made for the placket lap; therefore, buttons applied to decorate the placket are slightly off center when it is completed. To finish the left side of the placket (the overlap), cut a piece of bias fabric 1" (2.5 cm) wide by 6" (15 cm) long. Turn in both long edges ¼" (.5 cm) and blind stitch in place. (Fig. 7.15.)

To finish the right side of the placket (the under lap), cut a piece of bias fabric 1 ½" (1.5 cm) wide by 6" (15 cm) long. Press one long edge under ¼" (.5 cm). Set the other edge to the inside of the raw placket opening and stitch. (Fig. 7.15.) Turn the binding out and cover the seam with the folded edge. Blind stitch to close and secure the bottom of the placket with a hand bar tack. (Fig. 7.16.)

7 • JOIN BACK SECTIONS Stitch the back side sections to the center sections. Press the seams toward the sides and overcast. (Fig. 7.17.)

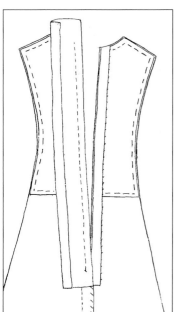

Fig. 7.15. *The placket facing (right side of drawing) is blind stitched in place. The under lap is stitched (left side of drawing) to the center back seam.*

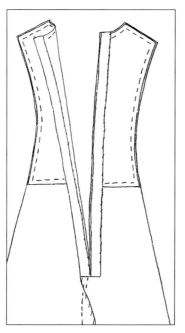

Fig. 7.16. *The under lap is folded over the raw edge of the seam and blind stitched in place.*

Fig. 7.17. *The side back sections, with their linings, stitched to the center section. The seams are turned and overcast. Note that the bottom of the placket is secured with a small hand bar tack.*

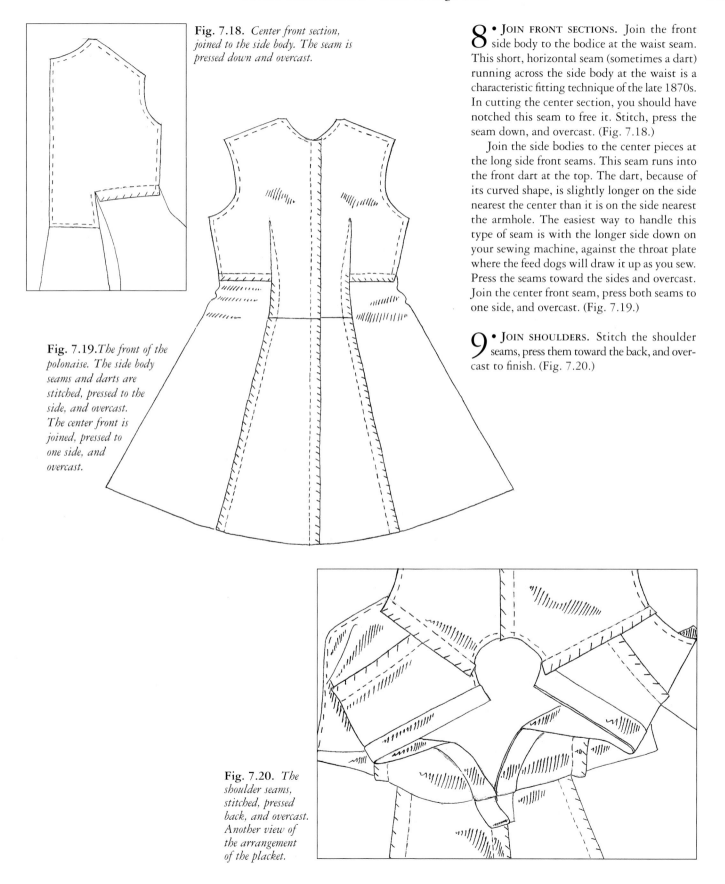

Fig. 7.18. *Center front section, joined to the side body. The seam is pressed down and overcast.*

Fig. 7.19. *The front of the polonaise. The side body seams and darts are stitched, pressed to the side, and overcast. The center front is joined, pressed to one side, and overcast.*

Fig. 7.20. *The shoulder seams, stitched, pressed back, and overcast. Another view of the arrangement of the placket.*

8 • JOIN FRONT SECTIONS. Join the front side body to the bodice at the waist seam. This short, horizontal seam (sometimes a dart) running across the side body at the waist is a characteristic fitting technique of the late 1870s. In cutting the center section, you should have notched this seam to free it. Stitch, press the seam down, and overcast. (Fig. 7.18.)

Join the side bodies to the center pieces at the long side front seams. This seam runs into the front dart at the top. The dart, because of its curved shape, is slightly longer on the side nearest the center than it is on the side nearest the armhole. The easiest way to handle this type of seam is with the longer side down on your sewing machine, against the throat plate where the feed dogs will draw it up as you sew. Press the seams toward the sides and overcast. Join the center front seam, press both seams to one side, and overcast. (Fig. 7.19.)

9 • JOIN SHOULDERS. Stitch the shoulder seams, press them toward the back, and overcast to finish. (Fig. 7.20.)

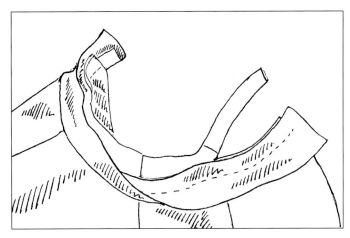

Fig. 7.21. *Finishing the neck edge. After stitching the binding on at ¼" (.5 cm), the seam is trimmed out to about ⅛" (.3 cm).*

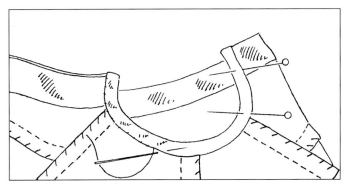

Fig. 7.22. *The neck edge binding, turned inside and blind stitched.*

10 • FINISH AND TRIM NECK EDGE.

The original garment is finished at the neck by a ⅛" (.3 cm) bias binding. The neck may also be finished with a bias facing turned inside or by a cord facing. Cord facings were becoming old-fashioned by the time this dress was made, but the dressmaker finished the armholes of the original dress with cord.

The neck seam has ¼" (.5 cm) allowed for consistency's sake. Cut the bias neck binding 7" (18 cm) long by 1" (2.5 cm) wide. Leave a short allowance to tuck in as you begin, and work the bias around the neck, right sides together, stitching at ¼" (.5 cm). When the seam is completed, trim the neck seam down to 1/8" (.3 cm). (Fig. 7.21.)

Turn the bias inside. Trim the bias so that it folds neatly, tuck in the raw edges, and close with a blind stitch. (Fig. 7.22.)

Make a pair of collars. Seam the outer edges, grade the seams and clip the corners. Turn. (Fig. 7.23.) Refer to Fig. 7.26 and the pattern for placement. The upper edge of the collar runs along the shoulder seam. This edge is tucked under ⅜" (1 cm) and blind stitched down. Be sure the raw upper edge is secure. The two lower points are then tacked in place. (Fig. 7.24—the small "x"s indicate where the collar is to be stitched.) The collar is otherwise left loose.

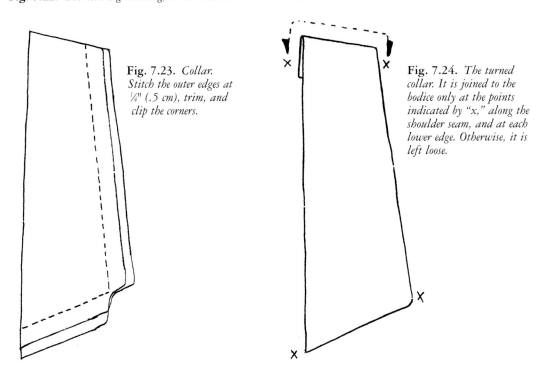

Fig. 7.23. *Collar. Stitch the outer edges at ¼" (.5 cm), trim, and clip the corners.*

Fig. 7.24. *The turned collar. It is joined to the bodice only at the points indicated by "x," along the shoulder seam, and at each lower edge. Otherwise, it is left loose.*

Fig. 7.25 illustrates the method of making the small, drooping bow that decorates the front of the collar. Ribbon was used on the copy because the faille used to make the collar itself was too heavy to make a pretty bow on this scale. The original dress has a bow of the same brown taffeta used to make the collar.

After stitching the collar in place, the neck is trimmed with a small ruffle of lace whipped to the inside of the bias neck binding. (Fig. 7.26.)

11 • JOIN SIDE SEAMS AND FINISH HEM. Join the side seams, press toward the back, and overcast.

The hem of the polonaise is bound to finish it. Make a piece of bias binding (in the main color) 1½" (4 cm) wide by 40" (101.5 cm) long, piecing as necessary. Set the right side of the binding to the wrong side of the hem and stitch at ¼" (.5 cm). (Fig. 7.27.) Wrap the binding around the hem, turning it to the right side, and arrange it smoothly. Baste the raw top edge. (Fig. 7.28.) Make a second strip (in the contrast color) 1" (2.5 cm) wide by 40" (101.5 cm) long. Turn both long edges under ¼" (.5 cm), yielding a bias strip ½" (.5 cm) wide. Set this strip over the hem binding, covering the raw top edge. Measure carefully to ensure that the applied strip is a uniform distance from the edge of the hem. Close both edges with a neat blind stitch. (Fig. 7.35 has a view of the inside of the hem.)

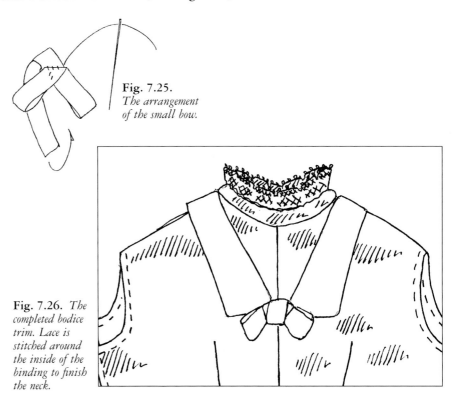

Fig. 7.25. *The arrangement of the small bow.*

Fig. 7.26. *The completed bodice trim. Lace is stitched around the inside of the binding to finish the neck.*

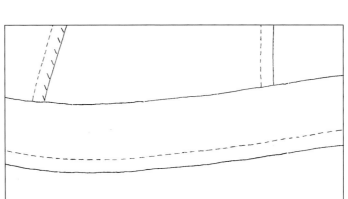

Fig. 7.27. *The hem of the polonaise. The right side of the applied hem is stitched to the wrong side of the skirt.*

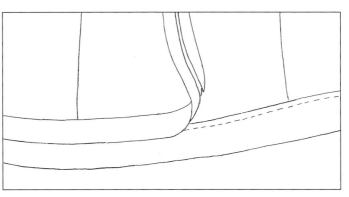

Fig. 7.28. *The hem binding is turned right side out and basted in place on the right side of the hem. The raw seam of the hem binding is covered with a strip of bias trim blind stitched along both its folded edges.*

12. **APPLY POCKET.** This large elaborate pocket dates this dress definitively at 1876 or shortly thereafter.

Cut all the pieces and identify them. The foundation should be cut from a medium-stiff interfacing or similar fabric. No seams are allowed on the foundation; the seams are allowed on the shell fabric only. Part "A" is first basted to the foundation. (Fig. 7.29.) The diagram shows the back side, with the seam allowances of "A" sticking over the edge of the foundation.

Next the middle section, part "D" is prepared by pressing down the side seam allowances (Fig. 7.30); it is blind stitched in place on the pocket, covering the raw seams of the edge sections. The trim, part "C" is likewise pressed and blind stitched in place. (Fig. 7.31.) The "flap" (part "B") is next prepared by pressing down its lower edges, and blind stitching it onto the pocket foundation. (Fig. 7.32.)

Draw the pocket seams over the edge of the foundation and press them in place.

(Fig. 7.33.) Lastly, press down the hem and secure it with a catch stitch through the hem and the foundation only, showing nothing on the outside of the pocket. (Fig. 7.34.)

Blind stitch the pocket to the outside of the polonaise, using the pattern as a guide. (Fig. 7.35.) A handkerchief is arranged to peek out of the pocket.

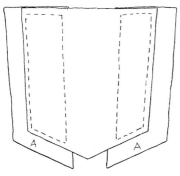

Fig. 7.29. *Construction of the pocket. A view of the "wrong side"; part "A" is basted to the lining along the sides of the pocket on the right side. Seams are allowed on the shell pieces only, in order to save bulk.*

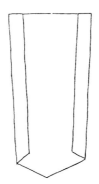

Fig. 7.30. *The center shell of the pocket, its seams turned under (part "D").*

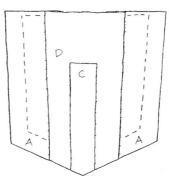

Fig. 7.31. *A view of the "right side"; the center shell piece of the pocket (part "D") blind stitched in place with its contrast trim (part "C").*

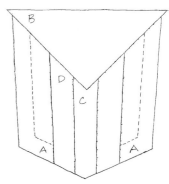

Fig. 7.32. *The upper pocket part (part "B") blind stitched in place. The hem is allowed on the shell part only.*

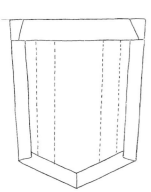

Fig. 7.33. *A view of the "wrong side," showing the hem side edges folded under.*

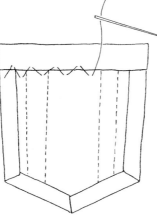

Fig. 7.34. *The pocket, hemmed with a catch stitch through the back of the hem and the foundation.*

Fig. 7.35. *Placement of the pocket.*

13• **Make and set sleeves.** Stitch the sleeves, turn the seams toward the undersleeve, and overcast. Turn the hem and close with a hem stitch. (Fig. 7.36.) Turn the sleeve out and steam (do not press) flat.

The sleeve detail is applied much like the pocket. Turn all the edges down as indicated on the pattern with the exception of the "under lap." Baste. (Fig. 7.37.) Cut a piece of bias fabric about ¾" (2 cm) wide by 5" (12.5 cm) long. Tuck in the short ends and fold the strip in half the long way. Set the strip behind the top of the detail, mitering the top neatly, and baste it in place. (Fig. 7.38.)

Set the cuff to the sleeve. The sleeve should just show at the lower edge. The point is aligned with the sleeve outseam. The raw "under lap" is on the undersleeve. The cuff laps over from the top sleeve, making the join inconspicuous. (Fig. 7.39.)

Blind stitch to close. The sleeve may then be trimmed with a ruffle of lace whipped to the inside hem. (The drawing shows this operation completed.) (Fig. 7.40.)

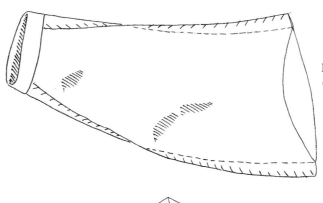

Fig. 7.36. *Construction of the sleeve. Seams are overcast for neatness and turned toward the under sleeve. The sleeve is finished with a turned hem.*

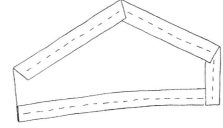

Fig. 7.37. *Sleeve trim. All the edges are turned under and basted as marked, except the under lap edge. The sleeve trim has a "left" and "right," as the seams are asymmetrical.*

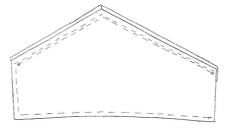

Fig. 7.38. *The sleeve trim. A narrow, folded piece of contrast trim is basted behind the upper turned back edge.*

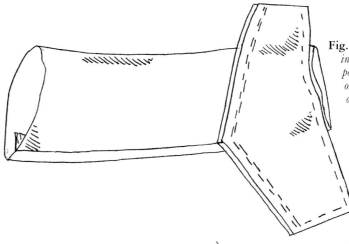

Fig. 7.39. *The trim, laid in place on the sleeve. The point is aligned with the outseam; the under lap is on the under sleeve.*

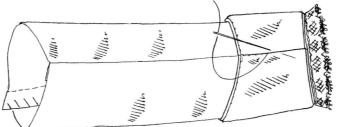

Fig. 7.40. *The trim, stitched in place. The cuff may be trimmed with a ruffle of lace.*

The sleeve set of the polonaise is made with a narrow cording around the armhole. Cording was much less used at this time—would in fact disappear during this period—and in the 1870s represents a personal stylistic choice of the dressmaker. The cording may be omitted if you don't like to put it in.

To make the covered cord, cut two pieces of cord 6" (15 cm) long, the approximate armhole circumference. Cut two pieces of bias fabric 6" (15 cm) long by 1" (2.5 cm) wide and stitch the cord inside. The stitches should fix the cord securely into the fold of fabric, but not tightly. Trim the folded fabric down to ¼" (.5 cm). (Fig. 7.41.) Beginning at the bottom of the armhole, lay the cording against the armhole and stitch it in place. The raw edges should be aligned to ensure that the cording is at ¼" (.5 cm), the width of the seam allowance. (Fig. 7.42.)

At the point where the cording laps itself at the bottom of the armhole, peel open the bias fabric and trim out the excess cord. Lap the fabric at the bottom (Fig. 7.43) and incline the raw edges into the armhole.

Turn the bodice inside out, and align the sleeve in the armhole. The outseam should be about ⅜" (1 cm) behind the shoulder seam. The inseam falls into the deepest point of the front armhole. Around the top of the sleeve, there is a small amount of excess, which should be eased. This is done with your fingers inside the *sleeve*, by pushing the sleeve toward the needle slightly as you sew. (Fig. 7.44.) This should allow you to take up slightly more of the sleeve than the armhole with each stitch, drawing up the sleeve without any apparent puckers. Around the bottom of the armhole, excess is made into a small, forward-opening pleat in the undersleeve. (Fig. 7.45.)

The sleeve may be reinforced with a blind stitch around the outside next to the cording. Turn the armhole out, trim the seam down to about ³⁄₁₆" (.45 cm) and overcast. (Fig. 7.46.)

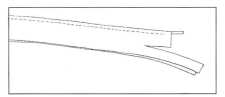

Fig. 7.41. *The construction of the cording.*

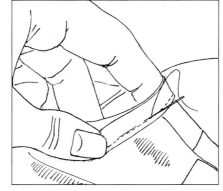

Fig. 7.42. *Setting the cording to the armhole.*

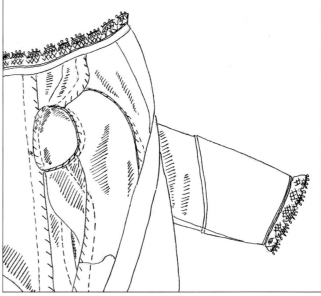

Fig. 7.43. *The cording at the armhole. The cording is opened out and the excess cord trimmed to reduce bulk at the point where the cording meets under the arm.*

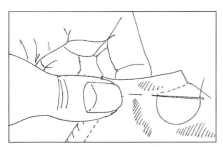

Fig. 7.44. *Setting the sleeve. The needle follows the bump of the cording, which can be felt through the fabric of the bodice.*

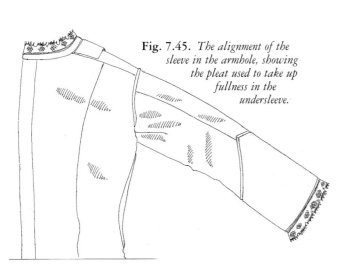

Fig. 7.45. *The alignment of the sleeve in the armhole, showing the pleat used to take up fullness in the undersleeve.*

Fig. 7.46. *The armhole seam is trimmed to ³⁄₁₆" (.45 cm) and overcast for neatness.*

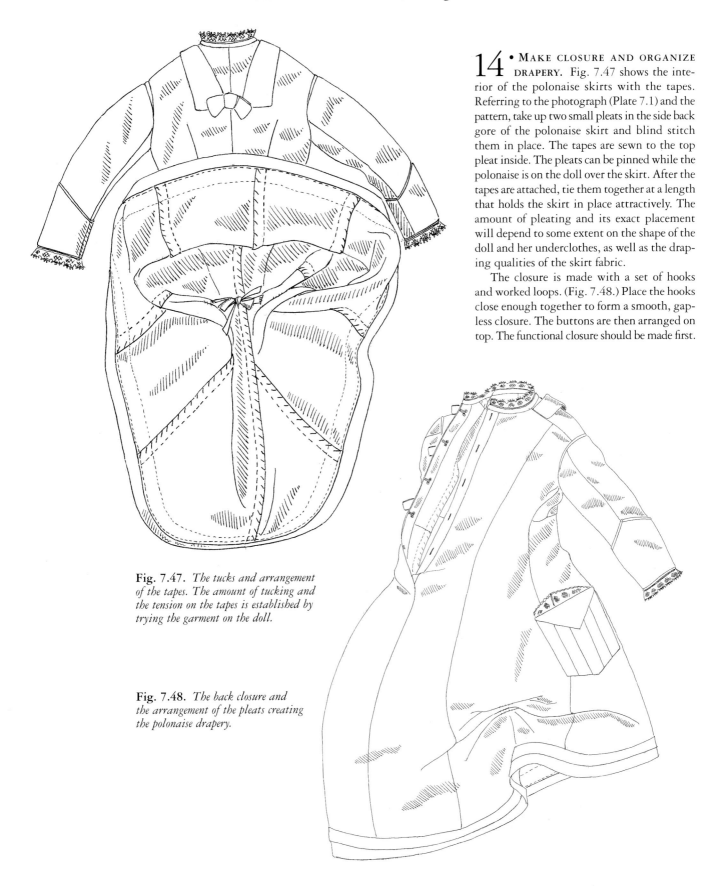

14 **· MAKE CLOSURE AND ORGANIZE DRAPERY.** Fig. 7.47 shows the interior of the polonaise skirts with the tapes. Referring to the photograph (Plate 7.1) and the pattern, take up two small pleats in the side back gore of the polonaise skirt and blind stitch them in place. The tapes are sewn to the top pleat inside. The pleats can be pinned while the polonaise is on the doll over the skirt. After the tapes are attached, tie them together at a length that holds the skirt in place attractively. The amount of pleating and its exact placement will depend to some extent on the shape of the doll and her underclothes, as well as the draping qualities of the skirt fabric.

The closure is made with a set of hooks and worked loops. (Fig. 7.48.) Place the hooks close enough together to form a smooth, gapless closure. The buttons are then arranged on top. The functional closure should be made first.

Fig. 7.47. *The tucks and arrangement of the tapes. The amount of tucking and the tension on the tapes is established by trying the garment on the doll.*

Fig. 7.48. *The back closure and the arrangement of the pleats creating the polonaise drapery.*

CHAPTER VIII

Edwardian Skirt and Waist

circa 1895–1910

THE gored skirt is one of the basic silhouettes of the Belle Époque. The model presented here is the successor to the fan-shaped skirt of the 1890s. Although it is cut less extravagantly, it presents a similar appearance, gracefully draping over the hips and spreading around the feet. This produces the attractive bell shape characteristic of the time. Although just before the First World War narrow skirts became fashionable, the bell-shaped skirt was worn throughout the 20th century's first decade.

The skirt is worn with the classic Edwardian blouse or "waist." The "skirt and blouse," introduced in the 1860s, has remained a staple in women's clothing repertoire ever since. The peculiar balloon-shaped bodice is an idiosyncrasy of the pre-World War I period; the fullness at the front was thought to add "stature" to the figure. The desired figure formed by the corset of the day was a "straight front," which thrust the chest forward and the buttocks back. The Pingree trousseau contains a very correct silk corset in fashionable "butterfly blue." (See Plate 47.) The waist was at its approximate natural level with the fullness of the blouse gathered into a band at the waist or shaped to ride on the hips.

Ladies were completely covered up in the daytime for most of this decade; sleeves were either full or three-quarter length and some standing collars were designed to go right up to the ears. The delicate appearance of these blouses is somewhat deceptive, as they were often made over a fitted and boned underlining. Lace collars were sometimes reinforced with wire or celluloid inserted into the tiny seams. Exquisite workmanship is the hallmark of the fine Edwardian ladies' blouse.

With the gored skirt in a handsome fabric, completed with a neat and finely made blouse, you can create an unfussy, classic ensemble for your doll. A two-piece dress can also be created with a plain or slubbed silk or very fine wool challis trimmed with buttons and lace and belted with contrast silk or velvet.

Plate 8.1. *Silk tweed skirt, interlined and lined, for the very stiff appearance of the late 1890s and turn of the century. The skirt was made from an old kimono and interlined with the original navy blue cotton lining. The silk taffeta lining has a pleated flounce to finish the hem, which makes the skirt stand away from the body. The blouse with jabot was made from an old set of linen napkins, using the original fil tiré designs in the shoulders.*

Plate 8.2. *The same skirt, made of a much softer silk tweed, interlined with new silk organza. The taffeta lining was made without a hem flounce, to allow the skirt to drape naturally. The blouse with collar tabs and tucked front is made of gray silk broadcloth.*

Skirt

PATTERN NO. 14

⇒ MATERIALS ⇐

F ROM 1900 to 1910, materials for dressmaking were becoming softer and more fluid. By the end of the decade, the rustling of stiff silk petticoats, thought to be fetching at the turn of the century, was deemed by the fashionable to be "vulgar."

Several combinations of finishing techniques are appropriate for the inside of the skirt; which you use will depend upon the fabric you select. The skirt has a full lining that makes it possible to omit a petticoat, to minimize bulk. The skirt may be finished either with a separate lining or by lining in one with the shell and then pinking or taping the interior seams. Both of the pictured examples (Plate 8.1 and Plate 8.2) are lined and underlined. Tape is cut from the lining fabric.

The choice of materials and their combinations is nearly limitless. The Pingree trousseau has versions of this skirt in wool serge, melton, chiffon and lace, velvet, linen, satin, and taffeta, styled with various pleats, tucks, panels, and many different arrangements of the gores. Some are lined and some are not. Taffeta is the best basic lining material easily available; it can be had in various degrees of "crispness" and many colors. Skirts made of linen may be unlined and worn over a cotton petticoat cut from the skirt pattern.

SKIRT CIRCA 1895–1905

Taffeta, raw silk, stiff but thin jacquards
Stout silk satins
Crisp, lightweight brocades
Wool flannel, serge
Heavier linen types
Velveteen

SKIRT CIRCA 1905–1910

Soft silk satins, old silk crepe,
silk broadcloth
Wool crepe, wool challis
Lighter linen types
Panne velvet, silk velvet

LINING

Taffeta

UNDERLINING

Organza
Batiste or other sheer cotton
Old coarsely woven cotton interlinings

NOTIONS

Thread (silk or cotton)
3-4 hooks
1 hook (belt, optional)

⇒ SUMMARY OF STEPS ⇐

SHELL

1. Close center back seam; apply placket.
2. Stitch remaining seams.
3. Apply hem.

LINING

4. Close center back seam; apply placket.
5. Stitch remaining seams.
6. Apply hem.

FINISHING

7. Apply waistband and closure.

GENERAL ⇒ CONSTRUCTION ⇐ NOTES

A FTER you have selected the fabric, decide how the inside of the skirt will be finished. Heavier fabrics such as serge and velvet are preferably lined. This makes them drape better, as well as being the cleanest way to finish them. You may want to pink as well as line to reduce interior ravelling. The skirt lining may be finished at the bottom with a pleated flounce if necessary to prevent the skirt shape from collapsing at the feet.

A fabric that ravels badly, like satin or jacquard-pattern silk, should be taped if it is not lined. Whether you underline and tape or line fully will depend on the drape of the fabric and what period you are trying to suggest. Plate 8.1 and Plate 8.2 show silk skirts typical of the early and later parts of the decade, respectively. Underlining increases the stiffness of the skirt and in most cases will not be appropriate for very soft drapey silks like charmeuse, since the underlining will overwhelm the natural hand of the fabric. However, pick a shell fabric with enough body to show the bell shape effectively; silks that are completely limp are unsuitable even with underlining. Softer silks are often better lined only—supported by the lining rather than being stiffened with underlining. Linings of skirts later in the decade will not call for a flounce, since the whole fashion line is softer.

⇒ INSTRUCTIONS ⇐

B EFORE beginning, decide how you will finish the interior seams. If you decide to pink, do each seam after it has been sewn, before it is pressed open. If you decide to use tape, bind all the long vertical seams at once before starting to sew. The center back seam should be bound only from the hem to the notch.

In either case, if the fabric is underlined, put the underlining and shell together first. Cut the underlining identical to the shell and baste each shell piece to its corresponding underlining around the edge so the two layers can be treated as one.

Fig. 8.1. *The back gores of the skirt, joined to the notch marking the end of the opening. The seams have been pinked to the notch to finish them, and the placket seams basted down.*

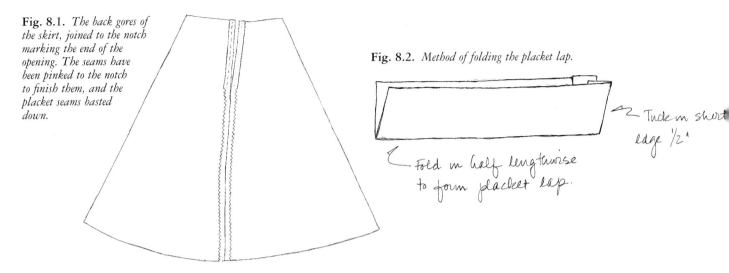

Fig. 8.2. *Method of folding the placket lap.*

Tuck in short edge ½"

Fold in half lengthwise to form placket lap.

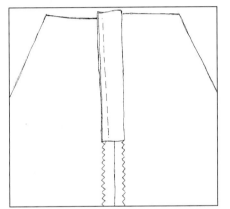

Fig. 8.3. *The lap, laid in place along the raw edge of the placket opening.*

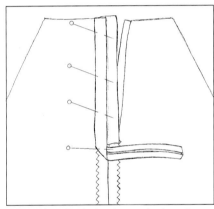

Fig. 8.4. *The placket facing, laid in place along one edge of the placket opening. Note the beginning of the turn at the bottom of the placket opening.*

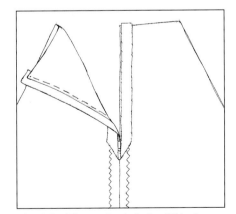

Fig. 8.5. *The completed placket. This drawing shows the placket of a skirt that has been underlined; both the inner and outer edges of the placket facing were blind stitched. If the skirt has no underlining, the outer edge must be closed with a small hem stitch.*

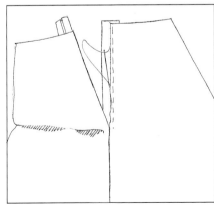

Fig. 8.6. *Blind stitching the lap from the outside to reinforce.*

SHELL

1 • CLOSE CENTER BACK SEAM; APPLY PLACKET. Stitch the back seam to the notch at the bottom of the placket. Press open, including the unsewn portion at the top. Baste the placket seams down to keep them smooth and straight. (Fig. 8.1.)

Make the "lap," which fills the placket opening. Cut a strip of self fabric 1½" (4 cm) wide by 4¾" (12 cm) long. (If you are working in a heavy fabric like velveteen, you may wish to make the lap from color-matched lining material. Take care to pick a fabric that is inconspicuous—it may show a little when the skirt is fastened up.) Tuck in one short edge to finish the bottom, and then fold the piece in half lengthwise. (Fig. 8.2.) Lay the lap against one raw seam of the placket edge (Fig. 8.3.), basting to hold it secure.

The placket facing is a 1" (2.5 cm) wide piece of bias fabric double-folded to make a ½" (1.5 cm) wide piece of tape. Use your taffeta lining fabric. Work the placket facing around the placket opening and stitch it in place. (Figs. 8.4 and 8.5.) Use a small hem stitch around the inside, a blind stitch at the placket opening edge. Then, from the outside, blind stitch the lap to reinforce it. (Fig. 8.6.)

2 • STITCH REMAINING SEAMS. Stitch the remaining long seams using the notches as a guide, and press them open.

3 • APPLY HEM. The skirt has an applied hem facing of bias tape. Make a piece of bias binding 1" (2.5 cm) wide by 40" (101.5 cm) long, piecing as necessary, and press the seams open.

Before stitching, turn one long edge of the facing down a scant ¼" (.5 cm) and press. Right sides together, stitch the facing to the skirt hem, stretching very slightly as you sew. (Fig. 8.7.) This will cause the facing to hug the skirt without ripples when it is turned under. If the bias is pulled too tight, however, it will draw the hem up. Turn the facing to the inside, favoring the shell, and close with a small hem stitch. (Fig. 8.8.) Alternatively, if you are making a sporty or tailored ensemble such as a tennis outfit or shirtwaist dress, the bottom may be finished with several parallel rows of machine topstitching. The topstitching of this period is close and very neat, made with a very small stitch.

LINING

☞ If you are omitting the lining, skip to step 7 below. The skirt pattern has a line indicating where the lining is to be cut if it is to have a pleated flounce around the bottom.

4 • CLOSE CENTER BACK SEAM; APPLY PLACKET. Stitch the center back seam to ¼" (.5 cm) below the notch at the bottom of the placket. The ¼" (.5 cm) allowance ensures that the lap on the shell side will clear the lining placket when the skirt is fastened. Pink the seam and press it open, including the unsewn portion at the top. Baste the placket seams down to keep them smooth and straight.

The lining placket facing is a 1" (2.5 cm) wide piece of bias fabric doubled folded to make a ½" (1.5 cm) wide piece of tape, just like the shell placket facing. (See Figs. 8.4, 8.5, and 8.6.) Use your self taffeta lining fabric. Work the placket around the opening as before and stitch it in place, by hand or machine.

5 • STITCH REMAINING SEAMS AND PRESS THEM OPEN. As above, at step 2. Pink to finish the lining seams.

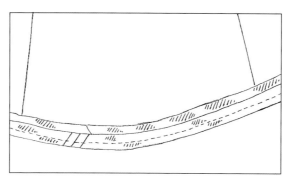

Fig. 8.7. *The folded hem facing stitched along the bottom of the skirt from the right side.*

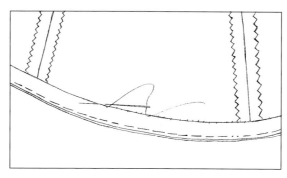

Fig. 8.8. *The hem facing turned inside the skirt, basted in place and hemmed down. At the very bottom edge, the shell has been favored in the turning, i.e., the hem is turned all the way inside so as to be completely invisible from the outside.*

6 • APPLY HEM. If the lining is to have a plain bottom, finish it with an applied hem just like the shell (step 3). It can be applied entirely by machine, including closing the hem.

If you are planning a flounce, make sure you have cut the lining at the appropriate level (the dotted line on the pattern). If not, you can trim it off now. To make the flounce, cut a strip of taffeta on the straight grain, 2" (5 cm) by 120" (304 cm). This is a generous estimate—how much you actually use will depend on the uniformity and depth of your pleats. Knife pleats are cut 3 times their finished length. Piece the strip on the straight as necessary; pink any joining seams and press them open.

Hem one long edge very narrowly, turning about ¼" (.5 cm) total (or a double ⅛" {.3 cm} fold). Stitch the hem by machine.

You can use a pleater or tuck the pleats up by hand. If you are able to introduce some small irregularities into the completed strip, it will look less "new." The pleats may look odd if they are too regular and "perfect." The pleats should be ¼" (.5 cm) wide or less.

After completing the strip, pin it to your ironing board and trim it off evenly to 1½" (4 cm). (Fig. 8.9.) Stay stitch by machine about ³⁄₁₆" (.45 cm) from the raw top edge. The seam will hide this. Set the raw edge of the pleated flounce along the bottom edge of the lining, right sides together, beginning at the center back. Overlap the beginning and end slightly, making a double fold to hide the raw edges at the ends of the pleated strip. (Fig. 8.10.) Cover the seam with a bias strip, 1 x 40" (2.5 x 101.5 cm), applied as described above for a taped hem. After stitching, open the flounce down and press the tape up into the skirt. Close with a machine stitch. (Fig. 8.11.)

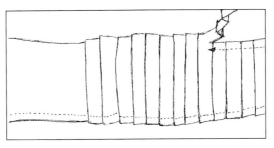

Fig. 8.9. *The lining hem flounce, showing its straightened bottom edge and trimmed off top.*

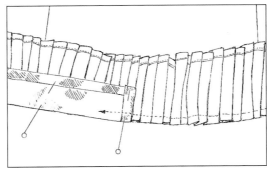

Fig. 8.10. *The lining hem flounce, set to the right side of the lining and covered with tape. The hem of the lining may be closed entirely by machine.*

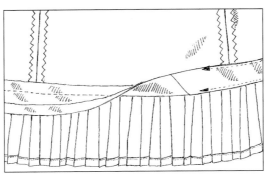

Fig. 8.11. *Closing the taped flounce seam.*

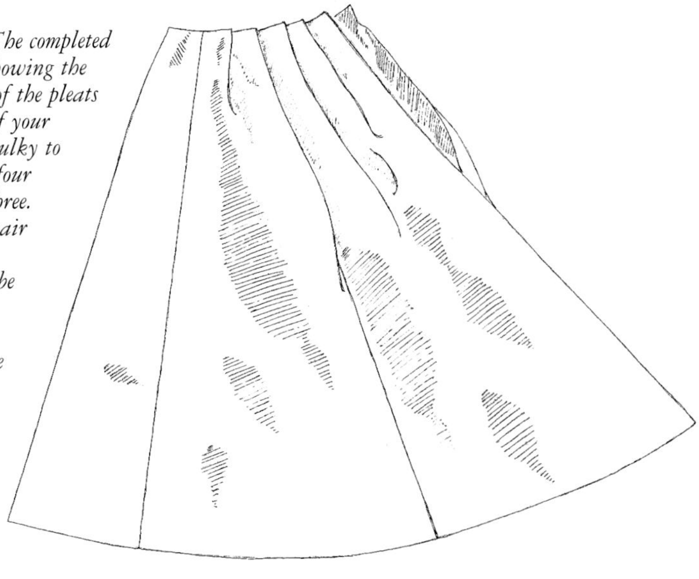

Fig. 8.12. *The completed skirt parts, showing the arrangement of the pleats at the back. If your fabric is too bulky to accommodate four pleats, take three. At least one pair (at the center back) should be about ½" (1.5 cm) in depth to create the proper set of the skirt across the derriere.*

FINISHING

7 • **APPLY WAISTBAND AND CLOSURE.** Both the lining and shell must be pleated on either side of the back closure to arrange the set of the skirt over the derriere. Full-size skirts of this period have pleats that artfully converge at the center back near the closure, but Betty Modish's dressmakers did not trouble to do this. First, determine the actual finished waist measurement of the doll over her underclothes, if any. The skirt waist seam itself will take up some space inside the waistband. The depth of the pleats will also depend upon the weight of the fabric you have chosen, which will make a difference on this small scale. You need three or four pleats, deeper at the back (about ½" or 1.5 cm) than at the sides (less than ¼" or .5 cm). (Fig. 8.12.) Do the skirt and lining separately, and then set the lining inside the shell. They should finish net to each other, except for the overhanging lap on the shell placket. The shell and lining are left loose at the placket.

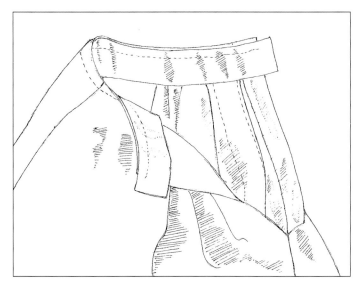

Fig. 8.13. *The waistband, placed inside the joined shell and lining and set on by machine.*

Fig. 8.14. *Waistband finishing.*

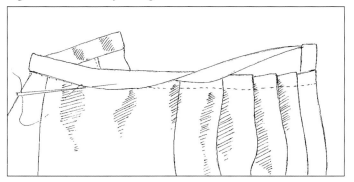

Fig. 8.15. *The back closure.*

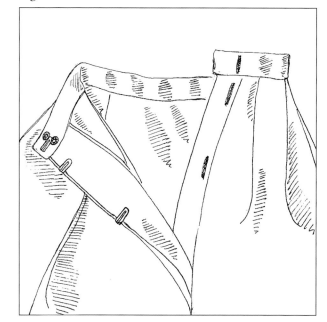

The waistband goes on more or less like a piece of binding. To save bulk, cut the waistband from taffeta, provided the finished waistband will be covered by a belt or the cummerbund of a blouse. Set the waistband inside the skirt and stitch through all the layers. (Fig. 8.13.) Turn the waistband out, tuck in all the raw edges, and stitch down, either by hand or machine. (Fig. 8.14.) The skirt will be closed with hook and worked bar. You may add auxiliary hooks and worked bars down the length of the placket as necessary if it gaps when put on the doll. Work a line of small loops on the lap. The hooks are sewn to the placket facing of the shell and are fastened from between the shell and lining. (Fig. 8.15.)

The Pingree trousseau contains several self-fabric belts that match the various skirts. They were made by topstitching around a double-folded strip of fabric. The "point" is rather bulky, since it is seamed straight at the end, turned, and folded down to make the tip. The belt fastens with hook and worked bar. (Fig. 8.16)

Fig. 8.16. *Self-fabric belt.*

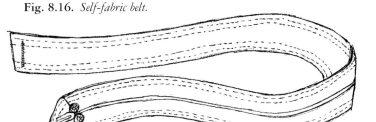

Waist

PATTERN NO. 15

The waist presented below is based on the unlined tennis blouse of the Pingree trousseau.
The original blouse has a standing collar with jabot and tabs; I have used tabs on one model and
the jabot on the other. I have also replaced the elaborate front fly with a simple center back closure.

Plate. 8.3. *Detail of blouse made from 1920s luncheon napkins.*

⨯MATERIALS⨯

THE classic blouse of the period is of white cotton, linen, or silk, trimmed with elaborate tucks, frills, and insertions of lace. Catalogues of the time also offer similar blouses in black silk. Additionally, cotton waists were offered in tiny checks, stripes, and pale colors; colored cotton blouses often were worn with separate collar and jabot, invariably white. Blouses with long sleeves could have detachable white cuffs as well.

Choose a soft but crisply draping fabric for the waist. The style of this period is dressy but smart, despite the intensely feminine trimmings. Old table linens are a good source for this type of project, since you may be able to use whole motifs that are very difficult for a modern needleworker to duplicate.

WAIST
Linen
Silk broadcloth
Cotton lawn
Lightweight striped or check shirtings
with small patterns

TRIMMINGS
Lace

NOTIONS
Thread to match (cotton or silk)
5 hooks

If it is to be the bodice of a two-piece dress, the blouse can also be made of more substantial fabrics like taffeta, duppionni, or wool challis. The cummerbund hides the join of skirt and waist; many authentic examples have a row of hooks at the cummerbund to hook the bodice securely to the skirt. The cummerbund may match or contrast with the blouse.

⨯SUMMARY OF STEPS⨯

8. Join shoulders and sides.
9. Set waistband.
10. Set collar and trim.
11. Make and set sleeves.
12. Make closure.

GENERAL ⨯CONSTRUCTION⨯ NOTES

IF you are assembling the blouse from old linens, it is extremely important to *plan carefully* before you start cutting. This is especially important if you have only a small amount of old fabric to work with. The blouse shown in Plate 8.3 was cut from a set of 1920s luncheon napkins. The original fil tiré design was placed on the shoulders like a yoke. Decorative details on the jabot were executed in a matching pin stitch, and old lace was added. To distribute the original worked design on the doll's garment attractively, it is useful to lay all the pattern pieces out and baste around the outlines. Although somewhat time-consuming, it is a simple procedure that ensures you have enough fabric, that you have allowed for a left and a right, etc.

The gray silk blouse shown in Plate 8.2 was made entirely from new fabric, but was assembled largely with the pin stitch—even the tucks—to suggest an antique piece.

Because of the small size of this design, it is not very helpful to try to assemble the blouse by machine. Appendix A (Sewing by Hand) contains suggestions for finishing hand-worked seams. The most practical for this project are French seaming, felling, or taping. Many blouses of this period are finished with bias strips of lightweight washing silk. After stitching, the seams are trimmed down to ⅛–³⁄₁₆" (.3–.45 cm) and bound or taped with bias silk applied like a bias binding over the raw edges of the seam.

⨯INSTRUCTIONS⨯

8 • JOIN SHOULDERS AND SIDES. Tucks down the front of a blouse should be executed before it is cut out. (Fig. 8.17.) Note that the gathering stitch at the front waist also secures the tucks in the proper position. When the waist is gathered into the band, the tucks should remain orderly.

Underline the back and front bodice pieces, if necessary. The underlining is cut identically to the shell. Join each piece to each underlining piece by basting around the edges. The shell and underlining are then treated as one.

Fold the center back turn-backs under and close with a small hem stitch or decorative stitch such as the pin stitch. Stitch the shoulder seams and side seams and finish. (The handling is easier if the shoulder seams are closed first.) Put a small gathering stitch between the notches along the front waist edge. Fig. 8.18 shows the seams of the blouse finished with bias strips of china silk.

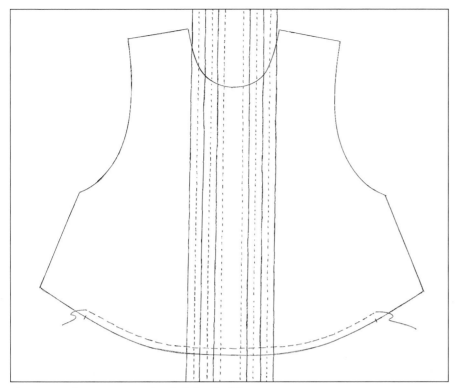

Fig. 8.18. *Unlined blouse with taped seams. The "notch" in the drawing indicates the top of the shoulder. The plackets have been hemmed with a decorative stitch.*

Fig. 8.17. *The arrangement of tucks before the fabric is cut.*

9 • SET WAISTBAND. The waistband is set on like a piece of binding, easing the bodice slightly around the back and sides and concentrating the gathering in the front. (Fig. 8.19.) Set the waistband to the inside of the bodice; turn, tuck in all the seams, and blind stitch to close from the outside.

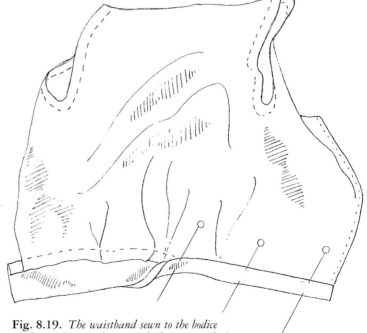

Fig. 8.19. *The waistband sewn to the bodice on the inside. It is then turned, the seams tucked in, and blind stitched to close from the outside.*

10 • SET COLLAR AND TRIM. The collar is also set on like a binding. The collar finishes ½" (1.5 cm) wide. Two collar treatments are explained below; they may be used together.

TABS: Tabs can be used in combination with a jabot, like Lady Betty's tennis blouse, or alone. They are slightly tricky to sew because they are so small. The easiest way to approach this is to sew the tabs into the edge of a larger piece of fabric, and then cut the excess away. (See Fig. 8.26.) The tabs are made by turning two edges up and hemming very narrowly. This can be done with a plain or decorative stitch. Unfortunately, tabs look odd if they are not perfectly square. If yours come out with little curves, they can be saved by cutting opposing curves in the seam edge. (Fig. 8.20.) When the seams are set into the collar, the tabs will look correct.

To set the collar tabs in, cut a pair of collars. The tabs are set into the collar seams at the center front. Lap the tab seams slightly so that the tabs touch when the collar is finished. (Fig. 8.21.) After basting in the tabs, the collar is assembled along the long edge, and can be treated as usual. (Fig. 8.22.)

Set the collar to the inside of the neck, clipping the neck seam as necessary to ease the collar in. No fullness is allowed, but the neckhole itself is a tight curve. (Fig. 8.23.) Turn the collar out, tuck in the seams, and blind stitch to the outside. (Fig. 8.24.)

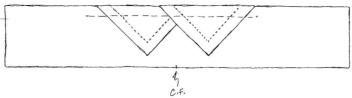

Fig. 8.20. *Collar tabs, showing the method of compensating for stitching error by cutting an opposing curve at the seam edge. If the tab edges curve in, cut the seam curving out, and vice versa.*

Fig. 8.21. *Collar tabs, basted to the edge of the collar.*

Fig. 8.22. *The two collar parts stitched, right sides together, at the upper edge. The tabs are caught in the seam.*

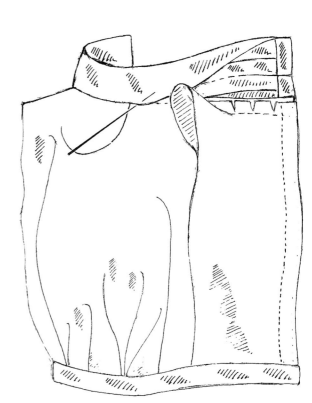

Fig. 8.23. *The collar, set to the inside of the neck. The neck seam is clipped to ease the collar on.*

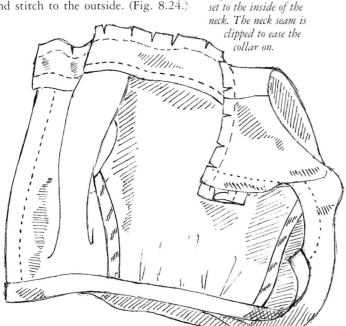

Fig. 8.24. *The collar, turned out, all seams tucked under, and blind stitched to close.*

JABOT: Various types of neck decorations fall under this heading; Lady Betty's tennis blouse has an embroidered square of lace-edged lawn tacked at the neck. A jabot can also be simply made from softly arranged loops of lace or a single elegant motif tacked at the neck. White jabot-and-collar inserts that were tacked or pinned to the neck and washed separately were also worn.

The easiest way to stitch the jabot is by cutting and working each edge one at a time. (Fig. 8.25.) In this way, the edge being worked is always clean and straight. This does require careful measurement, however, to ensure that when you are finished you have an approximate square. (Fig. 8.26.) Some digression from a perfect shape is tolerable, since the finished piece will be tacked by one corner and gathered into folds, but it will appear strange if it does not *look* square. In turning the hem, I used the useful pin stitch again, making about a ¾₆" (.45 cm) hem.

When applying the lace edging, you will have to "full" the lace around the corners. Normally, this is done by pulling one of the header threads in the lace, and self-gathering it slightly. However, old lace may be quite brittle and will disintegrate if you try this. To accomplish the fulling, run your sewing thread through the header of the lace, picking up two or three threads of lace at the edge and in effect taking tiny pleats. By taking very small stitches in the linen, you gradually draw the lace around the corner. (Fig. 8.27.)

Do not put lace around the corner by which the jabot will be tacked to the blouse. Begin and end at that corner, without going around it. To finish the jabot, turn the lace under at an angle and press to hold it. (Figure 8.27.) Form the small finished square into a set of soft diagonal pleats. If your linen is light enough, steaming may be sufficient. Heavier fabrics can be tacked with a tiny stitch drawn across the back, picking up one thread of linen as it travels along (Fig. 8.28.) Then tack the jabot to the base of the collar.

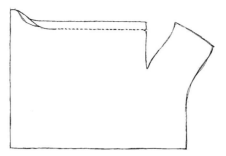

Fig. 8.25. *Stitching the jabot. The stitches extend only the planned finished length. The excess is cut away as marked.*

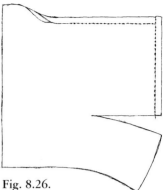

Fig. 8.26. *The next leg of the stitching.*

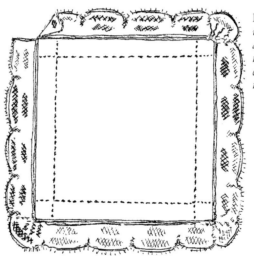

Fig. 8.27. *The jabot with lace whipped on. The lace is "fulled" around the corners. One corner is turned down to be pressed. This corner will be tacked at the throat of the blouse.*

Fig. 8.28. *The finished jabot, with brooch.*

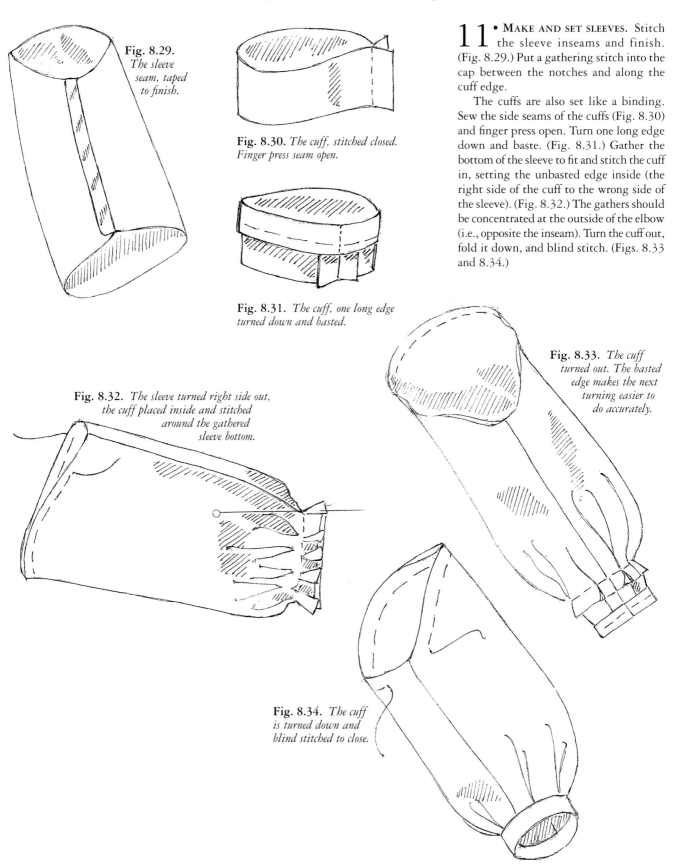

Fig. 8.29. *The sleeve seam, taped to finish.*

Fig. 8.30. *The cuff, stitched closed. Finger press seam open.*

Fig. 8.31. *The cuff, one long edge turned down and basted.*

Fig. 8.32. *The sleeve turned right side out, the cuff placed inside and stitched around the gathered sleeve bottom.*

Fig. 8.33. *The cuff turned out. The basted edge makes the next turning easier to do accurately.*

Fig. 8.34. *The cuff is turned down and blind stitched to close.*

11 • **MAKE AND SET SLEEVES.** Stitch the sleeve inseams and finish. (Fig. 8.29.) Put a gathering stitch into the cap between the notches and along the cuff edge.

The cuffs are also set like a binding. Sew the side seams of the cuffs (Fig. 8.30) and finger press open. Turn one long edge down and baste. (Fig. 8.31.) Gather the bottom of the sleeve to fit and stitch the cuff in, setting the unbasted edge inside (the right side of the cuff to the wrong side of the sleeve). (Fig. 8.32.) The gathers should be concentrated at the outside of the elbow (i.e., opposite the inseam). Turn the cuff out, fold it down, and blind stitch. (Figs. 8.33 and 8.34.)

Gather the cap of the sleeve between the notches. To align the sleeve in the armhole, set the center of the sleeve to the top of shoulder. This is slightly forward of the actual shoulder seam, which is set back. (The pattern is marked with a notch.) The sleeve seam goes to the deepest part of the front armhole. Stitch around the armhole. (Fig. 8.35.) Trim the armhole seam to about ¾₆" (.45 cm) and bind. Cut two pieces of bias binding ¾" (2 cm) wide by 6" (15 cm) long. The easiest way to set the binding is to put the tape inside the sleeve for the first seam. Turn the tape out, tuck in the raw edge, and blind stitch to close. In this way, you are always working on the "outside" of the armhole; your index finger is inside the sleeve to support the work.(Fig. 8.36.)

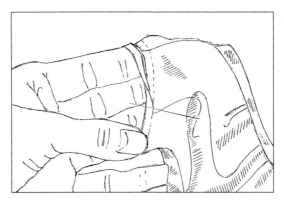

Fig. 8.35. *Sleeve set.*

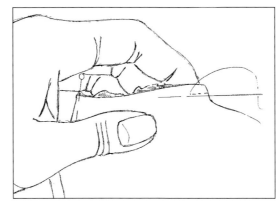

Fig. 8.36. *The tape is turned, raw edges tucked in, and blind stitched to close.*

12**· MAKE CLOSURE.** The blouse is closed with a set of hooks and worked loops. (Fig. 8.37.)

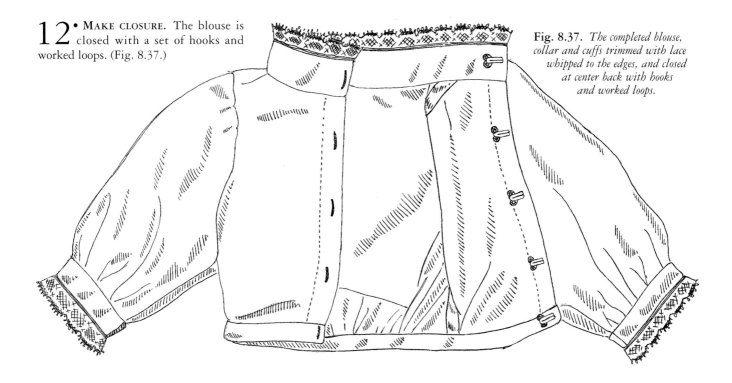

Fig. 8.37. *The completed blouse, collar and cuffs trimmed with lace whipped to the edges, and closed at center back with hooks and worked loops.*

CHAPTER IX

Bridge Dress

1911

PATTERN NO. 16

The dress presented in this chapter is based on the bridge dress, shown in at left, from Lady Betty Modish's trousseau. (Plate 51.)

The high fashion of around 1910 shows a strong Oriental influence, with long, straight lines, and deep, exotic colors. Metallic lace, fur, elaborate beadwork, hand-painted designs, and brilliant color are all used, often in the same garment. The bridge dress and its coordinating large toque are good examples of this style, luxe without being ostentatious or vulgar.

The bridge dress exemplifies modern women's clothes not only in its columnar lines, but in the fact that it was designed to be worn with a light, elastic "foundation" garment that signified the end of the corset.

MATERIALS

THE dress of the pre-War period is soft and fluid. Its simple lines make their statement by the layering of coordinating and contrasting materials. The finished look is rich, but it is a challenge to the reproduction dressmaker to accumulate all the necessary materials, especially if you are working in antique fabrics.

The shell, which forms the foundation, is appropriate in silks such as satin or crepe, medium weight silk jacquards, thin brocades, hand-painted novelty silks, and similar fabrics. A slightly crisp hand is acceptable, but choose nothing stiff. Limp fabrics are also inappropriate, since the skirt's gentle A-line will collapse and disappear. A matching lining of soft china silk is called for.

The shell is half covered with a drapery of gauze that forms an overskirt with a rosette behind the knee. I substituted a soft bow for the copy. A fabric of the same hue, but of a darker or lighter shade is appropriate for the overskirt, as is a related hue that forms a gentle contrast, as the original example with its rose and puce. Lace fabric also works, but it must be fine enough to make the small tucks at the shoulder. Black or white can be draped over nearly anything and may be combined with metallic laces on the rest of the garment.

The trimmings actually present the greatest challenge to completing this dress and hat correctly. The original garments are trimmed with four or five different laces, glass beads, fabric flowers, feathers (in this case, clipped feathers, a fashion peculiarity of the time), and fur. This is a difficult call for modern dressmakers and should be dealt with by study of period photographs and garments. If you must err, do so on the side of conservatism. A conservatively trimmed dress will work, but if you overtrim, the dress will look "flash," which would be quite wrong. Often an antique dress that has nearly disintegrated will have much useful trim on it, as the sturdy silk ribbon and cord from which it was constructed will have lasted much better than the fragile materials of the garment and you may be able to take the trimmings off whole.

Instead of lace, the sleeves, neck, and sash can be trimmed with bands of coordinating fabric and cord or bits of the Chinese silk embroidery that was so popular during this period.

SHELL
Satin
Lightweight brocades
Silk crepe
Medium weight silk jacquard

DRAPERY
Organza
Silk gauze
Lace fabric
Silk chiffon

LINING
China silk

TRIMMINGS
Beads
Period embroideries, especially "Oriental" varieties
Lace
Ribbon
Fabric flowers

Plate 9.1. The bridge dress made in old yellow crepe and draped with ivory organza. The sash is made from a scrap of old teal blue taffeta. The standing collar of the original design was omitted because the lace used in the copy was an edging type with a decorative, uneven edge.

SUMMARY OF STEPS

SKIRT
1. Sew and hem skirt shell and lining separately.
2. Apply trim to skirt.
3. Form skirt and lining placket.
4. Set lining into skirt.
5. Apply overskirt and its trim to skirt.

BODICE
6. Stitch bodice foundation seams (shell); apply bodice trimming; hem sleeves.
7. Make tucks in bodice drapery; stitch underarm seams; hem sleeves.
8. Stitch drapery to bodice foundation; trim sleeves.
9. Apply neckline trimming.

FINISHING
10. Set bodice to skirt.
11. Make sash.
12. Make closure.

GENERAL ☞CONSTRUCTION☜ NOTES

Tʜᴇ clothing of this period should look rather familiar, as it is made more or less the way modern clothing is made. The dress, for all its complicated effect, is essentially a bodice and skirt sewn together at the waist. The drapery makes it appear much more intricate than it really is. The closure at the back is asymmetrical, the bodice closing at center back, and skirt at the left. The offset is hidden by the sash. This is very typical of this period—many of the dresses of this time look as though they have no closure at all, as though they were assembled on the wearer from scratch. In fact, they are usually made like the bridge dress, the various layers wrapping around and around, and sewn to a "foundation," often the sash lining.

A pattern change from the original dress that should be noted here is the construction of the overskirt. The Pingree ladies simply draped a piece of gauze over the skirt and wound the excess into a rosette at the back of the knees. As this method seemed to me to leave a lot to chance, I took some liberties with the organization of the drapery. I have made the overskirt very similarly, but have provided a finished back with applied knot of fabric in place of the rosette.

Most of the seams of the bridge dress are finished by pinking. While the skirt and its lining are set wrong sides together, hiding the work completely, the bodice will have two seams under the arms that show inside the finished garment. If you have chosen a very ravelly fabric like a jacquard with long floats, you may prefer to finish the foundation with overcasting.

Fig. 9.1. *The panels of the skirt shell stitched together and the first turn of the hem.*

Fig. 9.2. *The hem, stitched in place and steamed to smooth out the fullness.*

Fig. 9.3. *The lace trim stitched onto the skirt. The high point of the trim is at the center back (not under the placket).*

☞ INSTRUCTIONS ☞

SKIRT

1 • **SEW AND HEM SKIRT SHELL AND LINING SEPARATELY.** Sew the long seams of the skirt shell and lining, with the exception of the left back, which is marked with a notch for the placket. Pink and press seams open. Note carefully which is the right and wrong side when you cut, since the shell and lining are contrary to each other.

To hem, press the bottom edge of the skirt up ¼" (.5 cm). Put a small running stitch into the pressed edge. (Fig. 9.1.) Stitch the remaining long seam, closing it up to the notch on the shell; on the lining, sew to ¼" (.5 cm) below the notch. The placket opening on the lining is slightly deeper than on the shell to ensure that the placket lap clears the lining when the skirt is fastened. Baste the seams down along the open placket to keep them neat. You can now turn up the hem where it is marked, matching the seams to keep the fullness evenly distributed. Draw up the basting thread to ease in the excess in the turned hem. Sew with a neat hem stitch and pull out the basting. The lining should be hemmed up about ¼" (.5 cm) shorter than the shell, to ensure that it doesn't show when the dress is worn.

To press, use the steam of your iron, without touching the silk, to smooth out the eased fullness at the hem stitching. (Fig. 9.2.) Be very careful not to press the actual hem flat. The steam should be used at the bottom of the skirt to make the hem hang gracefully, but it should not be creased.

2 • **APPLY TRIM TO SKIRT.** The original skirt has a band of metallic lace around the knees that accentuates the drapery and back detail. The bottom edge of the trim should be at the hem stitching in front, but the lace curves up as it goes around to the back of the skirt. At the center back, the bottom edge of the trim should be about ½" (1.5 cm) above the hem stitching. Stitch it all down, along both edges, with a neat blind stitch. You may have to ease the lace slightly at the curves. (Fig. 9.3.)

3 • **FORM SKIRT AND LINING PLACKET.** The actual placket lap of the skirt is applied to the left side of the opening. Cut a piece of shell fabric 4¼" (11 cm) long by 1½" (4 cm) wide; this forms the lap at the back when the placket is fastened. Tuck in one short edge, and then fold the whole in half lengthwise. (Fig 9.4.) This is then laid along the left edge of the

placket opening, with raw edges aligned. (Fig. 9.5.) Blind stitch in place from the outside along the edge of the seam. In both the shell and lining, take a pair of tucks at the center back, indicated by the notches on the pattern, and steam them in place to form a wide "box pleat." Baste the top to keep them neat while you work. (Fig. 9.6.)

Fig. 9.4. *The arrangement of the placket "lap."*

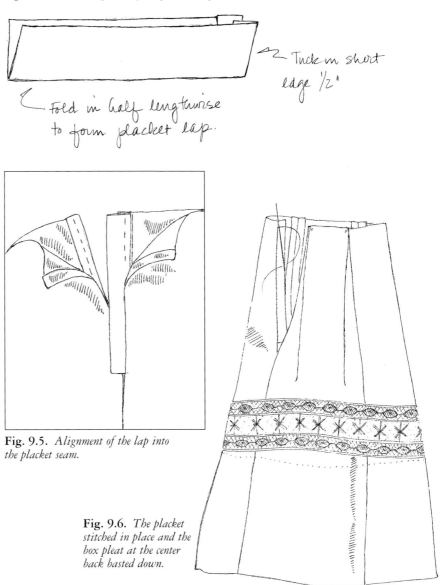

Tuck in short edge ½"

Fold in half lengthwise to form placket lap.

Fig. 9.5. *Alignment of the lap into the placket seam.*

Fig. 9.6. *The placket stitched in place and the box pleat at the center back basted down.*

4 • SET LINING INTO SKIRT Set the lining into the skirt. They should be net to each other, seam to seam. Baste in place along the upper edge. The plackets should now be joined by blind stitching the lining to the shell at the opening. Set the lining back slightly, to ensure that it doesn't show. If the placket pulls at the bottom, you can leave it open for a short way; this may provide sufficient ease for it to lie smoothly.

5 • APPLY OVERSKIRT AND ITS TRIM TO SKIRT. The overskirt consists of a piece of fabric 9 x 16" (23 x 40.5 cm), which is tucked and pleated, steamed to set the shape, and draped over the shell. It is slightly too long and too wide as cut; the excess will be trimmed off after the drapery is done. The finished effect should give the impression that the skirt is wrapped or bound, but should not actually draw up or pull on the foundation material. The look is enhanced by the detail behind the knee; the overskirt should appear to be drawn up into it and tied off behind the knee.

To make the overskirt hem, double fold the long bottom edge up narrowly, and press into place. Make a set of loose folds parallel to the bottom and steam them, being careful not to crease or crush them. They should give the illusion that they came about naturally. The Pingree ladies actually used the selvage edge of their gauze as the hem of the overskirt; if your fabric has an adequate, attractive selvage, you may do the same. Turn under the right-hand edge of the overskirt, and begin draping by laying the edge along the placket next to the lap. The hem of the overskirt should just cover the lace trim of the skirt. (Fig. 9.7.)

Lay the overskirt loosely around the foundation; the circumference of the overskirt is determined by the circumference of the skirt at the knee. It should touch the skirt all around without binding or drawing it in. The top edge will be trimmed off later.

When you have wrapped the overskirt all the way around to the placket, turn the left edge under and trim out any excess. Note that to follow the line of the trim, the hem of the overskirt curves up at the center back, but dips down again where it meets itself at the placket. The overskirt is sewn to the foundation on each side of the placket separately with a line of little backstitches that leave a row of tiny dimples and a slightly ruffled up edge. The hem is left loose.

The top edge is formed into soft pleats to take up the excess girth. A box pleat should be put in over the center back pleat of the foundation. At the front, form a pleat or a set of pleats approximately at the seams of the center front panel. Baste the top edge to the foundation all around the waist and trim off the excess fabric, making sure that you are not pulling on the drapery of the overskirt.

The detail at the back is actually a loose knot of fabric tacked over the *center back* of the overskirt at the hem. To make it, cut a piece of fabric about 12" (30.5 cm) long by 4" (10 cm) wide. Make a soft lengthwise double fold to enclose the raw edges and steam to hold them. (Fig. 9.8.) Form the length of fabric into a soft knot, tucking in all the raw edges; and tack the whole unit over the center back of the skirt drapery (not the seam). The knot is fixed high enough just to expose the bottom edge of the lace trim. (Fig. 9.9.)

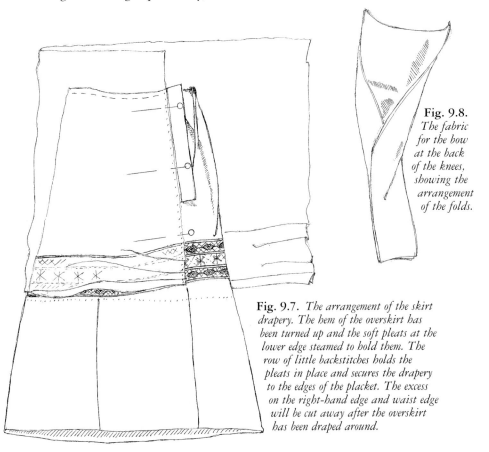

Fig. 9.7. *The arrangement of the skirt drapery. The hem of the overskirt has been turned up and the soft pleats at the lower edge steamed to hold them. The row of little backstitches holds the pleats in place and secures the drapery to the edges of the placket. The excess on the right-hand edge and waist edge will be cut away after the overskirt has been draped around.*

Fig. 9.8. *The fabric for the bow at the back of the knees, showing the arrangement of the folds.*

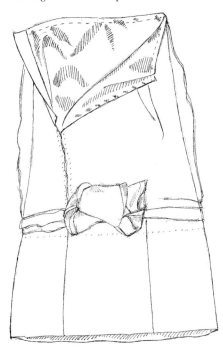

Fig. 9.9. *The bow, tacked into place at the back of the knees. It is attached at the center back, not under the placket where the edges of the drapery meet. The skirt lining has been set in place and basted in.*

BODICE

6 • STITCH BODICE FOUNDATION SEAMS; APPLY BODICE TRIMMING; HEM SLEEVES. Stitch the underarm seams of the bodice foundation. Pink and press open, using a ham of rolled fabric. (Fig. 9.10.) Hem the sleeves, taking a narrow double fold.

The bodice has a lace trim similar to the skirt, laid on in a shallow curving line and blind stitched in place. At the center front, the top edge is about ⅜" (1 cm) below the raw edge of the neck line. Under the arms, it touches the extreme point of the underarm seam. At the back, the lower edge is about ½" (1.5 cm) from the raw bottom edge of the bodice. The lower edge of the lace will have to be eased; this can be done by taking a tiny running stitch through the edge and drawing it up as you sew. Be careful not to draw up the foundation fabric itself. (Fig. 9.11.)

If the undersleeve is to have trimming, you may apply it now. The trimming of the sleeves is to some extent discretionary, depending on what you have and what effect you want to produce. The original garment is trimmed with two bands of lace, one applied to the undersleeve and other applied to the sleeve of the drapery. I trimmed only the over sleeve. Bands of fur, bead bobbles, and all kinds of embroidered trimmings are appropriate, but should be coordinated with the trim at the neck and/or the sash to give a unified appearance to the finished garment.

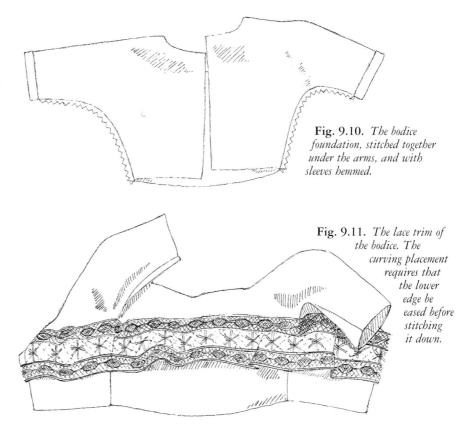

Fig. 9.10. *The bodice foundation, stitched together under the arms, and with sleeves hemmed.*

Fig. 9.11. *The lace trim of the bodice. The curving placement requires that the lower edge be eased before stitching it down.*

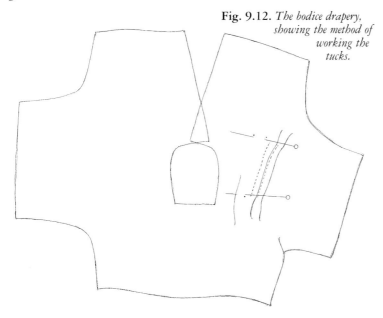

Fig. 9.12. *The bodice drapery, showing the method of working the tucks.*

7 • MAKE TUCKS IN BODICE DRAPERY; STITCH UNDERARM SEAMS; HEM SLEEVES. The bodice drapery has a set of small tucks on each shoulder to control the fullness across the bust. To make them, begin by first marking them very clearly with graphite pencil or dressmaker's pencil. Don't use anything permanent; the marks should disappear in the handling. To draw up a tuck accurately, stick a pin through the pair of marks at each end of the tuck, and draw the fabric together along the pin. Press the tuck with your fingers, and then stitch, using a fine running stitch, parallel to the fold, at the distance indicated by the dots. Take care that the tucks are as regular and neat as possible. Begin and end with a small, neat knot buried on the underside of the tuck. Press the tucks toward the sleeve. (Fig. 9.12.)

When the tucks are complete, close the side seams with a narrow French seam. The seam allowance is ¼" (.5 cm); you may add a small bit in the cutting if you can't execute both passes of the seam in that allowance. Or you may pink the seams, although it does not make as nice a finish. Hem the sleeves, adding any hem trimming that is to be sewn to the drapery only.

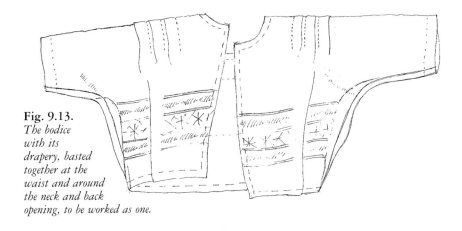

Fig. 9.13. *The bodice with its drapery, basted together at the waist and around the neck and back opening, to be worked as one.*

8 • STITCH DRAPERY TO BODICE FOUNDATION; TRIM SLEEVES. Stitch the bodice drapery to the foundation. Join the two parts all along the back opening and neckhole by taking a small running stitch in the seam allowance all the way around. Join the waist edges likewise, forming small pleats at the side front and back to take up the fullness under the tucks. Steam, but don't press, to set the folds. (Fig. 9.13.)

9 • APPLY NECKLINE TRIM. The neckline is finished with an applied bias tape. Cut the tape ¾" (2 cm) wide by about 18" (45.5 cm) long. Fold the raw edges together lengthwise and press. (Fig. 9.14.) Turn the neck and center back seams in ¼" (.5 cm), clipping as necessary, and baste the entire edge down. Beginning at the center back waist, blind stitch the tape over the basted seam, mitering the corners as you go around. (Fig. 9.15.)

The neckline is filled with a piece of lace about 1½" (4 cm) long. (Fig. 9.16.) The lace can be blind stitched to the tape as is, taking very small stitches to fix the cut edges securely, unless it is very ravelly. In that case, the edges should be turned under and stitched. The lower, finished, edge can be whipped on to the edge of the neckhole or placed inside. A piece of lace fabric can also be used for this operation, using one finished edge at the top and cut edges inside the neckhole all around.

The original garment also has a narrow standing collar of lace whipped to the edge of the neckhole and the upper edge of the lace insert. This will work only with an insertion lace having a straight upper edge. For a collar, use lace about ¼" (.5 cm) wide, whip stitching it finely all around and turning in the cut edges at the back.

Fig. 9.14. *The folding of the bias tape, which finishes the neck and center back edges.*

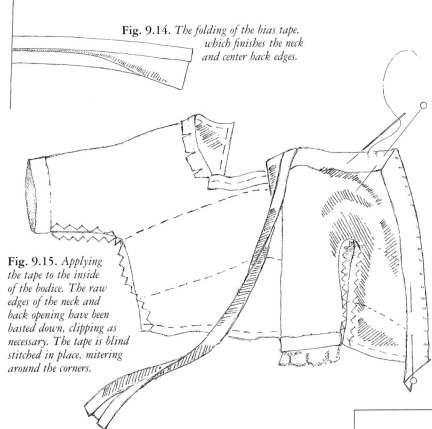

Fig. 9.15. *Applying the tape to the inside of the bodice. The raw edges of the neck and back opening have been basted down, clipping as necessary. The tape is blind stitched in place, mitering around the corners.*

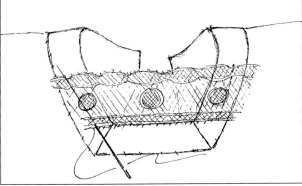

Fig. 9.16. *Filling in the neckline with lace. The straight, finished lace edge is whipped to the lower edge of the neck opening. At the sides, the lace is carried behind the tape and firmly tacked down.*

FINISHING

10. SET BODICE TO SKIRT. The bodice
and skirt are now joined. The pleats
on each part should line up symmetri-
cally—make sure they look well organized
on the finished garment. The back closure
is asymmetrical, a common arrangement on
clothing of this period. When assembling
these pieces, be careful to align the *center front*
and *center back*, letting the rest fall where
it may. Baste (Fig. 9.17) and try the garment on your doll to make sure there are
no fitting problems. You may then put in
a permanent stitch and tape the join. Cut
the tape 1" (2.5 cm) wide by 10" (25.5 cm)
long, and bind the waist seam. Cover the
overhanging offsets as well, enclosing them
completely. After closing the tape, turn it
up into the bodice and tack it in place at
the seams. Steam in place, if necessary.
(Fig. 9.18.)

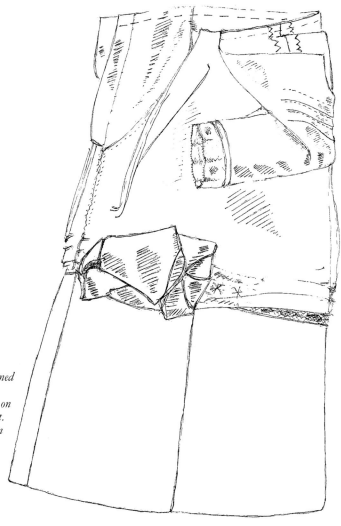

Fig. 9.17. *The bodice, properly aligned
to be stitched onto the skirt. On the
right, the skirt overhangs the bodice; on
the left, the bodice overshoots the skirt.
This will be covered by the sash when
it is sewn in place.*

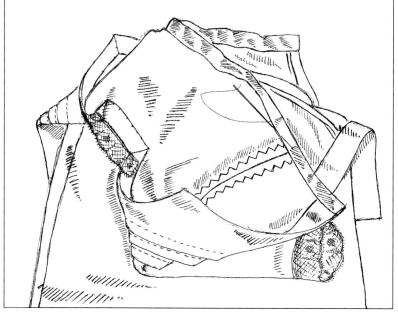

Fig. 9.18. *Taping the
waist seam. After the
tape is closed, it will be
tacked up into the bodice.*

Fig. 9.19.
*Arrangement
of the sash.*

11 • **MAKE SASH.** The sash is made from a piece of contrasting material about 2" (5 cm) wide by 10" (25.5 cm) long. Form it into a set of soft folds, tucking in all the raw edges. (Fig. 9.19.) Steam it to set the folds, but don't crease or press flat. Tack into place, covering the offsets at the center back entirely. Finish with a small tailored bow at center back. The original garment has a rather plain sash covered with a piece of lace coordinating with the sleeve and neckline trim. The bow at the back is covered with the same lace.

12 • **MAKE CLOSURE.** The back is joined with a set of hooks and hand-worked loops. (Fig. 9.20.)

Fig. 9.20. *The finished back of the garment, showing the placement of the sash bow, hooks, and worked loops.*

PATTERN 1

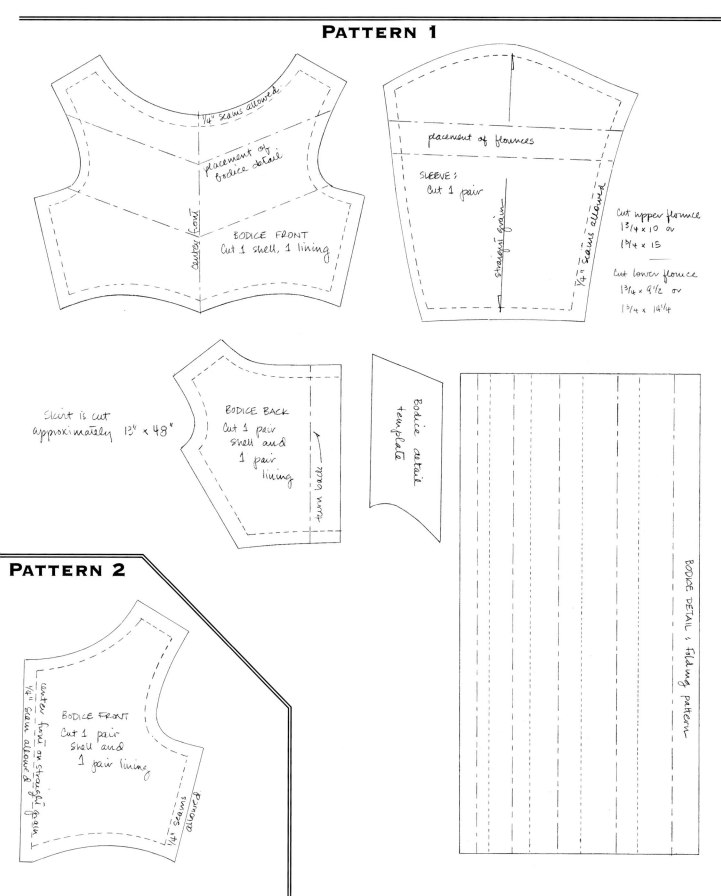

1/4" seams allowed

placement of bodice detail

center front

BODICE FRONT
Cut 1 shell, 1 lining

placement of flounces

SLEEVE:
Cut 1 pair

straight grain

1/4" seams allowed

Cut upper flounce
1³/4 x 10 or
1³/4 x 15

Cut lower flounce
1³/4 x 9¹/2 or
1³/4 x 14¹/4

Skirt is cut
approximately 13" x 48"

BODICE BACK
Cut 1 pair
shell and
1 pair
lining

turn back

Bodice detail
template

BODICE DETAIL: folding pattern

PATTERN 2

center front on straight grain

1/4" seam allowed

BODICE FRONT
Cut 1 pair
shell and
1 pair lining

1/4" seams allowed

PATTERN 3

PATTERN 4

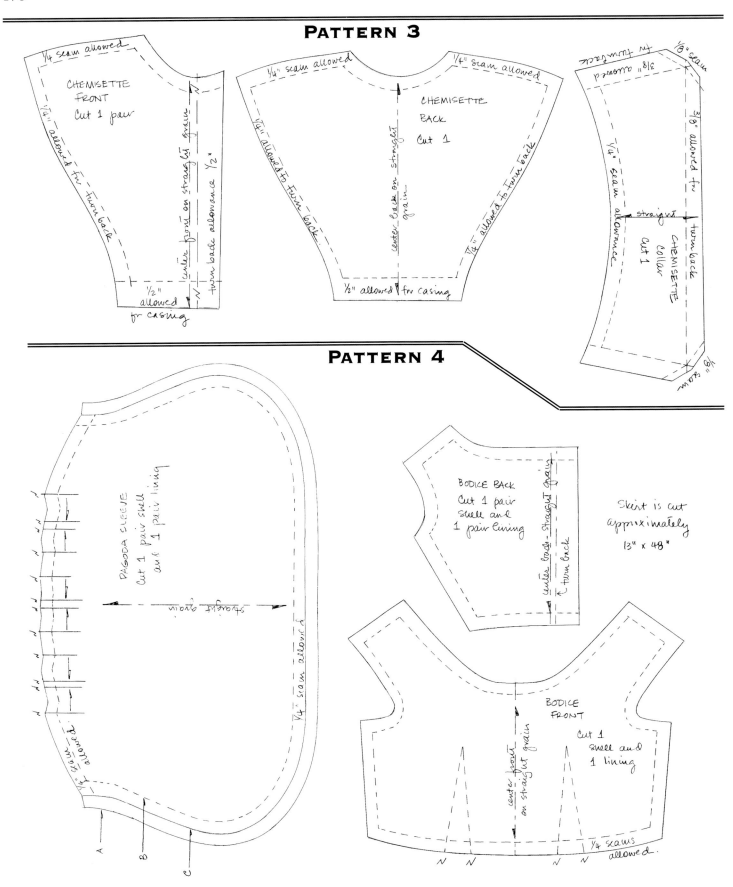

CHEMISETTE FRONT
Cut 1 pair

¼ seam allowed

¼" allowed for turn back

center front on straight grain

turn back allowance ½"

½" allowed for casing

CHEMISETTE BACK
Cut 1

¼" seam allowed

¼" seam allowed

¼" allowed to turn back

center back on straight grain

½" allowed for casing

CHEMISETTE COLLAR
Cut 1

⅛" seam for turnback

⅜" allowed for turn back

¼" seam allowance

straight grain

turnback

PAGODA SLEEVE
Cut 1 pair shell
and 1 pair lining

straight grain

¼" seam allowed

¼" seam allowed

A
B
C

BODICE BACK
Cut 1 pair
shell and
1 pair lining

center back - straight grain

turn back

BODICE FRONT
Cut 1
shell and
1 lining

center front on straight grain

¼" seams allowed.

Skirt is cut approximately 13" x 48"

PATTERN 5

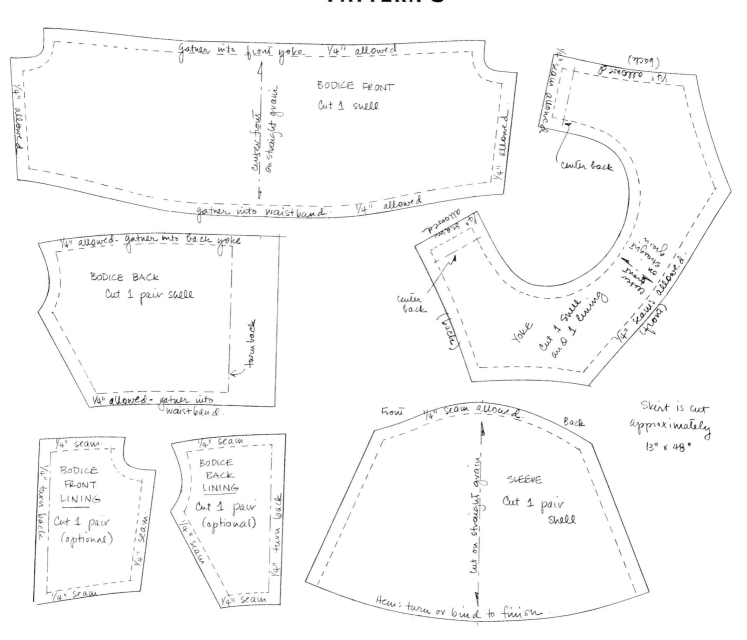

BODICE FRONT
Cut 1 shell

Gather into front yoke   1/4" allowed

center front on straight grain

gather into waistband   1/4" allowed

1/4" allowed

1/4" allowed

BODICE BACK
Cut 1 pair shell

1/4" allowed- gather into back yoke

turn back

1/4" allowed- gather into waistband.

center back

YOKE
Cut 1 shell and 1 lining

1/4" allowed (back)

1/4" allowed

1/4" allowed

center back

(back)

(front) center front on straight grain

1/4" seam allowed.

Skirt is cut approximately 13" x 48"

BODICE FRONT LINING
Cut 1 pair (optional)

1/4" seam

1/4" turn back

1/4" seam

1/4" turn back

1/4" seam

BODICE BACK LINING
Cut 1 pair (optional)

1/4" seam

1/4" seam

1/4" turn back

1/4" seam

1/4" seam

Front   1/4" seam allowed.   Back

SLEEVE
Cut 1 pair shell

cut on straight grain

Hem; turn or bind to finish.

PATTERN 6

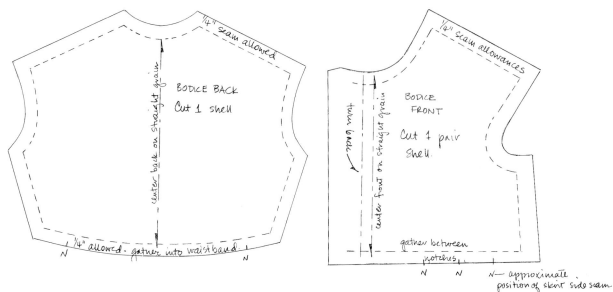

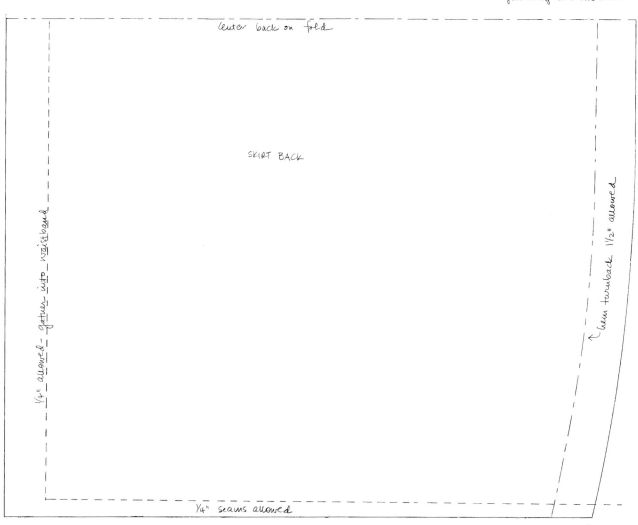

PATTERN 6

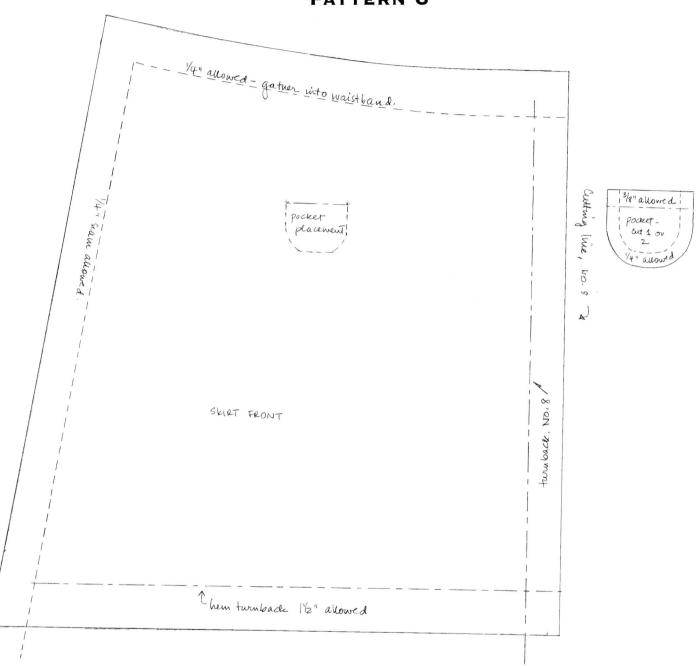

¼" allowed – gather into waistband.

pocket
placement

¼" seam allowed.

SKIRT FRONT

turnback, NO. 8

cutting line, no. 8

⅜" allowed

pocket –
cut 1 or
2

¼" allowed

hem turnback 1½" allowed

PATTERN 7

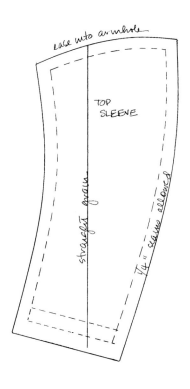

ease into armhole

TOP
SLEEVE

straight grain

¼" sleeve allowed

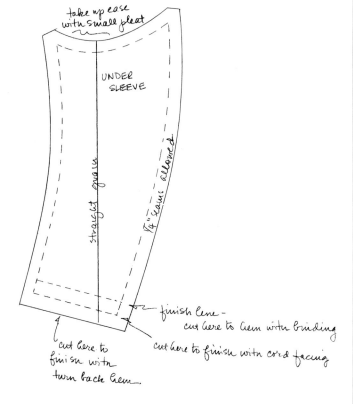

*take up ease
with small pleat*

UNDER
SLEEVE

straight grain

¼" seams allowed

*finish line —
cut here to hem with binding*

cut here to finish with cord facing

*cut here to
finish with
turn back hem.*

PATTERN 8

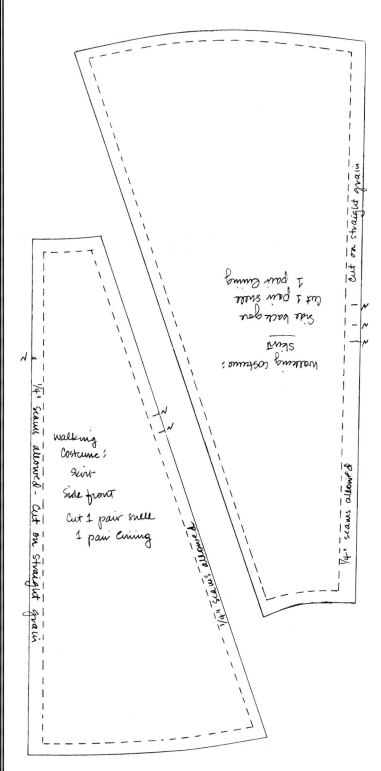

Cut on straight grain

*Side back gore
Cut 1 pair shell
1 pair lining*

*Walking costume:
Skirt*

*walking
Costume:
Skirt
Side front
Cut 1 pair shell
1 pair lining*

¼" seams allowed - Cut on straight grain

¼" seams allowed

¼" seams allowed

PATTERN 8

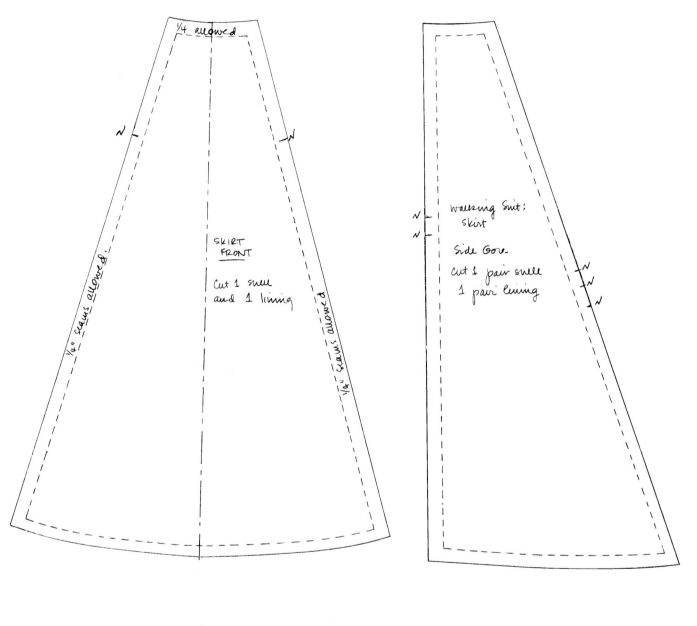

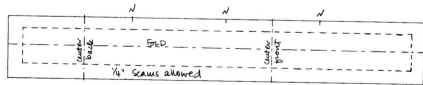

PATTERN 8

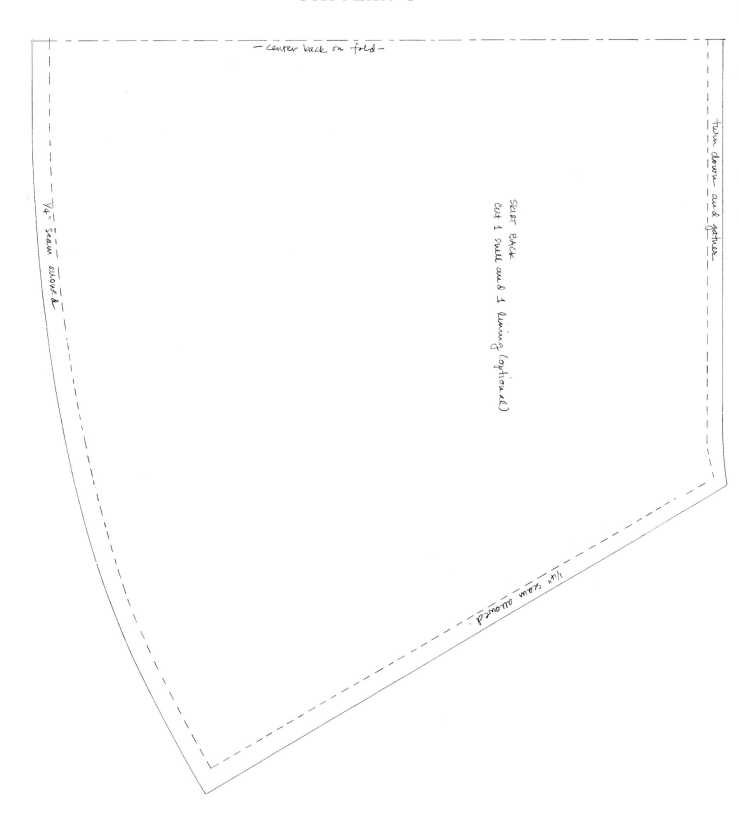

- center back on fold -

turn down and gather

SKIRT BACK
cut 1 shell and 1 lining (optional)

¼" seam allowed

¼" seam allowed

PATTERN 9

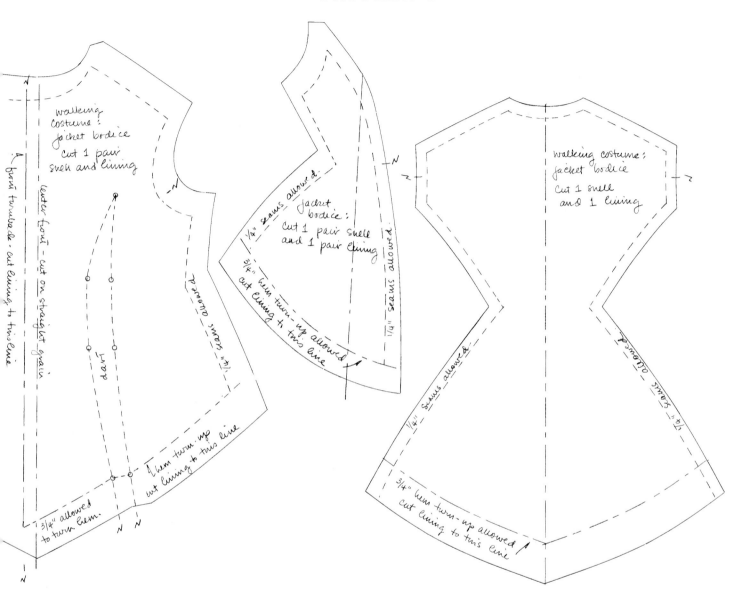

walking
costume:
jacket bodice
cut 1 pair
shell and lining

center front - cut on straight grain

front turnback - cut lining to this line

dart

3/4" allowed
to turn hem.

hem turn-up allowed
cut lining to this line

1/4" seams allowed

1/4" seams allowed

jacket
bodice:
Cut 1 pair shell
and 1 pair lining

3/4" hem turn-up allowed
cut lining to this line

walking costume:
jacket bodice
cut 1 shell
and 1 lining

1/4" seams allowed

1/4" seams allowed

3/4" hem turn-up allowed
cut lining to this line

PATTERN 10

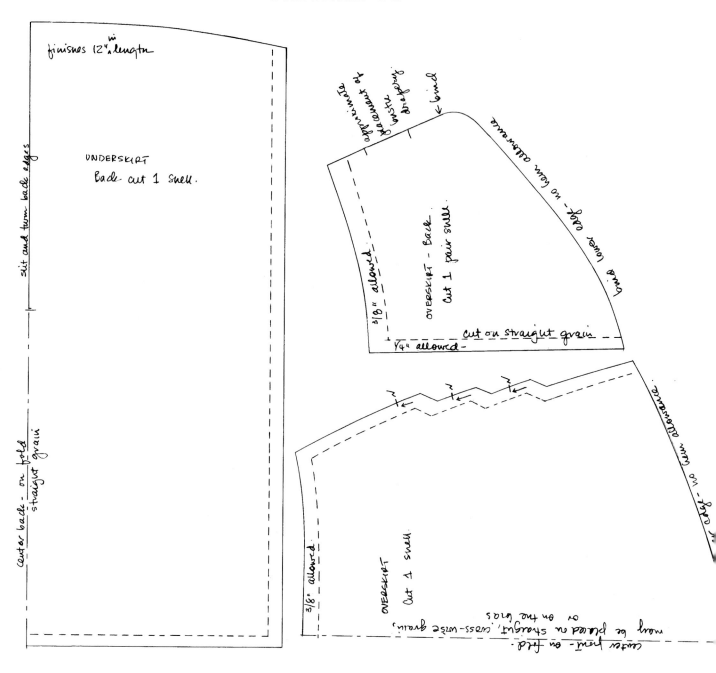

finishes 12" length

UNDERSKIRT
Back cut 1 shell.

slit and turn back edges

center back - on fold
straight grain

approximate placement of bustle drapery

← level

ornament from on lower edge allowed

3/8" allowed

OVERSKIRT - Back.
Cut 1 pair shell

cut on straight grain

1/4" allowed -

3/8" allowed

OVERSKIRT
Cut 1 shell.

ornament mm on lower edge allowed

may be placed on straight, cross-wise grain,
or on the bias

center seam - on fold

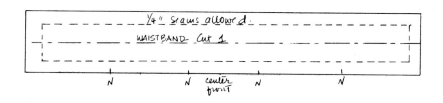

1/4" seams allowed.

WAISTBAND Cut 1

center front

PATTERN 10

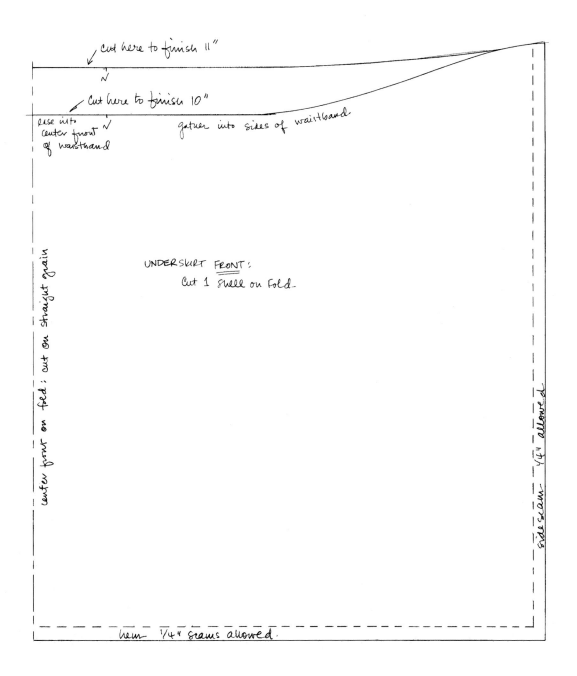

Cut here to finish 11"

Cut here to finish 10"

ease into
center front
of waistband

gather into sides of waistband

center front on fold; cut on straight grain

UNDERSKIRT FRONT:
    Cut 1 shell on fold.

side seam 1/4" allowed

hem 1/4" seams allowed.

PATTERN 11

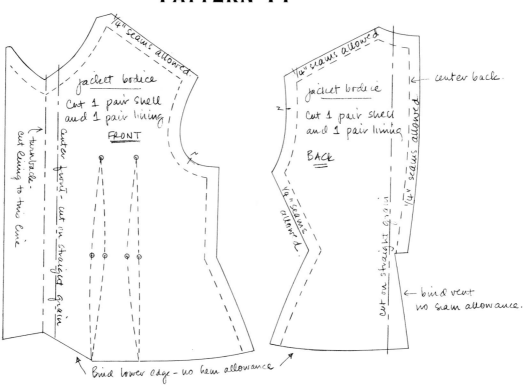

PATTERN 12

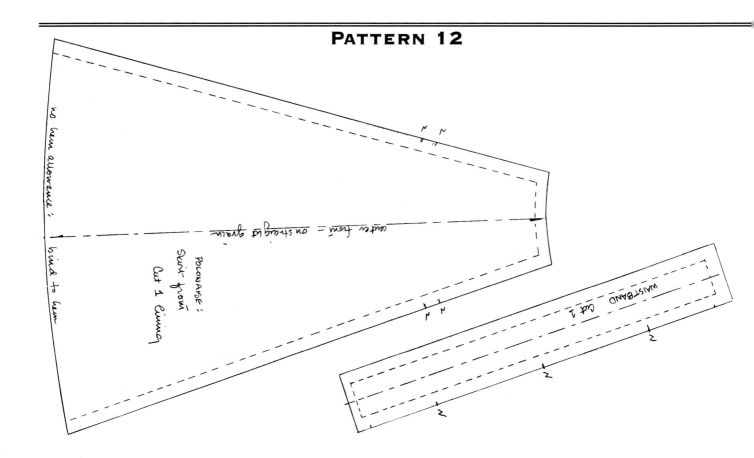

PATTERN 12

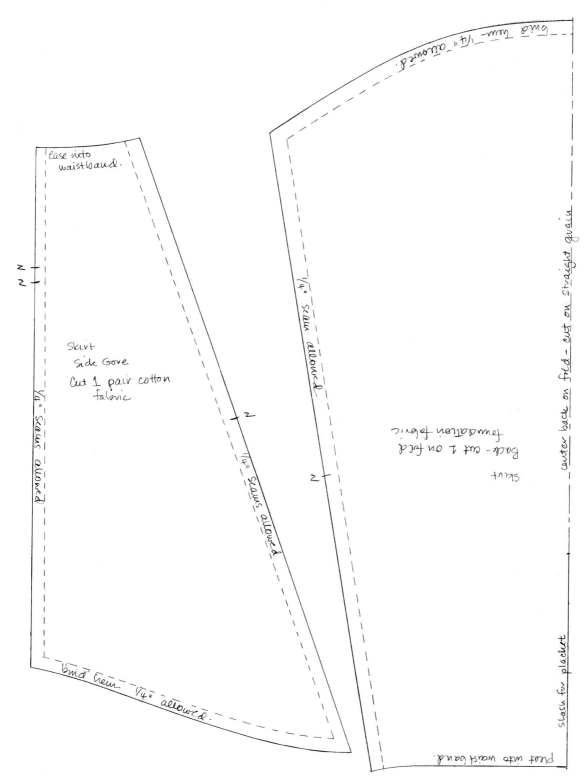

ease into waistband.

Skirt
Side Gore
Cut 1 pair cotton fabric

1/4" seams allowed

1/4" seams allowed

1/4" seams allowed

bmd hem — 1/4" allowed.

Skirt
Back-cut 1 on fold
foundation fabric

center back on fold — cut on straight grain

stash for placket

Pivot into waistband.

PATTERN 13

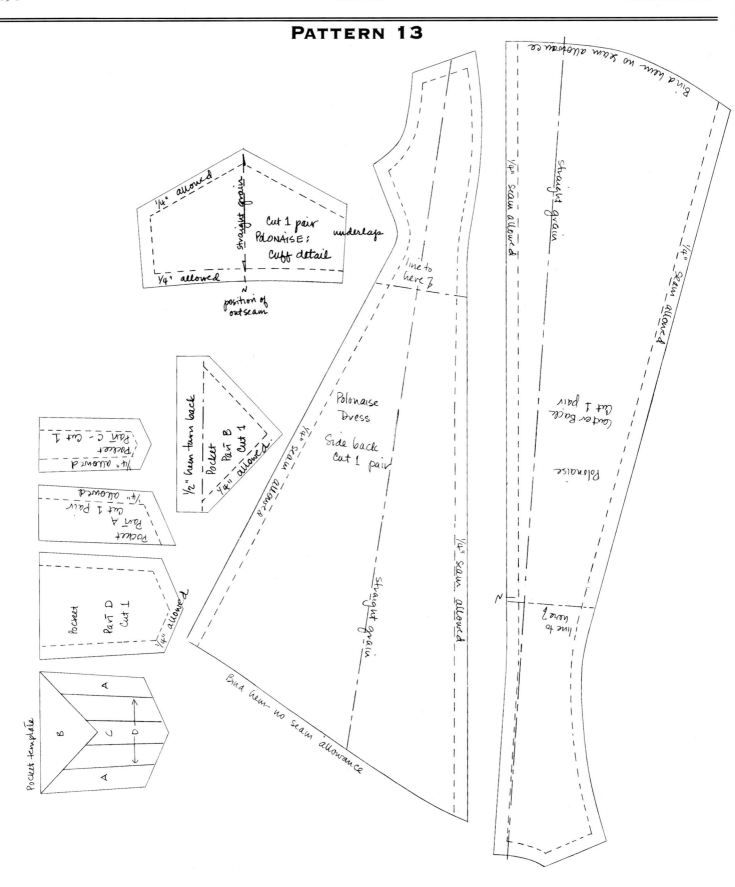

Cut 1 pair
POLONAISE;
Cuff detail

¼" allowed

¼" allowed

straight grain

N
position of outseam

underlap

line to here B

Pocket
Part C - Cut 1

¼" allowed

Pocket
Part A
Cut 1 Pair

¼" allowed

½" hem turn back

Pocket
Part B
Cut 1

¼" allowed

Pocket
Part D
Cut 1

¼" allowed

Polonaise
Dress

Side back
Cut 1 pair

¼" seam allowed

straight grain

¼" seam allowed

Bind hem no seam allowance

Pocket template

A

B   C   D

A

Bind hem no seam allowance

¼" seam allowed

straight grain

Polonaise
Cut 1 pair
Center Back

Polonaise

N

line to here J

¼" Seam allowed

PATTERN 13

PATTERN 14

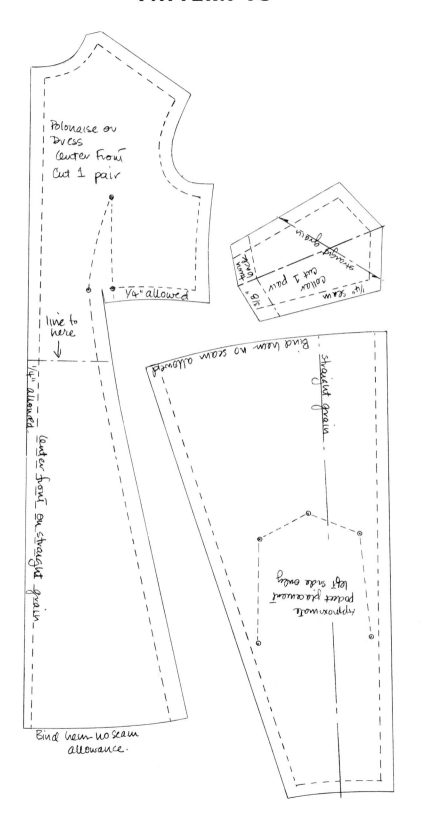

Polonaise or
Dress
Center Front
Cut 1 pair

¼" allowed

Collar
Cut 1 pair
straight grain
½" seam
¾

line to
here
↓

¼" allowed

Center front on straight grain

Bind hem no seam allowed

straight grain

Approximate
pocket placement
left side only

Bind hem no seam
allowance.

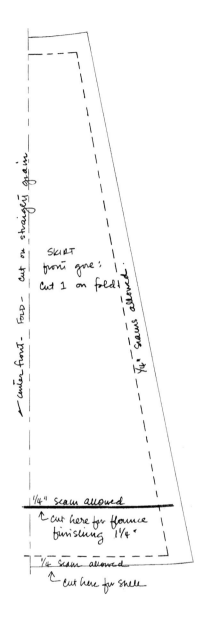

SKIRT
front gore:
Cut 1 on fold!

center front - FOLD - cut on straight grain

¼" seams allowed

¼" seam allowed
↰ cut here for flounce
finishing 1¼"

¼" seam allowed
↰ cut here for shell

PATTERN 14

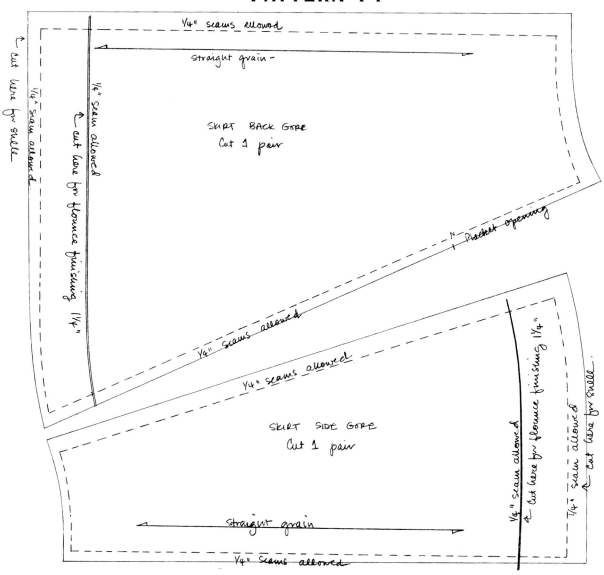

SKIRT BACK GORE
Cut 1 pair

SKIRT SIDE GORE
Cut 1 pair

PATTERN 15

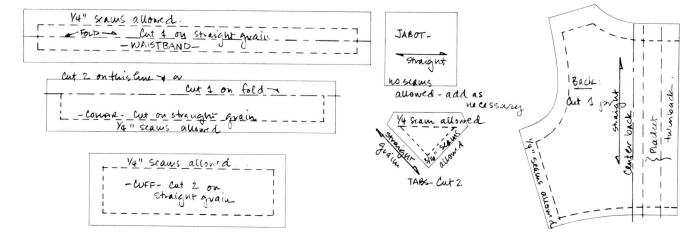

PATTERN 15

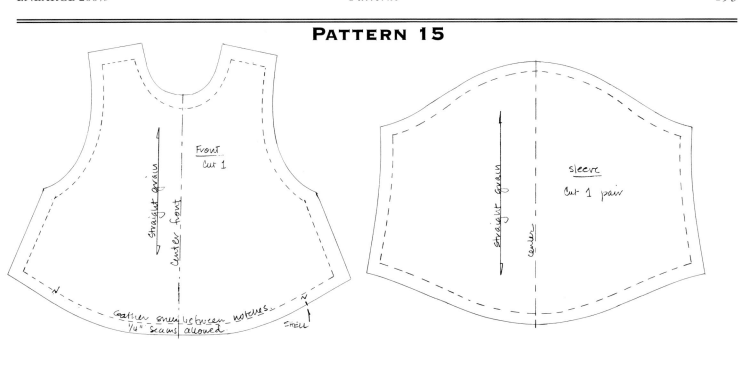

Front
Cut 1

Straight grain

Center front

Gather sleeve between notches
¼" seams allowed.

SHELL

sleeve
Cut 1 pair

Straight grain

center

PATTERN 16

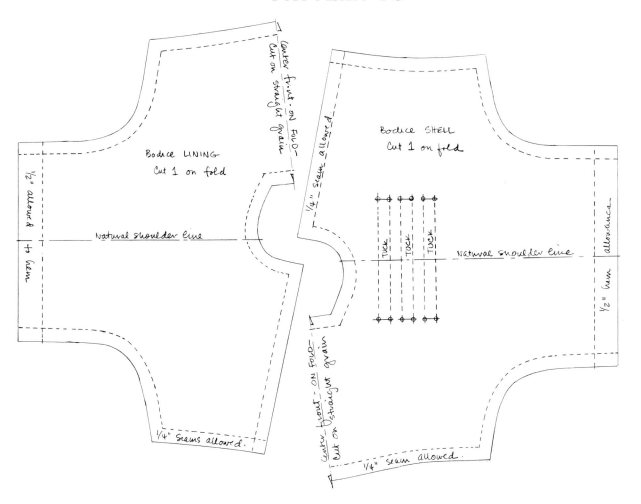

Bodice LINING
Cut 1 on fold

Center front - ON FOLD
Cut on straight grain

½" allowed to hem

Natural shoulder line

¼" Seams allowed.

Bodice SHELL
Cut 1 on fold

¼" seam allowed

TUCK TUCK TUCK

Natural shoulder line

½" hem allowance

Center front - ON FOLD
Cut on straight grain

¼" seam allowed.

PATTERN 16

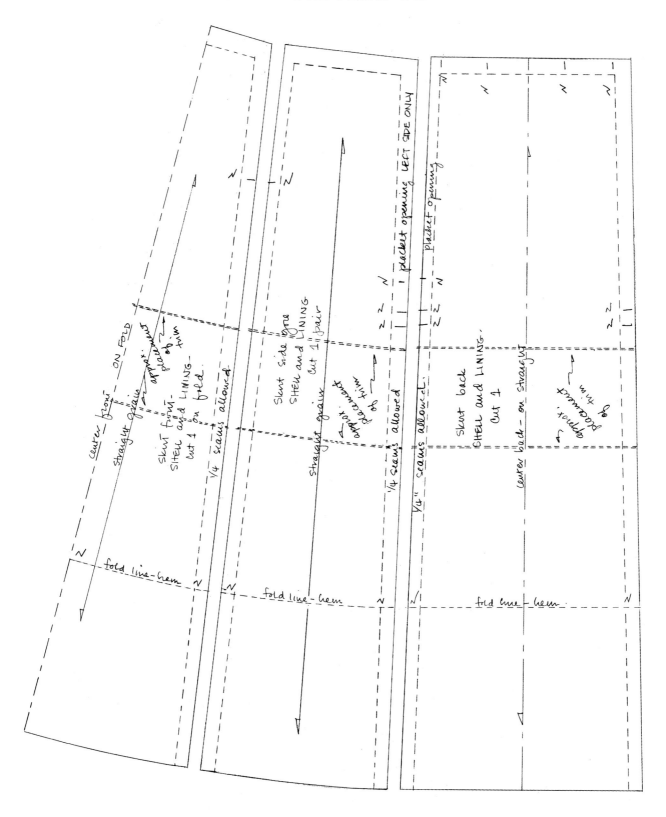

Sewing by Hand

SEWING BY HAND has been rendered obsolete for most worka-day purposes, although certain techniques have in recent years enjoyed a comeback among hobbyists. Technically, most garments fashionable before about 1860 should be put together by hand. After that date, machine sewing is commonly found in various combinations with handwork. As soon as the sewing machine became commonly available, women began to look for ways to achieve the style of handworked garments by the use of the machine. Dolls' clothes are something of a "special case," however, in that the scale of the garments may call for hand stitching where machine stitches would be visible, bulky, and intrusive.

Modern homesewers, who may seldom do anything by hand, may feel slightly intimidated by the concept of assembling an entire garment by hand. The biggest hurdle is to get used to making consistently small, even, stitches. This obviously gives a better looking result; in addition, the durability of hand stitches depends upon distributing as evenly as possible the strain they are bearing. Nothing need be done fast. Your project will be more fun if you think of it like a sampler, executed for enjoyment, rather than a mending job required by necessity.

In setting out to make a replica of an antique garment, or even a frank reproduction using an old style as a model, one is confronted with certain issues almost immediately. Anyone who comes into possession of an old object whose provenance makes it impossible to replace has some obligation to consider what responsibility she has for its survival. This is quite apart from its "market value." This applies to an old garment you may wish to cut up for authentic material or to an old doll whose authentic clothing you may wish to replace. There will never be any more milliner's models or French fashion dolls, and there will equally be no more Civil War era dresses or kid gloves.

New Fabric

IF you like the look of new, perfect garments, you can use new fabrics and laces of good quality, copying only the handwork techniques. This is a perfectly acceptable way to dress a reproduction, and by far the most practical, considering the cost of antique materials.

Whether an old doll must be clothed in old materials is another issue, and the subject of a good deal of disagreement among collectors. Unsurprisingly, established collectors with expensive collections of rarities and closets full of antique inventory tend to think that only the highest standards should be maintained. Beginners and more recreationally oriented collectors tend to disagree. It seems to me that a reproduction is still a reproduction no matter how many hours of labor you put into it; there is no legitimate reason to pass one off as an antique. Most people sew for their dolls because it's challenging fun. The only standard that should be observed is that the finished garment must "look right" on the doll. It is inevitable that the more time one spends looking at authentic pieces, the more exacting one's standards become. The quality of the materials and the care taken in making up, in other words, the "taste" evidenced in the choice and workmanship, is far more important than the actual age of the fabrics. Fine materials will age gracefully as the Victorian originals did, and in a very few years they too will be "old." On the other hand, nothing improves a badly researched or carelessly assembled project.

If you select your fabrics and other materials judiciously, they can be very well employed to dress an old doll. Old trims are espe-cially effective in lending verisimilitude to an otherwise new ensemble, since they are difficult to duplicate. Good quality silk taffeta, on the other hand, is nearly indistinguishable from old material, and, used skillfully, looks perfectly appropriate. Linings and interfacings, which are extremely difficult to come by in quantity, are invisible in the finished garment, and are a good place to compromise. Conversely, modern lace, although attractive in itself and not, perhaps, offensive on a reproduction doll, simply doesn't look like Victorian lace.

It is well to avoid the use of synthetics to the extent possible, although it is in some situations unavoidable. "Cotton" laces, for instance, generally have a small amount of nylon in them to make the thread strong enough to be woven on high-speed modern machines. In general, although there is a place in the world for synthetics, this is not it. In addition to being more difficult to work with, synthetics often do not press very well. Moreover, as your eye becomes more discriminating and your taste educated by study of authentic period work, you will probably come to feel that synthetics, no matter how well employed, look "wrong" on an antique doll, or even a replica of one. An exception to this is certain fabrics and trimmings made of rayon, or "artificial silk" as it was then called, which was invented in the 1880s. Although it is a "synthetic," it is not "artificial," being made today mostly of pine sap. It was originally based on mulberry sap and used to replace expensive silk tassels and soutache, but was impractical as a fabric until the 1920s. Since it looked very rich but did not wear well, it was used to line coffins in the late 19th century. (I am indebted to Nancy Rexford for this bit of late-Victorian fabric lore.) Modern blends of silk and rayon can look extremely convincing and are much less costly than pure silk.

Perhaps most importantly, synthetic fabrics and fabric finishes age unpredictably. Conservationists often use synthetics because the object of the exercise is to prevent, to the extent possible, any further change in the condition of a garment. Conserved garments are stored in controlled climatic conditions that expose them to as little light and handling as possible. Most doll collectors, however, like to handle and display their acqui-

sitions. And for a great many people, the use of the doll as a venue for creating replicas of historic costume is half the fun. Synthetics, therefore, mixed with authentic old fabrics in combination with new analogs may come to look quite strange over time. As the "natural" components of an ensemble gracefully fade, they may appear tacky next to a chemically neutral synthetic trim that may not change at all for the next 200 years. On the other hand, an experimental fabric finish may turn black and destroy a dress in a year. I expect my work to be permanent, and therefore use only the best materials I can get, not necessarily old, but "real."

Old Fabric

AN alternative to creating an entire garment by hand is to re-work antique pieces. This is actually the preferred method for dressing an old doll, since it takes some skill not merely to duplicate the quality of antique workmanship but to make it look correct on an antique doll. Antique stores, second-hand shops, and estate liquidators often have old garments and household linens that can be cut up and recycled for dolls' clothes. Some shops specialize in old handworked pieces, but you will pay a premium for a laundered, perfect, or professionally restored piece. There are some conservation issues to consider in deciding to cannibalize a perfect piece of antique hand workmanship to dress a doll. Many doll collectors have no qualms about doing so; but it is possible to become so absorbed in one's own area of interest that perspective is lost. It is, at any rate, an issue that ought to be addressed, even if the ultimate decision is to cut.

Rather than using first quality pieces for dolls' clothes, soiled or damaged pieces can be used, as you need only a small piece for most garments, assuming you can get it clean. Not only is soiled fabric unpleasant to sew on, but it may be carrying oils and microorganisms that can harm a doll, especially a stuffed doll made of organic materials. You should be sure that you can clean anything that has been starched, as well, since starch, while it makes a garment look good, provides a very attractive medium to pests. This actually applies to new fabrics as well; be sure to wash anything washable to remove any fabric finishes or preservatives.

The cleaning method will depend upon the fiber. Anything too fragile to clean is probably too frail to justify your sewing effort. If you can't decide how strong a fabric really is, find a small hole and gently try to push your finger through it. If it tears easily or falls apart, it is unsuitable. Remember that after you have spent your hours of labor, the fabric will still continue to deteriorate, and fairly soon it could look terrible. The stress of the sewing process will accelerate this.

You can safely launder white cotton or linen fabric that is basically sound. Be extremely careful before laundering any old fabric with a printed pattern on it. The dyes are very likely non-color-fast, and washing may effectively ruin it. Test a small piece first, to see how it will fare. Conservationists refer to "laundering" as "wet cleaning" and use it only as a last resort.

Most advisors in this area avoid the mention of chlorine bleach, but many people use it. Personally, I prefer to bleach old white fab-

ric, which may be a stranger's aged underwear. Bleach is a strong solution similar in chemical composition to lye and therefore must be used with great care. Use chlorine bleach in a light solution. If necessary you can wash a piece two or three times; this is preferable to leaving a delicate piece of handwork soaking for long periods in a strong solution. Soak the piece for a few minutes, and rinse carefully.

Not only is bleach a rather aggressive solvent, but left in the fabric will cause it to disintegrate, so if your water is hard, use a water softener in the rinse to improve its solubility. Keep flushing the piece through clean water until the bleach smell is out. It may be advisable to invest in a few gallons of distilled water; this is what conservation studios use. If your water is very hard, you may consider using distilled water for the washing process as well, since hard water can cause normally safe soaps to leave acid salt deposits on fabric, which will harm it over the long term.

There are several pH neutral soaps on the market. Wool washes and similar preparations are safe for most washable fibers, but are not great for taking out stains or a fusty smell.

Non-chlorine bleaches based on hydrogen peroxide or sodium perborate are generally safe (again with the proviso regarding printed fabrics). Instead of attacking soil by chemically smashing it up as chlorine does, they work by oxidation. Commercial non-chlorine bleaches may also contain fluorescing agents which make things appear "whiter" by reflecting more light.

White cotton or linen fabric may also be lightly bleached by laying it in the sun. As this is an "uncontrolled" method, use it with care. It is, however, one of the classic methods of whitening things.

Several dealers I buy from swear by commercial "rust removers." These are very aggressive solutions designed to take rust out of new white cottons. The manufacturers of these products do not recommend them for use on fragile old fabrics, nor for ordinary laundry purposes. They are for stain removal only. I mention this only because it seems to be one of those "trade secrets" that people pass on; whether you use this approach on your own antique materials depends upon how much risk you like to assume. Professional conservationists recommend the contrary approach, that is, using the mildest solution that will do the job, and upping the ante only if it doesn't work. Besides, "perfect white" is not the effect you are necessarily looking for.

After laundering, air dry your pieces, if possible spread flat on a towel. If you are short of space, drape over a non-metal hanger or rod, distributing the weight of the wet garment evenly; don't pin to a line. Spread the piece over several hangers if necessary to avoid straining the fabric with its own soaked weight.

When the fabric is dry enough to be light in weight, it can be hung in the conventional manner on a padded hanger. Small details can be pressed into shape with your fingers. Sound fabric can be ironed when it is just damp to the touch. It will require less handling with the iron and help shape lace more crisply than if you try to press when the fabric is bone dry. You can lightly sprinkle dry clothes and roll them up to dampen them before you press, like your grandmother used to do. Some people advise storing the sprinkled fabric in the refrigerator to make it easier to press; when I tried it, I was unable to decide whether it helped or not.

Old white or light-colored lace is frequently found in an extremely grubby condition but can usually be laundered with a small amount of preparation. If the cleaning is done carefully, it prepares the lace for use without any pulling or straining, and without subjecting it to the heat of an iron. Wrap a large, clean, empty jar with white cotton fabric that has already been washed to remove sizing and other surface treatments, and secure the fabric with a few basting stitches. Carefully wrap the lace flat around the jar without stretching it, and lightly baste the end of the lace to the jar as well. Submerge the entire works in your solution. It is inadvisable to use bleach for this job because of the difficulty of rinsing it out thoroughly. You can very gently pass your fingers across the surface of the lace to work soil loose. Rinse very thoroughly, and set the jar aside to dry. When the lace is removed from the jar, it should be ready to use.

You may consider dry cleaning wool or silk, which when new are generally safe with this process. However, commercial dry cleaners do not typically handle garments in a manner that you would want your old fabric subjected to, and you should therefore try to find someone willing to do the work by hand. Commercial dry cleaners use an agitator-type machine for washing; garments are dried with heat. If the dry cleaning solvent is not clean, the heat may, in addition to the intrinsic damage it does, cook deposits into the fabric; this may be more damaging than the soil you originally were concerned with. Before dry cleaning anything, check to see if any trims are attached with glue, which may be dissolved by the solvent. Pearls and sequins may also disintegrate.

To cut your old fabric, section off the pieces you intend to use very carefully, using the patterns and finished drawings as a guide. The individual instructions explain how the photographed pieces were created; obviously, there are unlimited permutations. Although this approach saves you some of the handwork, and is most appropriate for dressing a doll that is old, it presents its own challenges, as you must adapt your sewing style so that all of the recombined parts are compatible with each other and with other bits you may have taken from other pieces. Small damages can be worked right into the design; but avoid large ones. Careful planning will enable you to use worked hems and other borders by taking them off whole. Sewing thread and other trims must be chosen carefully to present a unified design. Naturally, once you have cut your old fabric, you are committed, so unless you are lucky enough to have a generously large piece, you may have no room for error. In this situation, I very carefully trace each and every piece I am cutting onto the fabric with basting stitches. You may actually have to section up the pattern itself to get all the parts of the dress out of a small, irregularly shaped scrap, and it is very easy to forget about the seams, to cut two rights and no left, etc. Although basting is time-consuming, it is not difficult, and I like the assurance that I have not forgotten something. It is advisable to sew a muslin if you have made major pattern changes, to be sure the garment still fits correctly. There are several dresses shown in the color plates that were pieced from scraps.

NOTE: If you are working with old fabrics it is important to label your work indelibly. It really is important in a market where there are many amateurs looking for that special "find." Regrettably, there are sellers whose ethical standards are somewhat flexible; they are not necessarily intending to deceive, but may represent a costume as genuinely old when they don't actually know. No one should be able to mistake your perfectly lovely sewing project for an authentic 19th century item. Remember the old dealer's warning: "It's later than you think."

Tools

Handsewing is a low-tech activity, but all jobs are easier with the right tools. In case your local sewing supply shop does not have everything you need, I have included several tools and notions suppliers in the appendix.

NEEDLES. If you are inclined to try any fine work, size 11 or 12 needles are recommended. Once you get used to using a really fine needle, you may find your ordinary sharps feel very awkward.

THIMBLE. I don't like to use a thimble for most jobs, but occasionally it is good to have help driving a hand needle through several layers of fabric. I recommend getting a "tailor's thimble," with an open top. This provides you with the protection you need while permitting you the use of the tip of your finger.

PATTERN SCRIBER. Tailors' suppliers often carry them, but pattern scribers are hard to find otherwise. A scriber looks like a metal pencil with a long, pointed blade like an awl. It is wider at the base and narrower and sharper at the point than an typical awl, however. Patternmakers use a scriber to transfer the points of a design through the heavy manila-type paper used for commercial patterns. Sewers use them for making small holes for eyelets and for unpicking threads.

BEESWAX. Very helpful for work with fine cotton threads, beeswax not only discourages the thread from tangling and knotting, but also makes it slightly tacky, which holds stitches in place as you work. The thread is drawn lightly through the wax before starting to sew.

WEIGHTED CUSHION. Used as a "third hand," a weighted cushion is very helpful in holding down one end of your work, which can either be placed underneath the cushion or pinned to it. A weighted cushion can be made at home. Any small flat shape stuffed with wadding will work. The best thing to use for "weights" are bird shot or small BBs, which are enclosed in a fabric bag inserted between the layers of stuffing as they go in. A pair of buttons, linked together through the cushion, will help preserve its shape. I also like to attach a piece of sturdy ribbon as a means of securing the occasional awkwardly shaped piece of work to the cushion. (Fig. A.1.)

STEAM IRON. Although it seems obvious, you must have a reliable steam iron and use it. Pressing is necessary to make a garment, especially a tiny garment, hang correctly. The directions for each garment indicate how it is to be pressed, but it may be helpful to review generally how to press correctly. First off, the minimum pressing equipment you need is a sleeve board and a press cloth. Hams are useful but not necessary. A press cloth is very important to avoid harming your fabric, especially an old fabric, with the soleplate of your iron. Any thinnish white cotton fabric—calico, muslin, batiste, even a piece of lightweight interfacing—will do. The fabric should be washed to remove sizing and preservatives.

Before starting, test a piece of your antique fabric to determine how much heat and steam it will tolerate. With an old silk fabric, you will likely find it is not much.

To press, arrange the fabric on your board correctly, wrong side up, and lay the press cloth over the area. Wool is best pressed by dampening the press cloth and allowing the iron to drive the moisture through it. Other fabrics can be lightly steamed through the cloth. After pressing the wrong side, turn the fabric over, replace the press cloth, and press the right side. The iron should merely be placed on the fabric, not dragged back and forth across it.

Many small constructions, like sleeves, are best steamed when they are completed to avoid crushing them. In this case, the seams should be basted in the correct alignment. The sleeve is turned, steamed, and the basting pulled out. It may be useful to make a small roll of cotton fabric to use as a tiny ham.

If you are trying to simulate the appearance of an old garment, you can use your steam to "crush" gathers and trimmings slightly. This is also a help in arranging folds and ribbons just the way you want them. To do this, pin the fabric into the shape you want on your board or over a ham, and lightly pass your iron over it with the steam running. Don't touch the soleplate to the garment, but merely let the steam "set" the fabric. As the fabric starts to cool, pull the pins out.

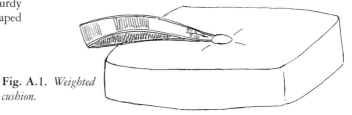

Fig. A.1. *Weighted cushion.*

Stitches

T HE following brief explanations present the hand stitches necessary to complete the projects in this book. Some of them are still in general use today; others have disappeared with handsewing generally. The pattern instructions give very explicit directions for duplicating the style of the original garments; it is helpful to review this section to see how a Victorian dressmaker approached her task.

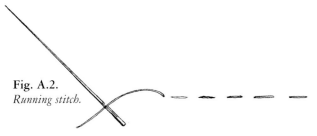

Fig. A.2.
Running stitch.

RUNNING STITCH. Many dolls' clothes of the antebellum period were put together entirely with running stitch. The running stitch is made two or three at a time, the needle picking up four or five threads of the fabric each time it goes in and out. (Fig. A.2.) Gauging and cartridge pleating are made with the running stitch.

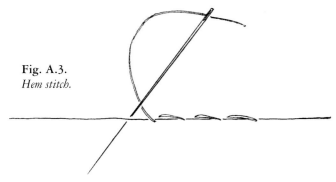

Fig. A.3.
Hem stitch.

HEM STITCH. Hem stitches should be neat and even, since they usually show slightly on the right side of the completed garment. Hemming is done along a folded or taped edge, joining it to the fabric underneath. The thread is carried along the surface; the stitches should therefore be small, so they are less likely to be snagged in wearing or putting on a garment. The needle picks up one or two threads of the fabric underneath and a bit of the edge or tape with each stitch. (Fig. A.3.)

Fig. A.4.
Blind stitch.

BLIND STITCH. Essentially a hem stitch, but carried out in the opposite fashion. The thread picks up a small bit of a folded edge, but the stitch "travels" on the back side of the fabric underneath, or between two layers. Only the single, tiny stitch shows on the surface, and it may be made nearly invisible if care is taken in the sewing. (Fig. A.4.)

Fig. A.5.
Catch stitch.

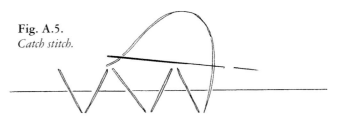

CATCH STITCH. Catch stitch is used to join or stitch down edges invisibly. It is often used as a hem in tailored jackets, for instance, where the edge is sewn down and then the lining is blind stitched on top. The stitches of the catch stitch run over the edge instead of through it. (Fig. A.5.) A variant of this is the cross stitch. (Fig. A.6 and Fig. A.7.)

Fig. A.6. *Cross stitch, in progress.*

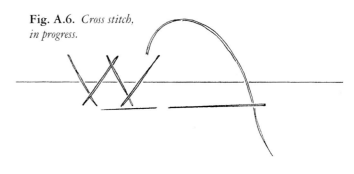

Fig. A.7. *Cross stitch, in progress.*

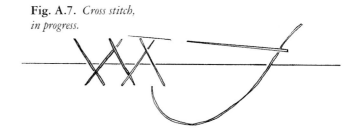

Fig. A.8. *Pin stitch.*

Fig. A.9. *Pin stitch.*

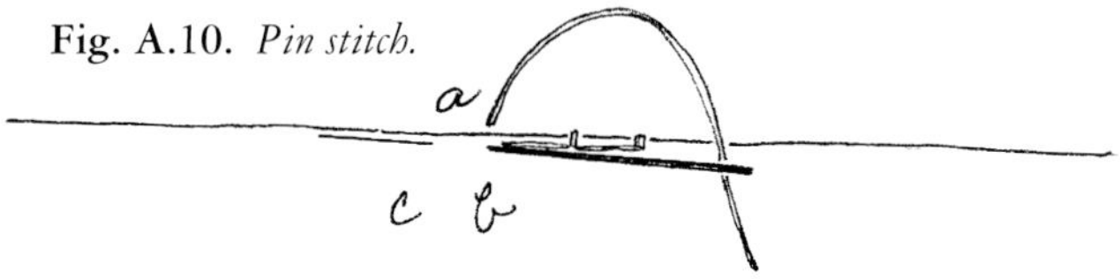

Fig. A.10. *Pin stitch.*

Fig. A.11
Feather stitch.
The "dotted lines"
are imaginary,
but may be basted
onto the as a
stitching guide.

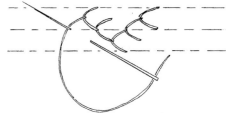

FEATHER STITCH. Used throughout the period covered by this book as a decorative technique on underthings. White, pink or red woolen calf-length petticoats with hems decorated with contrast silk feather stitch are an early Victorian classic. Feather stitch is also a useful white-on-white technique for later underthings. It is an extremely easy stitch, very economical with the sewer's time.

Fig. A.11 illustrates the alignment of the stitches. Feather stitch needs to be well organized across the surface of the fabric or the pattern appears to fall apart. The dotted lines on the drawing are imaginary, but if you have a great deal of difficulty, they can be basted across the garment as a guide and then pulled out.

PIN STITCH. This is one of those neat techniques that give a very satisfying result with a very modest effort on the part of the sewer. It is used principally on hems and other edges, but is also an elegant way to finish a felled seam or to make tucks. It is a simple and very economical way to join lace to fabric either as an edging or as a free-standing cut-work motif. The pin stitch is useful for handling seams and hems in old fabrics, since it is ubiquitously found on old linens of all kinds.

First, the edge must be established. When pin stitch is used to finish a straight edge, care should be taken to place the fold and the stitches along the grain of the fabric. The thread initially comes up from beneath the folded edge, at *a*, and a small stitch is taken, about four threads of the fabric, *bc*. (Fig. A.8.) Next, the needle goes back down into the same hole at *b*, and up at *d*. (Fig. A.9.) Pull on the thread gently; this will draw the fabric together, creating two tiny holes. This produces the characteristic pattern. On the other side of the work, the stitches form a line of tiny herringbones. Now you are at the beginning again (that is, at *a*), and ready to take the next stitch. (Fig. A.10.)

To join lace to fabric with pin stitch, the edge of the lace is treated as the fold of fabric. The stitching creates a decorative row of holes along the edge. When the lace has been joined, the fabric underneath is cut away 2–3 threads from the seam.

Fig. A.12. *Back stitch.*

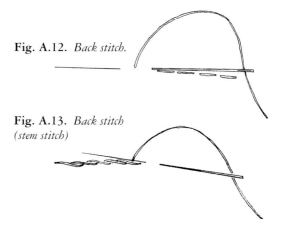

Fig. A.13. *Back stitch (stem stitch)*

BACK STITCH. Back stitching is used to make very secure seams. It was used extensively in making clothes before the machine era. Although it is much less used on dolls' clothes (as it is a more time-consuming stitch than the running stitch), it is a useful technique to know for certain operations, for instance, setting sleeves, where you may want a stronger join than a running stitch provides. It is also helpful to take an occasional back stitch while executing a seam by other means, as a way of securing your work in sections. (Fig. A.12.) The "back side" of the back stitch should look like the stem stitch. (Fig. A.13.) The stitch can be executed in either fashion.

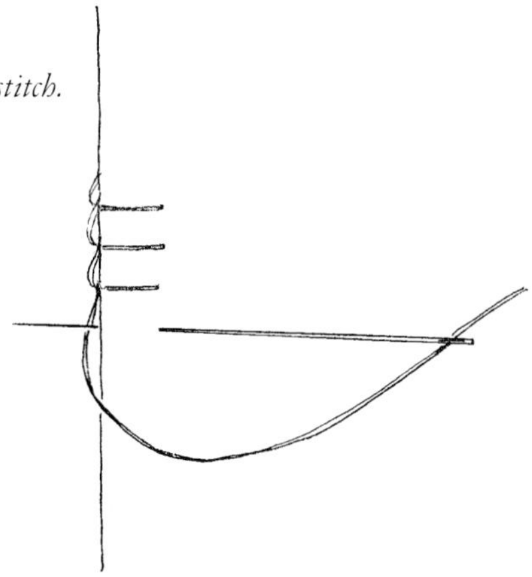

Fig. A.14.
Buttonhole stitch.

Fig. A.15. *Whip stitch.*

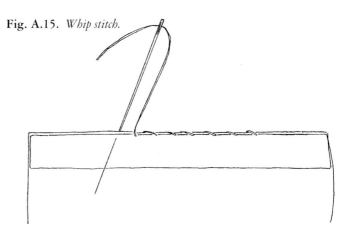

BUTTONHOLE STITCH. Buttonhole stitch is typically executed along an edge to bind and finish it. Broderie anglaise and many other types of cut work are based on this technique. In some styles of work, the fabric is cut first and the embroidery worked over the edge. Mid-Victorian ladies could buy lengths of fabric pre-cut with stamped dies for use in making embroidered edgings. In other styles of work, the embroidery is worked first and then the fabric cut away. When the piece is washed and ironed, the cut ends disappear into the embroidery, leaving a clean finish. (Fig. A.14.) Individual stitches are generally made close enough to just touch. In needle-made laces, the outline of the design is often reiterated with "cordonnet," a row of buttonhole stitches packed tight enough to form a raised pattern. When the stitches are made with visible space left between them, this stitch is sometimes called "blanket stitch."

WHIP STITCH. The most common use of the whip stitch is for attaching edgings and insertions to fabric. The edging is laid along the edge of the fabric to which it is to be joined, right sides together, and the two edges whipped together. The lace and fabric are then opened out and pressed. (Fig. A.15.) In reproduction work with old materials, it is sometimes more advisable simply to lay the pieces edge to edge and whip. This stresses the materials less.

Fig. A.16.
*Seam finished
with overcasting.*

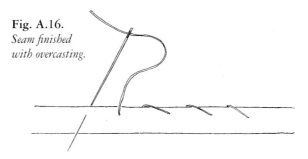

OVERCASTING. This provides a surprisingly effective seam finish. Seams are overcast with a long whip stitch. The edge should be trimmed of ragged bits and loose threads before beginning to stitch. (Fig. A.16.)

Seams

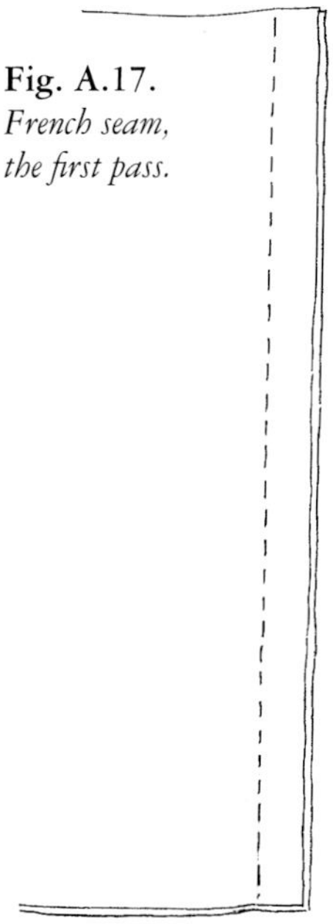

Fig. A.17.
*French seam,
the first pass.*

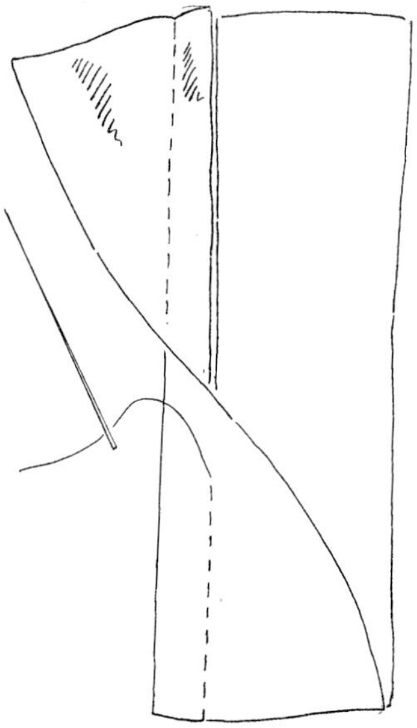

Fig. A.18. *French seam,
the second pass.*

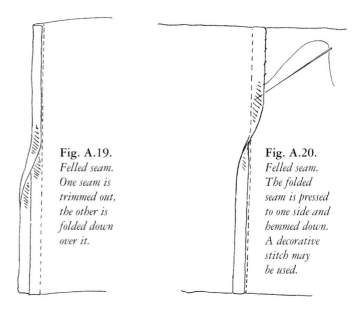

Fig. A.19.
*Felled seam.
One seam is
trimmed out,
the other is
folded down
over it.*

Fig. A.20.
*Felled seam.
The folded
seam is pressed
to one side and
hemmed down.
A decorative
stitch may
be used.*

FRENCH SEAM. French seams may be executed by machine as well as by hand, although a hand seam is more fluid than a machine seam. The French seam has traditionally been used to finish fine lingerie and blouses that are loose-fitting and delicate but require frequent washing. The seam is made in two passes. If ¼" (.5 cm) is allowed for the total seam allowance each pass must use slightly less than ⅛" (.3 cm), since some of the allowance is lost in the turning. A small amount may be added before cutting if you need a wider allowance. French seams are typically made with the running stitch; strength is provided by stitching twice.

First, unlike most construction seams, the fabric is joined with wrong sides together. (Fig. A.17.) Turn the seam; press if necessary, but usually the warmth of your hands will do. The second pass is sewn next to the inner seam allowance, enclosing it neatly. (Fig. A.18.)

FELLED SEAM. Another seam made in two passes that provides a clean finish inside the garment. A felled seam is stitched down to the shell fabric of the garment usually on the inside. The lap seam is the most common type of felled seam. The second pass, which, unlike the French seam, shows outside the garment, may be made with a small hem stitch or a decorative stitch such as the pin stitch. When this seam is done in the factory on a lap seam machine (in making blue jeans, for instance), the seam allowances must be carefully planned, since one seam must be wide enough to fully enclose the other. In doing this seam by hand, especially on dolls' clothes scale, this is unnecessary.

Stitch the seam at the normal allowance, typically ¼" (.5 cm) or wider. Trim out the under seam to about ⅛" (.3 cm), and fold the upper seam over it, enclosing it. The raw edge of the wider seam is brought down parallel to the stitching, nearly touching it. (Fig. A.19.) Press the seam down with your fingers, and stitch it down. (Fig. A.20.)

Lap seams have "direction," that is, they are asymmetrical, since the stitching shows on the right side of the garment. If you use this seam to finish a garment, bear in mind as you trim that you need to consider whether you need a "left" and "right."

ROLLING, WHIPPING, AND GATHERING. This is a specialized technique that has hardly any application at all beyond French handsewing hobbyists. It was in widespread use during the 19th century for fine underclothes, ladies' wear, baby garments, and table linens. Rolling, whipping, and gathering are used most frequently to finish decorative rather than structural seams. This includes flounces and other frilled edgings, insertions, and puffings.

To begin, establish a clean edge. This may be a straight edge, but a convex curve, such as a gored petticoat hem, may also be rolled. Rolled edges should be very even. Experienced sewers are generally able to judge the evenness of a rolled hem by observing the woven threads of the fabric they are working. This takes a great deal of practice, however, and in the meanwhile, to ensure that your rolled edge is uniform, it may be helpful to place a line of basting stitches about ¼" (.5 cm) from the raw edge to use as a gauge.

To start the rolling, moisten the fingers of one hand slightly to allow you to get a purchase on the fabric. (Most people use spit.) Place the needle against the fabric, and roll the fabric around the needle. (Fig. A.21.) The needle is then inserted under the roll and brought up through the top of the roll. If you have difficulty getting started, you can incline the fabric in the right direction by rolling between the fingers of both hands. (Fig. A.22.)

The stitching proceeds, whipping the thread around the roll by inserting the needle under the roll and bringing it out at the top. In addition to being sewn down, the roll is being inclined toward the back of the work. (Fig. A.23.) One hand is continually making the roll while the other whips it down. The roll should be as tight as possible; it should feel as though there is a very fine cord in the center. Take care in rolling, however, that you do not stretch the fabric. The edge of fabric that precedes the needle is always a short bias strip. (Fig. A.24, at *ab*.) When lace insertion or other constructions are joined to this edge, they are generally sewn to the right side with the whip stitch. When the seam is opened out, the rolled edge is pushed to the back of the work, where the seam should secure it.

Gathering by this method is done generally at a ratio of 2:1; that is, the edge to be gathered is cut twice as long as the edge to which it is to be joined. In joining, for instance, a petticoat flounce to the skirt of the petticoat, section off the various pieces before starting to gather. The flounce and the skirt are divided into quarters, eighths, or some other manageable proportion, and marked with tailor tacks that can be pulled out after the work is completed.

Begin by rolling the edge as usual. After completing two or three inches of rolling, the edge is gathered by sliding the work down the thread to the appropriate distance. (Fig. A.25.) This should be done in short sections to keep the work even. (Fig. A.26.) Use the tip of your needle to stroke the gathers into place. Tie off at each tailor tack.

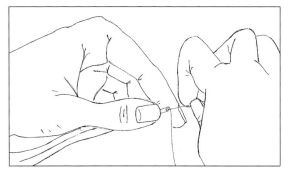

Fig. A.21.
Rolled edge. The needle is used to aid in beginning the roll.

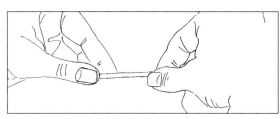

Fig. A.22.
Two hands may be used to roll the edge neatly.

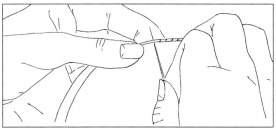

Fig. A.23.
The needle is inserted under the roll; the edge is caught down with a whip stitch.

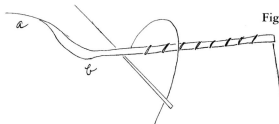

Fig. A.24.
The rolled and whipped edge.

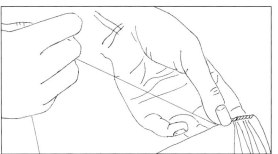

Fig. A.25.
The gathering is done in short sections of a few inches each. The gathers are stroked into place with the needle.

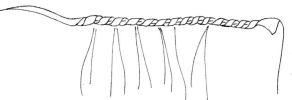

Fig. A.26.
The rolled, whipped, and gathered edge.

ROLLED SEAM. This is a very fine interior finish used for delicate lingerie items. It is in essence an elegant felled seam and is used principally on transparent fabrics. Join the seam as usual with the running stitch, and trim as though to make a lapped seam. Instead of lapping, however, roll the longer seam allowance down to the stitching and whip, enclosing the trimmed seam neatly inside as you go. (Fig. A.27.)

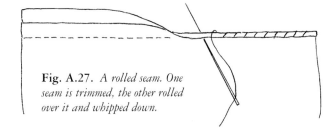

Fig. A.27. *A rolled seam. One seam is trimmed, the other rolled over it and whipped down.*

INSERTING CORD INTO SEAMS. Cording or "piping" was used extensively at the beginning of the period covered by this book. It was used less after about 1860, becoming a discretionary trim rather than a required construction method, and over the next 20 years gradually disappeared. Armholes were often finished with cording into the late 1870s. Cording can make seams bulky, but with proper trimming, it makes a very smart finish. It requires several steps, but is not difficult, and in fact may help in finishing seams by hand.

I recommend acquiring a large spool of cotton carpet warp for use as the actual cord. Pearl cotton may also be used, but its softer texture, while yielding a more flexible finished seam, is harder to cope with in sewing. Corded seams are sewn using the ridge the cord creates in the fabric as a guide for the needle, and carpet warp provides a more definite line.

The cord is covered with a strip of fabric cut on the true bias for maximum flexibility in working. Cut the fabric about 1" (2.5 cm) wide by whatever length you need. The fabric may be pieced, but on dolls' clothes scale, fabric and cord can be cut for each seam without much waste, and this is the easiest way to handle it, avoiding the need to deal with seams wrapped around the cord. Fold the fabric in half, and stitch the cord into the fold. Place the stitches close to the cord, but not tight against it. (Fig. A.28.) The fabric is then trimmed to provide a ¼" (.5 cm) seam allowance.

To set the cording into a seam, place the raw edge of the cording against the edge of the seam, and baste it in place. The cord itself is now lying along the garment seam allowance. (Fig. A.29.) The seam is then joined as usual, following the line of the cord, which you can feel through the fabric, with the needle. These stitches are placed as close as possible to the actual cord, to make a clean, tight join. The seams are then graded to reduce bulk and turned all one way. They can be overcast, felled, or covered with a lining to finish. (Fig. A.30.)

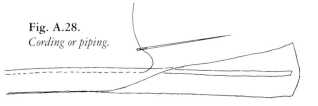

Fig. A.28. *Cording or piping.*

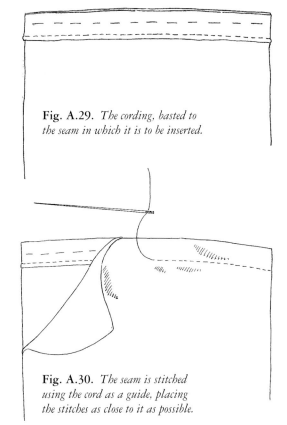

Fig. A.29. *The cording, basted to the seam in which it is to be inserted.*

Fig. A.30. *The seam is stitched using the cord as a guide, placing the stitches as close to it as possible.*

CORD FACINGS. This is another one of those old techniques that has disappeared entirely from modern usage. It began to be abandoned when cording became less popular as a finishing technique. Cord facings provide a clean finish for all kinds of edges, such as pocket hems, cuffs, and necklines. It is applied in a somewhat counter-intuitive fashion, but it is not difficult to do and is an extremely useful technique.

To prepare an edge for a cord facing, put a line of basting along the seam at ¼" (.5 cm). This provides a guide for your stitching. Measure the basted seam and cut a piece of cord at that length. Cut a piece of bias fabric 1" (2.5 cm) wide by the length of the cord plus two seam allowances. (Or, for example, to finish a neckline that measures 6" (15 cm) around the basting, cut the cord 6" (15 cm) long and the bias fabric 1" (2.5 cm) wide by 6 1/2" (16.5 cm) long.) Tuck the short edges of the bias fabric over the cord, and fold one edge down ¼" (.5 cm). Stitch the cord into the fold. The other edge of the bias strip is folded up so the raw edges meet. Baste. (Fig. A.31.)

The wrong side of the cord facing is laid against the edge of the right side of the garment, so that the cord runs along the basted line. The facing is joined to the edge with a running stitch placed right against the cord. (Fig. A.32.) Then it is turned inside. Clip the seam of the garment to ease the seam and let the facing lie flat. Close with a small blind stitch or hem stitch. (Fig. A.33.)

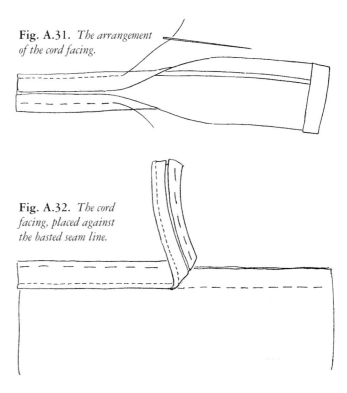

Fig. A.31. *The arrangement of the cord facing.*

Fig. A.32. *The cord facing, placed against the basted seam line.*

Fig. A.33. *The cord facing, turned in and blind stitched to close. The seam may be clipped, if necessary, to ease the turning.*

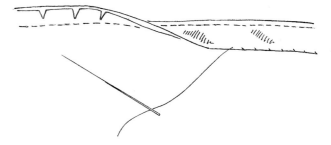

Closures

Fig. A.34. *Button and thread shank.*

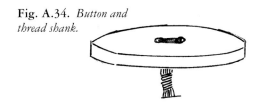

BUTTONS. Functional buttons should be provided with a thread shank to prevent strain when the garment is fastened up. (Decorative buttons obviously bear no strain.) When sewing the button, leave a small amount of slack in the thread as you go in and out. Before tying off, wrap the threads round several times to provide a thread shank. (Fig. A.34.)

Fig. A.35. *Hook. The actual hook should be sewn down to distribute the strain as much as possible and keep the closure neat.*

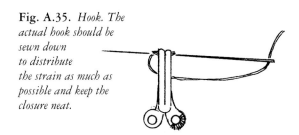

HOOKS. Hooks should be sewn flat, not left hanging loose inside a garment. Be sure in sewing a hook in place to take a few stitches through the hook itself. (Fig. A.35.)

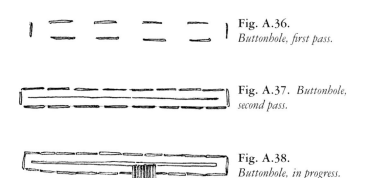

Fig. A.36. *Buttonhole, first pass.*

Fig. A.37. *Buttonhole, second pass.*

Fig. A.38. *Buttonhole, in progress.*

Fig. A.39. *Completed buttonhole. The bar at the bottom of this buttonhole is an optional finish for longer buttonholes, such as on a coat or jacket front.*

BUTTONHOLES. Although it is scary to cut a hole in your finished bodice, buttonholes are not as difficult as they are made out to be. The key is to learn to make small, regular stitches at a close but uniform distance. You can do the buttonhole stitch over a folded edge of fabric to develop a "rhythm," but, needless to say, before you take your buttonhole cutter to the front of a dress, you will want to do some practice holes.

You must go around a buttonhole several times to complete it. A single thread used without tying off is the most efficient way to do it.

First, determine the length of the buttonhole. Measure the button, allowing not only for diameter but also thickness. Mark the buttonhole with a pair of dots or faint line. Using a single thread, go around the outside of the buttonhole marks with small running stitches. You will probably have to execute these stitches one at a time, punching through and through to make sure all the layers are caught and the stitches are even. (Fig. A.36.) Then go around again, filling in the gaps. (Fig. A.37.) This provides a stable foundation for the buttonhole and will discourage the fabric from ravelling while you work. Cut the buttonhole. The cut, not the stitching, is the actual finished size of the buttonhole opening.

Begin to cover the running stitches with buttonhole stitches, placing them just close enough to touch. If the stitches are too far apart, the buttonhole will fray. If they are too close together, the edge will be ripply and unattractive. (Fig. A.38.) Fig. 39 shows a completed buttonhole. The square bar at one end is optional; it is usually worked on longer buttonholes in heavier materials, generally in jackets or coats where the buttonholes run horizontally across the garment and have a definite direction. A small buttonhole worked vertically down the center of a blouse or camisole may be rounded at both ends. When you have finished covering the buttonhole, draw the thread to the back side of the work and very neatly tie off.

WORKED BARS AND LOOPS. Often, a hook is paired with a thread bar or loop rather than a metal eye in old clothing. It is a neat and inconspicuous way to make a closure. This technique is also used to make the bars or "brides" of many types of needle-made laces.

To begin, lay down three or four threads to form a small bar. A very small amount of slack should be allowed, so the bar is not pulled tight against the fabric. To begin, take a tiny back stitch to secure the threads. (Fig. A.40.) Buttonhole stitches are then worked over the threads. (Fig. A.41.) At the bottom of the bar, the thread is drawn to the back side and tied off.

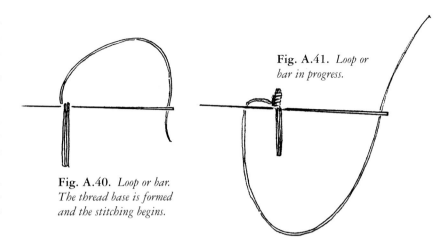

Fig. A.41. *Loop or bar in progress.*

Fig. A.40. *Loop or bar. The thread base is formed and the stitching begins.*

EYELETS. Eyelets, in addition to carrying laces in corsets and fabric shoes, may also be paired with hooks to make a smooth back or front closure. Buttonhole twist or ordinary silk machine thread should be used, depending upon the weight of the fabric and the size of the hole. A pattern scriber is a good tool to have for making the actual hole. The point should be placed against the fabric and worked through gently. In this way, the threads of the fabric may be spread apart rather than torn. Work the scriber into the fabric all the way down to the bit.

Begin with a waste knot. If the garment being worked on is lined, run the needle between the lining and shell and come up next to the hole. If there is no lining, run the needle to the hole with a set of small running stitches, and travel beside the hole for a short distance. (Fig. A.42.)

Begin covering the edges of the hole. This is done with whip stitches made close together. The needle goes down through the hole and up through the fabric beside it. This draws the edge of the hole to the back side of the work. Pull the stitches snug, working your way around the hole and covering the end of the thread as much as possible. (Fig. A.43.) When the circle is completed, draw the thread to the back side and tie off neatly. Cut the remaining thread from the beginning of the work and pull out the knot. (Fig. A.44.)

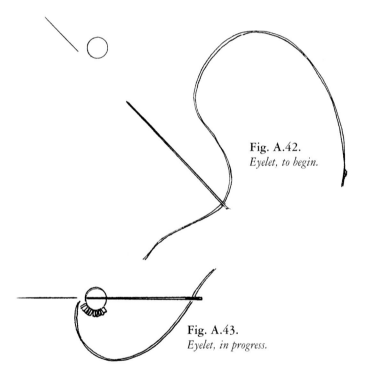

Fig. A.42. *Eyelet, to begin.*

Fig. A.43. *Eyelet, in progress.*

Fig. A.44. *Completed eyelet.*

Making Things Fit

Fig. C.1.

The basic measurements required for fitting a doll's garment.

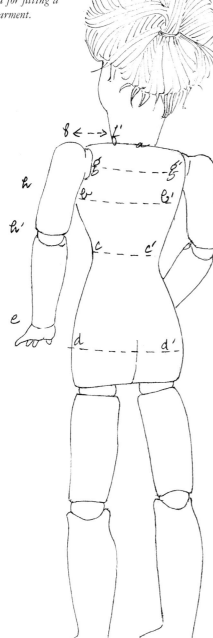

CP to floor (*a*): *The "**CP**" or "cervical point" is found on a person by bending the head forward and finding the bump at the back of the neck. Dolls do not have an actual cervical point, of course, but the drape from this point and the shoulders determines how a garment will hang and many measurements are taken using it as a reference.*

SHOULDER DEPTH (*ab*): *The distance from the cervical point to the bottom of the armhole.*

WAIST LENGTH (*ac*): *The distance from the cervical point to the natural waist.*

WAIST TO FLOOR (*c*–floor): *Should be measured at center front rather than at the back for most purposes, since the skirt styles of most of the periods covered in this book are slightly longer at the back than in front. The waist to floor measure in front therefore establishes the functional hem. The pattern instructions will indicate otherwise where applicable.*

NECK CIRCUMFERENCE (around at *a*): *Measure around, running through the cervical point.*

CHEST GIRTH (around at *b*): *Measure at the bottom of the armhole.*

WAIST GIRTH (around at *c*): *Measure at the "natural waist"; use the narrowest point.*

SEAT GIRTH (around at *d*): *Measure at the widest point.*

WRIST (spread fingers) (around at *e*): *Measure the smallest dimension above the hand, and note the measure of the spread fingers. The latter measure may be significantly larger and require adjustment so the sleeve will go on the doll.*

BICEP (elbow) (around *h* and *h'*): *Important for three-quarter sleeves, especially on a doll with ball joints. These heavy joints may be larger around than the limb sections they are connected to.*

SLEEVE (*afe*): *Measure the sleeve from the cervical point to the wrist over the shoulder when the arm is down.*

SHOULDER LENGTH (*f*–*f'*): *Measure from the base of the neck to the arm join. This is a rather short measure on a jointed composition and wood body, since the ball joint is better placed into the sleeve.*

CROSS-BACK WIDTH (*g*–*g'*): *This determines the width of the garment back at the approximate mid-point of the shoulder depth. On a person, the measure of the cross-back width is made by finding the small folds of flesh at the sides of the back when the arms are hanging loosely down. Although you need to use your imagination to find this measure on your doll, it is somewhat important, since it determines whether the arms can extend forward when wearing the garment. It establishes the back edge of the armhole; on the front, the armhole is slightly deeper at this point.*

Fig. C.1 illustrates the method of taking the measurements.

The models for each chapter of reproduction styles were chosen because they represented "typical" or "average" types of dolls for each period. The models are all more or less 18" (45.5 cm) tall. Although the dolls of the 19th century certainly belong to "types," they vary widely even within a type. Lady Betty Modish, for instance, is apparently wearing the forearms of a somewhat smaller doll. She is in her original condition; perhaps the factory was running low on her size forearms that day, or it may be sheer error. There is a good deal more of this kind of variation among old dolls than modern ones. In addition, although I have used a single model for each fashion period, there were many types of dolls for sale at any time in the past. For example, in this book the clothing of the period 1865-1880 has all been made for a Parisienne, but Parians and chinas, often assembled at home, were popular as well and would have been dressed similarly. The usefulness of the measurements given above, therefore, is principally that you can compare them to the patterns to see how the dresses in the pattern instructions fit. They are basically a place to start.

CH. I: The model for this chapter is a KPM reproduction with body made to approximately naturalistic proportions. The legs are made in one with the body, without a hip joint.

CH. II–IV: The model for these chapters is a china shoulderplate doll made about 1855. Her light pink lustre arms are also of the period. The body was made to approximately naturalistic proportions, jointed at the hip.

CH. V–VII: The model for these chapters is a reproduction body made about 1920, very artfully distressed to appear authentic. The head is an authentic head of about 1870 with a replacement mohair wig.

CH. VIII–IX: The model for these chapters is a Kestner 162 in original condition, including her mohair wig.

MEASUREMENT	CH. I	CH. II-IV	CH. V-VII	CH. VIII-IX
HEIGHT	18" (45.5 cm)	17½" (43 cm)	18" (45.5 cm)	18" (45.5 cm)
CP TO FLOOR (*a*–floor)	15½" (38 cm)	15½" (38 cm)	14½" (35.5 cm)	14" (35.5 cm)
SHOULDER DEPTH (*a*–*b*)	2¼" (5 cm)	2¼" (5 cm)	2½" (5 cm)	1¾" (2.5 cm)
WAIST LENGTH (*a*–*c*)	4" (10 cm)	4" (10 cm)	4¾" (10 cm)	3¾" (7.5 cm)
WAIST TO FLOOR (*c*–floor, at center front)	11" (28 cm)	11" (28 cm)	10" (25.5 cm)	10½" (25.5 cm)
NECK CIRCUMFERENCE (around *a*)	4" (10 cm)	4¼" (10 cm)	4¾" (10 cm)	5" (12.5 cm)
Chest girth (around *b*)	12" (30.5 cm)	12" (30.5 cm)	10" (25.5 cm)	9" (23 cm)
WAIST GIRTH (around *c*)	7" (18 cm)	7" (18 cm)	7" (18 cm)	6¼" (16 cm)
SEAT GIRTH (around *d*)	11" (28 cm)	11" (28 cm)	10" (25.5 cm)	9" (23 cm)
WRIST (spread fingers) (around *e*)	2½" (5 cm) [3½" or 7.5 cm]	1½" (2.5 cm) [1½" or 2.5 cm]	2" (5 cm) [2¼" or 5 cm]	2¼" (3 cm)
BICEP (elbow) (around *b* and *b'*)	3" (7.5 cm) [2½" or 5 cm]	3½" (7.5 cm) [2¾" or 5 cm]	2½" (5 cm) [3½" or 7.5 cm]	3½" (7.5 cm)
SLEEVE (*afe*)	7¼" (18 cm)	7¼" (18 cm)	8" (20.5 cm)	7½" (18 cm)
SHOULDER LENGTH (*f*–*f'*)	2½" (5 cm)	2½" (5 cm)	2" (5 cm)	¾" (1 cm)
CROSS-BACK WIDTH (*g*–*g'*)	4½" (10 cm)	4½" (10 cm)	4" (10 cm)	3" (7.5 cm)

THERE are several ways to approach pattern alteration. These suggestions are necessarily general, since you may be dealing with any number of "special circumstances" having nothing to do with style, such as an oddly shaped shoulderplate or a homemade body with peculiar proportions.

Doll measurements differ from people in one important respect. Dolls are proportionate representations of some "ideal" female figure. In other words, although your actual example may not be "ideal," a 16" (40.5 cm) doll and an 18" (45.5 cm) doll are, in theory, different sized versions of the same concept. You should, therefore, be able to make some of your pattern alterations simply by photocopying the pattern at the correct size.

The most difficult part of the patternmaker's job is the fit of the garment at the shoulder/breast/neckline area. Therefore, to determine the change you need to make, compare the chest measurement of your doll with the model. For example:

$$\frac{\text{Your doll}}{\text{Model}} = \frac{8" \ (20.5 \text{ cm})}{10" \ (25.5 \text{ cm})} = 80\%$$

Although you have used only the chest measurement for the comparison, copy the entire pattern so its various parts are in the same proportion. After you have made this adjustment, assess the pattern for fit. If it seems close enough, make a muslin. This is the easiest way to determine the fit of the bodice over the whole torso of the doll. (It will have to be done eventually no matter how you have chosen to alter the pattern, since there is no line on any doll labeled "chest girth.") Trim off the neckhole and armhole seam allowances when you cut out the muslin; at this stage they only get in the way.

Now you should be ready to alter the actual pattern. If you have a trifling change to make, you may be able to deal with it simply by adding or subtracting at the seams. However, only a minor change can be made in this fashion. For alterations amounting to any significant change, or several changes together, it is a better approach to split the pattern up and add or subtract fabric from the center, leaving the seam edges alone. In this way you don't disturb the perimeter, which determines the "style" of the garment. As a general rule, the pattern should be split somewhere in the middle of where you want to add or remove fabric from the garment. Usually, it is best to make your cuts along the straight or crosswise grain so that the garment drapes the same way it was designed. This is less important on dolls' clothes than on full-size garments, because the garments are not only very small, but the fabric itself is a bit out of scale to begin with.

One exception to this is the neckline. In a full-size pattern, a very careful alteration would be made preserving the shape of the shoulders and the exact shape of the neckhole, but on dolls' clothes scale, these intricacies are often moot. If your pattern almost fits, except at the neck, you may be able to get the fit you need by adding or subtracting a small amount all around. (Fig. C.2.) Be extremely careful in doing this, however. If you trim off ⅛" (.3 cm) all around, you may have actually enlarged the neck by 1" (2.5 cm). It is important that there be no bunching or pulling at the neck; it can make an otherwise well-fitting garment look awkward.

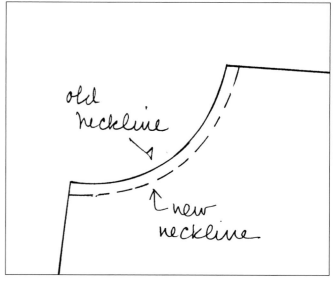

Fig. C.2. *One-quarter of a neckhole, showing the alteration. The dotted line, made ⅛" (.3 cm) in from the original, solid, line, makes the new neckhole nearly ¼" (.5 cm) larger. The whole neckline, therefore, is nearly 1" (2.5 cm) larger.*

In working with the pattern itself, it can be helpful to trim off the seam allowances and turn-backs, so that you are working with the garment only. Just don't forget to put them back on.

It is important to preserve the original pattern in some fashion, so that you have a reference and do not go too far afield. When I do this job, I divide the pattern, lay it out on a piece of paper the way I think it should be, and trace around. The drawings of each successive alteration are retained for a record.

Sleeves can also be altered by splitting them down the center; the alteration on a two-piece sleeve usually should be divided equally between the top sleeve and under sleeve. Fig. C.3 and Fig. C.4 illustrate two methods of altering the armhole seam of the sleeve: one narrows the entire sleeve; the other changes only the top, near the armhole itself.

Fig. C.5 illustrates points where the bodice may be split. The darts are being ignored for the time being. After making the whole alteration, draw the darts back in. When you make a new muslin, you can often do an ad hoc alteration to the darts. Several muslins and rounds of alteration may be needed to achieve the correct result.

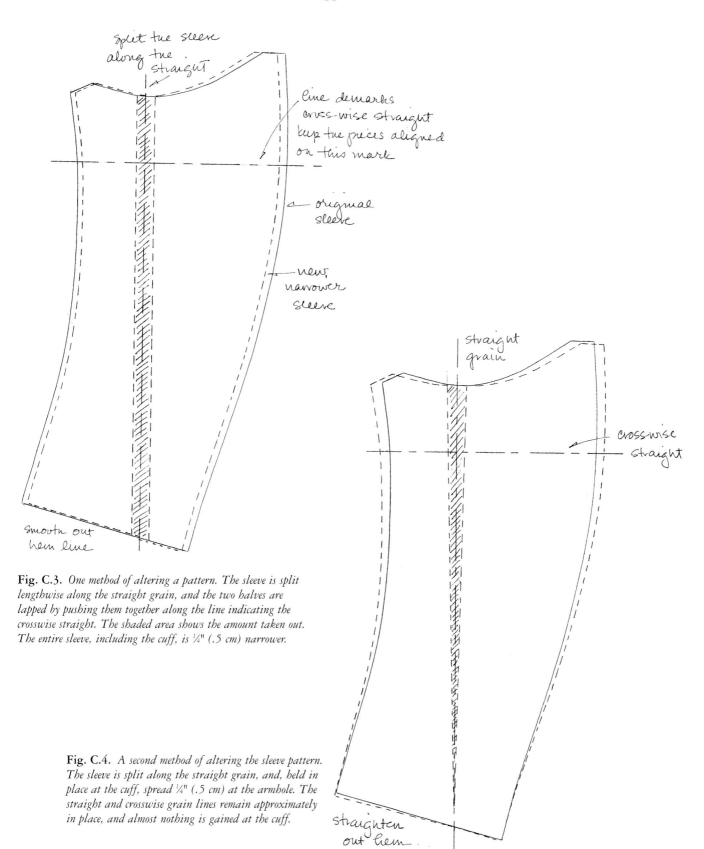

split the sleeve along the straight

line demarks cross-wise straight keep the pieces aligned on this mark

original sleeve

new narrower sleeve

smooth out hem line

straight grain

cross-wise straight

straighten out hem

Fig. C.3. *One method of altering a pattern. The sleeve is split lengthwise along the straight grain, and the two halves are lapped by pushing them together along the line indicating the crosswise straight. The shaded area shows the amount taken out. The entire sleeve, including the cuff, is ¼" (.5 cm) narrower.*

Fig. C.4. *A second method of altering the sleeve pattern. The sleeve is split along the straight grain, and, held in place at the cuff, spread ¼" (.5 cm) at the armhole. The straight and crosswise grain lines remain approximately in place, and almost nothing is gained at the cuff.*

Fig. C.5. *Suggested points at which to split a bodice pattern for alteration. It is important to remember that changes at one point may affect the pattern at another point. For instance, lengthening or shortening the shoulder depth also changes the waist length. Any of the sections indicated in this drawing may be moved either along the straight (as in Fig. C.3) or with a pivot-type wedge (as in Fig. C.4).*

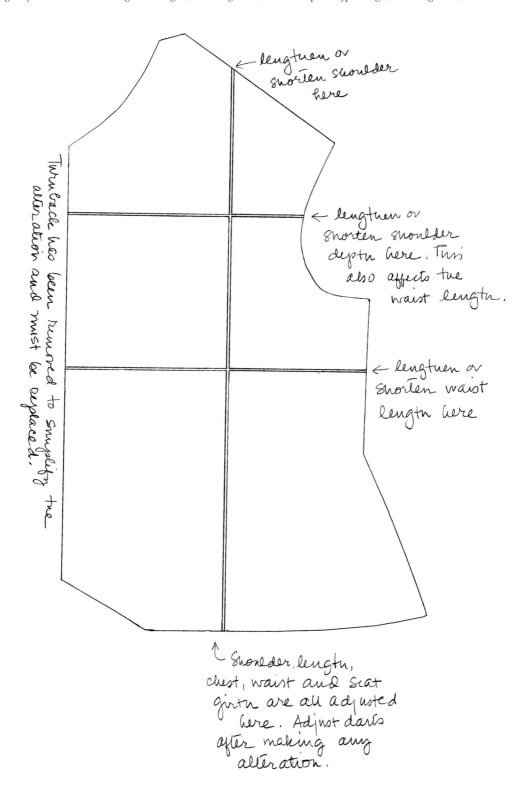

← lengthen or shorten shoulder here

← lengthen or shorten shoulder depth here. This also affects the waist length.

← lengthen or shorten waist length here

Turn back has been removed to simplify the alteration and must be replaced.

↳ Shoulder, length, chest, waist and seat girth are all adjusted here. Adjust darts after making any alteration.

Glossary

armscye. Armhole.

balayeuse. A "dust ruffle" applied to the hem inside a skirt with a train, to protect the skirt from soil and abrasion. Plate 23 and cover.

basque. Skirt-like jacket tails; popular off and on through the Victorian period in dresses made in two pieces. They were cut in various styles and lengths, but usually made in shaped sections. Sometimes skirt draperies are used to simulate basques. Plate 21 and Plate 23.

batiste. A fine, even-weave fabric, typically cotton.

bavolet. The curtain at the back of a bonnet that covers a lady's neck. Plate 1 and Plate 3.

beret sleeve. A short "puffed" sleeve made in one circular piece with the "cuff" made by a slash through the center. The outer edge of the circle is gathered up to set it into the armhole. Plate 9.

bertha. A wide, gathered collar popular during the middle years of the 19th century used to embellish low-necked dresses. The bertha was typically made of a long and wide piece of lace arranged to fall over the bosom and cover the short evening sleeve. Plate 6 and Plate 16.

bishop sleeve. A loose gathered sleeve with cuff; the fullness is pulled into puffs or other decorative arrangements with flounces, straps or other embellishments. Plate 4.

bretelle. A decorative shoulder strap. Plate 20.

brocade. A jacquard-woven fabric with more than one color in the pattern. Plate 47.

broderie anglaise. A type of fine cut work, generally but not exclusively white on white, based on the buttonhole stitch. The fabric in a pattern of scallops and holes. In the 1850s broderie anglaise had largely replaced techniques such as Ayrshire; broderie anglaise was much simpler and faster to work, and could be done not only by a competent amateur but also by machine. Ayrshire and other lace-like methods of embroidery had been the basis for an entire professional industry of hand embroiderers in northern England.

bullion. Heavy applied decoration made of twisted and knotted threads. Plate 33.

busk. Rigid stiffener placed into the front of a corset to keep the corset smooth and the figure erect. Busks were generally metal during the Victorian period, although even in the most tightly corsetted period, there were corsets made to be relatively comfortable (i.e., buskless). The shape of the busk often determined the finished look of the corset.

bust. A tailor's term, meaning to open seams out and press them flat.

cambric. A fine, even-weave fabric typically of cotton or linen.

carpet warp. A tightly twisted, string-like cotton yarn used in sturdy weaving applications.

cartridge pleats. Small, even pleats formed by gathering fabric very regularly on thread.

casquette. A small pillbox hat popular in the mid- to late 1860s worn tipped onto the forehead; variations include the pork pie and the Lamballe plateau. Plate 27.

cervical point. The prominent bone at the base of the back of the neck; a useful pattern drafting reference point, since garments hang from the shoulders around this point.

chemise. A woman's traditional undergarment until nearly the end of the 19th century. The chemise is a knee-length, short-sleeve garment of cotton or linen worn under the corset or stays.

chemisette. An undergarment fashionable through the 1840s, although still occasionally worn later, consisting of a collar with shoulders and terminating below the breasts. It was fastened around the body with strings running through casings and tied under the arms. The chemisette was used to fill in the neckline of dresses for day wear. It served the auxiliary function of protecting the often unwashable dress from body soil. Plate 1.

chiffon. A soft, sheer, even-weave fabric of silk. Plate 44.

Circassienne. A style of applied bodice drapery that forms a waist-deep pleated "V" across the bosom; fashionable in the mid-1830s. Plate 1, left.

corsage. Neckline; the upper bosom of a dress.

cross-back width. The distance across the back of a garment measured at a point halfway between the base of the neck and the bottom of the armhole.

damask. A jacquard-woven fabric, all of one color, whose pattern is formed by threads carried across the surface. Plate 7.

dentelles. Tooth-shaped embellishments. Lace can be made in the shape of dentelles; fabric may also be cut into a tooth-edge shape.

doupioni (*also* **duppionni**). A silk with crisp, lightly slubbed texture, formed by thick and thin silk yarns woven together.

dressing saque. A ladies' loose-fitting, often richly made jacket like a short dressing gown for wear in the bedroom or boudoir.

drill. A thin but stout twill-weave cotton fabric akin to ticking, but usually in a plain color.

en coulisse. Shaped or closed with a drawstring, as a neckline "en coulisse."

engageante. Undersleeve, generally a separate piece tied or tacked into the armhole of a dress with a short or open sleeve.

faille. A woven fabric whose surface is formed into small crosswise ribs. Plate 34.

favor. In turning a seam, to cause one side of the garment to show cleanly at the expense of the other. Usually, the outside of the garment is favored, with the seam pulled to the inside.

fell. To stitch down an interior seam to the shell so that it lays flat. This may be done invisibly by hemming or blind stitching, or it may be accomplished with a decorative stitch like the pin stitch. See Appendix A (Sewing by Hand).

fil tiré. A decorative filling stitch, commonly white on white, in which threads of the fabric are pulled into a crosshatch pattern by the thread. It is executed much like the pin stitch. Often the pattern is worked in the shape of a medallion with a design standing out in unworked relief in the center.

flounce. An applied, gathered band of fabric or lace. Plate 4, right.

French seam. A narrow seam sewn in two passes. The raw edges are enclosed, finishing cleanly. See Appendix A (Sewing by Hand).

gauge, gauging. Most commonly used to control the fullness of the mid-19th century skirt. The fabric is run with long gathering stitches, pulled up and arranged very neatly in a line of tiny pleats. Gauging was an innovation of the 1840s.

Gautier, Gaultier, F.G. A French manufacturer (or manufacturers) of fashion dolls and bébés, active about 1860-1915. There are French dolls variously marked F. Gautier, Gaultier Freres, A. Gautier, and Gaultier & Fils. These firms' relationship to each other is unknown.

gigot sleeve. A sleeve with very full head, often forming a large balloon, which narrows dramatically to fit the forearm closely. Gigot sleeves of various types were fashionable in the 1830s; a gigot-like sleeve came back into fashion in the late 1880s. Plate 1, left.

giraffe. A hair style popular in the romantic 1830s, in which loops or braids of hair, often false, were arranged in upstanding coils, sometimes supported by interior wires. A variation of the "Apollo knot." Plate 4, right.

godet. A wedge-shaped slice of fabric inserted into a seam, commonly on a jacket or coat, to increase fullness at the hem in a controlled fashion. Plate 48.

gore. A wedge-shaped slice of fabric inserted into a seam, commonly on a skirt or dress, to widen the hem in a controlled fashion. The late crinoline-style skirts of the 1860s were gathered and cut with gores. Typically, the gore is asymmetrical, having one straight edge and one slanted edge. Plate 21.

Greiner. An American manufacturer of papier-mâché dolls' heads. Founded in Philadelphia in the early 1850s by Ludwig Greiner, the firm was later operated by his sons and ultimately acquired by Knell Brothers. The firm was active until about 1900; it held the first known patent for a doll's head in the United States (mid-1850s). Some heads were sold alone, to be assembled to a body at home; others were commercially finished with bodies by Lacman. Plate 9 and Plate 36.

gusset. A small wedge of fabric inserted into a seam to provide close-fitting ease. Typically, a gusset might by let into an underarm seam to provide motion for the arm without increasing the apparent fullness in the sleeve. Gussets were inserted into the breast and hip areas of corsets to create a rounded form while retaining a skin-tight fit. Plate 2.

gutta percha. An easily malleable substance made from latex, like rubber, and used in the second half of the 19th century for making dolls. It is workable at very low temperatures, but can become brittle when exposed to air over time.

header. Loosely speaking, the top of a flounce or edging-style lace. Confusingly, texts on lace use "header" and "footer" interchangeably.

interlining. A reinforcing, padding, or shaping fabric sewn to the shell of a garment. Generally the entire inner surface of the shell fabric is interlined to the edges; shell and interlining are worked as one piece. After making up the garment, the interlining may be clipped out of the seams to reduce bulk.

jabot. A small, shaped decoration made to trim the neckline of a blouse. Plate 43.

jacquard. A fabric made with complex manipulation of the warp threads to create a pattern in the weave, rather than printed on the surface. Joseph Marie Jacquard invented the first automatic loom for this method of weaving in 1801. His loom, operating on a similar principle to computer punch cards, used a system of wooden plaques to carry the design. Brocade and damask are jacquard-woven fabrics.

jean. A stout twill-woven cotton fabric used to make corsets and lightweight ladies' footwear. Plate 2.

jockey. An embellishment of fabric mounted over a sleeve as a trimming. Plate 32 and Plate 33.

Jumeau. One of the outstanding manufacturers of dolls of porcelain and composition. Founded in 1840, the firm ultimately was succeeded by the Société Française de Fabrication de Bébés et Jouets, which survived into the 1920s. Plate 34, left.

J.D. Kestner. A German manufacturer of dolls. Founded in 1805, the firm survived into the 1920s. Kestner is best known as a manufacturer of progressively modelled designs of about 1890–1915, including character babies, ethnic children, and the Gibson girl. Plate 42 and Plate 43.

kimono. The traditional garment of Japan, made with straight lengths of fabric and without a shoulder seam. The only shaped pieces are two wedges of fabric stitched to the front to provide the V-shaped neck opening and the front lap.

Lacman. An American manufacturer of cloth doll bodies, active about 1860–1883. Lacman bodies typically wear leather boots made in one with the feet, often in brilliant colors. Lacman was the principal supplier of commercial bodies to the Greiner company. Plate 36.

lappet. A decorative, hanging tongue of fabric or lace, used on cloaks and caps, especially. Plate 1 and Plate 6.

lawn. A finely made, even-weave, semi-sheer cotton fabric with slightly crisp hand. Plate 43.

Mameluke. A style of gigot sleeve fashionable in the mid-1830s, having a very full, pleated head, and narrow, fitted cuff. Plate 1, left.

melton. A tightly woven, fine-textured woolen fabric with a slight but very dense surface nap; used as coating or suiting, depending upon the weight. Plate 45, left.

muslin. A trial run made in an appropriate waste fabric to see whether a garment will go together correctly and whether it will fit. Pattern drapers refer to a draped design in work as a "muslin." In the 19th century, cotton "muslin" was a fine, nearly sheer fabric often elaborately embroidered to make ladies' dresses and dressy underwear.

net. With reference to seams, a patternmaker's term, meaning that two seams are the same length, especially if they are not the same shape. We say, for example, that a sleeve is net to the armhole to mean that it is set in without any ease.

organdie. A slightly stiff sheer cotton even-weave fabric.

organza. A crisp, very fine, sheer, even-weave silk.

ottoman. A heavy twill-like silk with woven pattern. Plate 46, top.

pagoda sleeve. A wide, bell-shaped sleeve popular in the third quarter of the 19th century. Early pagoda sleeves were typically open in front from just below the armscye; this type of sleeve was always worn with some sort of lace or cotton undersleeve. In the 1870s when they became fashionable again, they often were open at the back from wrist to elbow. Plate 13.

papier-mâché. An inexpensive composition material made from various forms of organic paste, waste paper, and/or wood shavings. Papier-mâché was a fashionable material in the 1820s and 1830s. When china dolls became commercially feasible in the 1840s, papier-mâché became the material of cheaper, less fashionable toys. It was a low-tech material well-suited to small commercial firms. It is, however, highly perishable, not only from changes in heat and humidity, but also the depredations of vermin. Plate 9, left, and Plate 36, left.

Parian. A fine grade of unglazed china used to make highly detailed decorative objects. In the 1860s and 1870s it was also used to make shoulderplate dolls. Plate 16 and Plate 17.

passementerie. Applied decoration of tape or braid, generally used to trim borders. Plate 9 and Plate 21.

pearl cotton. A loosely twisted, glossy, cotton yarn, used principally for embroidery.

pelerine. A small shoulder cape, often made with long hanging lappets in the front, used to complete a dress. Pelerines were popular from the late 1820s through the early 1840s, and might be made either of dress fabric, or of lace, embroidered lawn, or other delicate material. Plate 1.

picot. A bead-shaped stitch used to ornament lace and edges. Plate 49.

Pierotti. Perhaps the premier manufacturer of English poured (as opposed to dipped) wax dolls. Founded in 1780, the firm remained in business into the 1920s. Plate 39 (although identification is not documented).

placket. A strip of fabric used to finish a slash or the edge of an open seam. Loosely speaking, the opening itself.

plastron. A bib-like false front, a decorative rather than functional detail. Plastrons may be mounted on separate pieces of fabric buttoned into an open dress front like a stomacher, or they may be applied at the neckline like a jabot. Plate 34 and Plate 35.

poet sleeve. A loose, wide sleeve, closely gathered or pleated at both the shoulder and cuff. Plate 20.

polonaise. Generally, a coat-like bodice of a two-piece ensemble, typically knee-length or longer, with the back drawn up and tied with interior tapes. Plate 31 and Plate 36.

puffing. A raised surface embellishment formed by gathering a strip of fabric and stitching the gathered edges to a foundation. Plate 29, right.

revers. Turn-back lapels, typically opening high on the chest.

Rohmer. A French dollmaker active from 1855 through the mid-1880s. Mlle. Rohmer's dolls were unusual at this date because she used Parian or glazed china heads frequently with set-in glass eyes, gusseted kid bodies and dressed her dolls with hair wigs. Plate 17.

ruche, ruching. A narrow strip of gathered or pleated fabric, lace, or ribbon used as an applied embellishment. Plate 44.

satin. A fabric with a shiny surface made by carrying threads across it during weaving.

shell. The outside, or fashion fabric, of a garment.

shoulder depth. The distance from the base of the neck to the bottom of the armhole, measured down the center back.

Simon & Halbig. A German manufacturer of principally porcelain, but also composition and celluloid, dolls' heads. They were supplied to a very large number of different dollmakers, including Jumeau. Founded in 1870, the firm remained in business into the 1920s. Simon & Halbig's character and ethnic heads are especially fetching. Plate 52.

soutache. Braid used to trim a garment, usually being formed into intricate patterns and stitched in place. Traditionally made of silk or rayon. Plate 45.

stock. A shaped neck covering like a cravat. Plate 43.

stomacher. A stiff, usually highly decorated piece used to fill the open fronts of robes of the 18th century.

suppression. Fabric taken out of a garment by curved seams, darts, pleating, etc., which causes the garment to fit the body more closely.

taffeta. A crisp, even-weave silk fabric with glossy surface.

tournure. The fashion name given to the bustle in the 1880s.

trapeze cut. A tent-like shape, generally used with reference to a short garment with a spreading hem like a jacket or short dress. The trapeze shape is achieved with shaped pieces of fabric rather than gathering. Plate 21, rear.

tulle. A net fabric of cotton or silk.

waist length. The length from the base of the neck to the natural waist, measured down the center back.

warp print. A fabric whose pattern is printed onto the warp threads before it is woven. The weaving process causes the finished pattern to have a soft, slightly wavering appearance. Plate 6.

Bibliography

THE following books were consulted in researching this book. Many of them would be useful additions to the library of any dressmaker interested in historic reproduction.

Fashion plates are somewhat problematical as references for costume reproduction and should be used with discretion, since they do not look like real 19th century people any more than contemporary fashion drawings look like us. The clothing in fashion plates normally represents a fashion fantasy rather than a practical choice for real women and children. Moreover, it is not necessarily appropriate to dress an old doll in a miniature version of high fashion. Nevertheless, fashion plates are useful for organizing your understanding of silhouettes, trimmings, and so forth, in addition to being a fascinating study in their own right. For the reproduction sewer, period photographs, which show real people in real settings, are much more useful.

Old catalogues are helpful, since they show styles that were actually for sale, and they normally are geared to a representative, middle-class buyer rather than the beau monde buying limited edition couture clothes. We are so used to material plenty that we have lost an appreciation for the novelty that real mass production represented 150 years ago. Catalogues are especially useful in their clear depictions of untrimmed hats, lingerie and stocking styles, clothing that is usually less fully covered by conventional fashion histories, but necessary in developing a complete ensemble for your doll.

Old instructional manuals are likewise a good way to learn how the Victorian sewer approached her task, although reference to authentic examples is important. A modern reader may sometimes be led to believe that a highly idealized recommendation was the way a job was typically handled. The advice writers of yesteryear, like those of today, had an editorial viewpoint.

Ames, Kenneth L. *Death in the Dining Room, and Other Tales of Victorian Culture.* Philadelphia: Temple University Press, 1992.

The Anchor Manual of Needlework. Hong Kong: Interweave Press, 1990. (First published, 1958.)

Anderson, Nancy Fix. *Woman Against Women in Victorian England.* Bloomington and Indianapolis: Indiana University Press, 1987.

Arnold, Janet. *Patterns of Fashion I: Englishwomen's dresses & their construction c.1660–1860.* London: MacMillan London Limited, 1977. (First published, 1964.)

Arnold, Janet. *Patterns of Fashion 2: Englishwomen's dresses and their construction c.1860–1940.* London: MacMillan London Limited, 1977. (First published, 1966.)

Baclawski, Karen. *The Guide to Historic Costume.* New York: Drama Book Publishers, 1995.

Baker, Jean H. *Mary Todd Lincoln, A Biography.* New York: W.W. Norton & Company, 1989. (First published, 1987.)

Barbier, George et al. *Parisian Costume Plates in Full Color (1912–1914).* New York: Dover Publications, Inc., 1982.

Barry, Kathleen. *Susan B. Anthony: A Biography of a Singular Feminist.* New York: Ballantine Books, 1988.

Bellocq, E. J. *Storyville Portraits: Photographs from the New Orleans Red-Light District, Circa 1912.* New York: The Museum of Modern Art, 1970.

Ben-Yusuf, Mme. Anna. *Edwardian Hats: The Art of Millinery (1909).* R.L. Shep, ed., with additional illustrations from *Correct Dress: Fall & Winter 1908–9* (Franklin Simon & Co., New York). Mendocino, California: R.L. Shep, 1992.

Bloomingdale Brothers. *Bloomingdale's Illustrated 1886 Catalog: Fashions, Dry Goods and Housewares.* Nancy Villa Bryk, ed. New York: Dover Publications, 1988. Published in association with Henry Ford Museum & Greenfield Village, Dearborn, Michigan.

Blum, Dilys. *Illusion and Reality: Fashion in France 1700–1900.* Houston, Texas: The Museum of Fine Arts, 1986.

Borger, Mona. *Chinas, dolls for study and admiration.* San Francisco: Borger Publications, 1983.

Bradfield, Nancy. *Costume in Detail: Women's dress 1730–1930*. Boston: Plays, Inc., 1968.

Briggs, Asa, with Archie Mills. *A Victorian Portrait: Victorian Life and Values as Seen Through the Work of Studio Photographers*. New York: Harper & Row, Publishers, 1989.

Brumberg, Joan Jacobs. *Fasting Girls: The History of Anorexia Nervosa*. New York: Plume (Penguin Group), 1989.

Brumgardt, John R., ed. *Civil War Nurse: The Diary and Letters of Hannah Ropes*. Knoxville, Tennessee: The University of Tennessee Press, 1993. (First published, 1983.)

Bryk, Nancy Villa, ed. *American Dress Pattern Catalogs, 1873–1909*. New York: Dover Publications, Inc., 1988. Published for Henry Ford Museum & Greenfield Village.

Buck, Anne. *Victorian Costume and Costume Accessories*. Carlton Bedford (England): Ruth Bean, 1984. (First published, 1961.)

Bushman, Richard L. *The Refinement of America: Persons, Houses, Cities*. New York: Alfred A. Knopf, 1992.

Caldwell, Mark. *The Last Crusade: The War on Consumption, 1862–1954*. New York: Atheneum, 1988.

Calvert, Karin. *Children in the House: The Material Culture of Early Childhood, 1600–1900*. Boston: Northeastern University Press, 1992.

Chafe, William H. *The Paradox of Change: American Women in the 20th Century*. New York: Oxford University Press, 1991.

Clinton, Catherine and Nina Silber, eds. *Divided Houses: Gender and the Civil War*. New York: Oxford University Press, 1992.

Cogan, Frances B. *All-American Girl: the Ideal of Real Womanhood in Mid-19th-Century America*. Athens, Georgia: The University of Georgia Press, 1989.

Coleman, Dorothy S., Elizabeth A. and Evelyn J. Coleman. *The Collector's Book of Dolls' Clothes, Costumes in Miniature: 1700–1929*. New York: Crown Publishers, Inc., 1975.

Coleman, Elizabeth Ann. *The Opulent Era, Fashions of Worth, Doucet and Pingat*. New York: Thames and Hudson, 1989.

Cotkin, George. *Reluctant Modernism: American Thought and Culture, 1880–1900*. New York: Twayne Publishers. 1992.

Cunnington, C. Willett. *English Women's Clothing in the 19th Century*. New York; Dover Publications, 1990. (First published by Faber and Faber, London, 1937.)

Cunnington, C. Willett and Phillis Cunnington. *The History of Underclothes*. New York: Dover, 1991. (First published by Michael Joseph Ltd., London, 1951.)

Dally, Ann. *Women Under the Knife: A History of Surgery*. New York: Routledge, Chapman and Hall, 1992.

Dalrymple, Priscilla Harris. *American Victorian Costume in Early Photographs*. New York: Dover Publications, 1991.

Degler, Carl N. *At Odds: Women and the Family in America from the Revolution to the Present*. New York: Oxford University Press, 1981. (First published, 1980.)

D'Emilio, John and Estelle B. Freedman. *Intimate Matters: A History of Sexuality in America*. New York: Harper & Row, 1989. (First published, 1988.)

Dillmont, Therese de. *The Complete Encyclopedia of Needlework*. Philadelphia: The Running Press, 1972. (First published by the DMC Company, late 19th century.)

Douglas, Ann. *The Feminization of American Culture*. New York: Anchor Books, 1988. (First published by Alfred A. Knopf, 1977.)

Dreher, Denise. *From the Neck Up, An Illustrated Guide to Hatmaking*. Minneapolis: The Madhatter Press, 1981.

Druesedow, Jean L. *In Style: Celebrating Fifty Years of the Costume Institute*. New York: The Metropolitan Museum of Art, 1987.

Dugan, James. *The Great Iron Ship*. New York: Harper & Brothers, 1953.

Earnshaw, Pat. *The Identification of Lace*. Aylesbury, Bucks (UK): Shire Publications, 1989. (First published, 1980.)

Epstein, Barbara Leslie. *The Politics of Domesticity: Women, Evangelism and Temperance In 19th-Century America*. Middletown, Connecticut: Wesleyan University Press, 1981.

Evans, Sara M. *Born for Liberty: A History of Women in America*. New York: The Free Press, 1989.

Finch, Karen, O.B.E., and Greta Putnam. *The Care & Preservation of Textiles*. London: B.T. Batsford Ltd., 1985. (First published by Barrie & Jenkins as *Caring For Textiles*, 1977.)

Fischel, Dr. Oskar and Max von Boehn. *Modes & Manners of the 19th Century, as Represented in the Pictures and Engravings of the Time*, in three volumes. London: J.M. Dent & Co., Aldine House, 1909.

Frank, Katherine. *A Passage to Egypt: The Life of Lucie Duff Gordon*. Boston: Houghton Mifflin Company, 1994.

Garber, Marjorie. *Vested Interests: Cross-Dressing & Cultural Anxiety.* New York and London: Routledge: 1992.

Geller, Jeffrey L. and Maxine Harris. *Women of the Asylum: Voices from Behind the Walls, 1840–1945.* New York, New York: Anchor Books, Doubleday, 1994.

Gernsheim, Alison. *Victorian and Edwardian Fashion, A Photographic Survey.* New York: Dover Publications, Inc., 1981. (First published by Faber and Faber, London, under the title *Fashion and Reality, 1840–1914,* 1963.)

Gilman, Charlotte Perkins. *The Yellow Wallpaper and Other Writings.* New York: Bantam Classics, 1989.

Gimbel Brothers. *Gimbel's Illustrated 1915 Fashion Catalog.* New York: Dover Publications, 1994.

Godey's Lady's Book. *Fashions and Costumes from Godey's Lady's Book.* Stella Blum, ed. New York: Dover Publications, 1985.

Goldthorpe, Caroline. *From Queen to Empress, Victorian Dress 1837–1877.* New York: The Metropolitan Museum of Art, 1988.

Gordon, S.S. *Ladies' Tailor-Made Garments, 1908.* Jules & Kaethe Kliot, eds. Berkeley, California: Lacis Publications, 1993. (First published by the Jno. J. Mitchell Co.)

Griffith, Elisabeth. *In Her Own Right: The Life of Elizabeth Cady Stanton.* New York: Oxford University Press, 1985. (First published, 1984.)

Grossberg, Michael. *Governing the Hearth: Law and the Family in 19th-Century America.* Chapel Hill: The University of North Carolina Press, 1985.

Harrison, Michael. *In the Footsteps of Sherlock Holmes.* New York: Drake Publishers, 1972.

Harrison, Michael. *Clarence: The Life of H.R.H. The Duke of Clarence and Avondale (1864–1892).* London and New York: W. H. Allen, 1972.

Havighurst, Walter. *Annie Oakley of the Wild West.* Lincoln, Nebraska: The University of Nebraska Press, 1992. (First published, 1954.)

Hawes, Joseph M. *The Children's Rights Movement, A History of Advocacy and Protection.* Boston: Twayne Publishers, 1991.

Heywood, Colin. *Childhood in 19th-Century France: Work, health and education among the 'classes populaires.'* Cambridge: Cambridge University Press, 1988.

Harper's Bazaar. *Victorian Fashions & Costumes from Harper's Bazaar: 1867–1898.* Stella Blum ed. New York: Dover Publications, 1974.

Hill, Margot Hamilton and Peter A. Bucknell. *The Evolution of Fashion: Pattern and Cut from 1066 to 1930.* New York: Drama Book Publishers, 1987. (First published, 1967.)

Himmelfarb, Gertrude. *The Idea of Poverty: England in the Early Industrial Age.* New York: Alfred A. Knopf, 1984.

Himmelfarb, Gertrude. *Marriage and Morals Among the Victorians and other essays.* New York: Vintage Books, 1987. (First published by Alfred A. Knopf, Inc., 1986.)

Himmelfarb, Gertrude. *Poverty and Compassion: The Moral Imagination of the Late Victorians.* New York: Vintage Books (A Division of Random House), 1992. (First published by Alfred A. Knopf, Inc., 1991.)

Himmelfarb, Gertrude. *Victorian Minds.* New York: Alfred A. Knopf, Inc., 1968. (First published, 1952.)

Homberger, Eric. *Scenes from the Life of a City: Corruption and Conscience in Old New York.* New Haven & London: Yale University Press, 1994.

Johnson, Paul E. and Sean Wilentz. *The Kingdom of Matthias.* New York: Oxford University Press, 1994.

Jordan, Marsh and Company. *Jordan, Marsh Illustrated Catalog of 1891, an Unabridged Reprint.* New York: Dover Publications, 1991. Published jointly with The Athenaeum of Philadelphia.

Kaye, Georgina Kerr. *Millinery for Every Woman.* Berkeley, California: Lacis Publications, 1992. (First published by The John C. Winston Company, 1926.)

Kemper, Rachel H. *Costume.* New York: Newsweek Books, 1977.

Kevill-Davies, Sally. *Yesterday's Children: The Antiques and History of Childcare.* Woodbridge, Suffolk: The Antique Collectors' Club, Ltd, 1994. (First published, 1991.)

Kidwell, Claudia B. *Cutting a Fashionable Fit: Dressmakers' Drafting Systems in the United States.* Washington, D.C.: Smithsonian Institution Press, 1979.

King, Charles R. *Children's Health in America, A History.* New York: Twayne Publishers, 1993.

King, Constance Eileen. *The Collector's History of Dolls.* New York: St. Martin's Press, 1978. (First published, 1977.)

Kurella, Elizabeth M. *The Secrets of Real Lace.* Plainwell, Michigan: The Lace Merchant, 1994.

Lansdell, Avril. *Fashion à la Carte 1860–1900: A study of fashion through cartes-de-visite.* Princes Risborough: Shire Publications, 1992. (Part of the "History in Camera" series; first published, 1985.)

Laver, James. *The Concise History of Costume and Fashion.* New York: Charles Scribner's Sons, 1969.

Lord, Walter. *The Night Lives On.* New York: Jove Books, 1987. (First published by William Morrow & Company, Inc., 1986.)

Lord, Walter. *A Night to Remember.* New York: Bantam Books, 1956. (First published by Holt, Rinehart & Winston, 1955.)

Mac Neil, Sylvia. *The Paris Collection.* Cumberland, Maryland: Hobby House, 1992.

Marcus, Steven. *The Other Victorians: A Study of Sexuality and Pornography in Mid-19th-Century England.* New York: Basic Books, Inc., 1966.

Massie, Robert K. *Dreadnought: Britain, Germany, and the Coming of the Great War.* New York: Random House, 1991.

McDowell, Colin. *Dressed to Kill: Sex, Power and Clothes.* London: Hutchinson (Random Century Group Ltd.), 1992.

Mitchell, Reid. *The Vacant Chair: The Northern Soldier Leaves Home.* New York: Oxford University Press, 1993.

National Cloak & Suit Co. *Women's Fashions of the Early 1990s.* New York: Dover Publications, 1992. (First published, 1909.)

Noble, John. *A Treasury of Beautiful Dolls.* New York: Hawthorn Books, Inc., 1971.

Oates, Stephen B. *A Woman of Valor: Clara Barton and the Civil War.* New York: The Free Press, 1994.

Patton, Phil. *Made in U.S.A.: The Secret Histories of the Things That Made America.* New York: Grove Weidenfeld, 1992.

Pearsall, Ronald. *The Worm in the Bud: The World of Victorian Sexuality.* Toronto: The Macmillan Company, 1969.

Perry, Dame & Co. *Women's and Children's Fashions of 1917: The Complete Perry, Dame & Co. Catalog.* New York: Dover Publications, 1992. (Originally published as *Catalog No. 67, New York Styles, Spring and Summer 1917.*)

Pond, Gabrielle. *An Introduction to Lace.* New York: Charles Scribner's Sons, 1973.

Pool, Daniel. *What Jane Austen Ate and Charles Dickens Knew: From Fox Hunting to Whist The Facts of Daily Life in 19th-Century England.* New York: Simon & Schuster, 1993.

Ribbon Art Publishing Company. *Old-Fashioned Ribbon Art: Ideas and Designs for Accessories and Decorations.* New York: Dover Publications, 1986. Published through the cooperation of The Center for the History of American Needlework. (First published, c.1920s.)

Rice, Edward. *Captain Sir Richard Francis Burton: The secret agent who made the pilgrimage to Mecca, discovered the Kama Sutra, and brought the Arabian Nights to the West.* New York: Harper Perennial, 1991. (First published by Charles Scribner's Sons, 1990.)

Riley, Glenda. *The Female Frontier: A Comparative View of Women on the Prairie and the Plains.* Lawrence, Kansas: University of Kansas Press, 1988.

Roberts, Edna H. *How to Know Laces.* New York: Dry Goods Economist, 1925.

Rothman, David J. *The Discovery of the Asylum: Social Order and Disorder in the New Republic.* Boston: Little, Brown and Company, 1990. (First published, 1971.)

Rothman, David J. *Conscience and Convenience: The Asylum and its Alternatives in Progressive America.* Boston: Little, Brown & Company, 1980.

Rose, Clare. *Children's Clothes.* London: B.T. Batsford Limited, 1989.

Rose, Phyllis. *Parallel Lives: Five Victorian Marriages.* New York: Alfred A. Knopf, 1983.

Rumbelow, Donald. *The Complete Jack the Ripper.* Boston, Massachusetts: The New York Graphic Society, 1975.

Ryan, Frank, M.D. *The Forgotten Plague: How the Battle Against Tuberculosis Was Won—and Lost.* Boston: Little, Brown and Company, 1993. (First published in the United Kingdom as *Tuberculosis: The Greatest Story Never Told,* 1992.)

Schlereth, Thomas J. *Victorian America: Transformations in Everyday Life, 1976–1915.* New York: HarperCollins Publishers, 1992. (First published, 1991.)

Smart, Carol, ed. *Regulating Womanhood: Historical essays on marriage, motherhood and sexuality.* London & New York: Routledge, 1992.

Smith, Barbara Clark and Kathy Peiss. *Men and Women: A History of Costume, Gender and Power.* Washington, DC: National Museum of American History, 1989.

Smith, F.B. *Florence Nightingale: Reputation and Power.* New York: St. Martin's Press, 1984. (First published, 1982.)

Smith-Rosenberg, Carroll. *Disorderly Conduct: Visions of Gender in Victorian America.* New York: Oxford University Press, 1986.

Stansell, Christine. *City of Women: Sex and Class in New York, 1789–1860.* Urbana and Chicago, Illinois: University of Illinois Press, 1987. (First published by Alfred A. Knopf, Inc., 1982.)

Steele, Valerie. *Fashion and Eroticism: Ideals of Feminine Beauty from the Victorian Era to the Jazz Age.* New York and Oxford: Oxford University Press, 1985.

Stevenson, Louise L. *The Victorian Homefront: American Thought and Culture, 1860–1880.* New York: Twayne Publishers, 1991.

Taylor, A.J.P. *The First World War: An Illustrated History.* New York: Perigee Books, 1980. (First published by Hamish Hamilton, 1963.)

Theriault, Florence. *In Their Fashion: Doll Costumes and Accessories, 1850–1925.* Annapolis, Maryland: Gold Horse Publishing, 1994.

Theriault, Florence. *The Trousseau of Blondinette Davranche: A Huret Doll and her Wardrobe, 1862–1867.* Annapolis, Maryland: Gold Horse Publishing, 1994.

Theriault, Florence. *The Way They Wore: Doll Costumes and Accessories, 1850–1925.* Annapolis, Maryland: Gold Horse Publishing, 1993.

Thieme, Otto Charles, Elizabeth Ann Coleman, Michelle Oberly, and Patricia Cunningham. *With Grace & Favour: Victorian & Edwardian Fashion in America.* Cincinnati: The Cincinnati Art Museum, 1993.

Thompson, Mrs. F.E. *Garment Patterns for the Edwardian Lady.* Jules and Kaethe Kliot, eds. Berkeley, California: Lacis Publications, 1991. (Originally published, 1905.)

Trulock, Alice Rains. *In the Hands of Providence: Joshua L. Chamberlain and the American Civil War.* Chapel Hill: The University of North Carolina, 1992.

Vallone, Lynne. *Disciplines of Virtue: Girls' Culture in the Eighteenth and Nineteenth Centuries.* New Haven: Yale University Press, 1995.

Wade, Wyn Craig. *The Titanic, End of a Dream.* New York: Viking Penguin, 1986. (First published by Rawson Associates, a division of The Scribner Book Companies, Inc., 1979.)

Washington, Peter. *Madame Blavatsky's Baboon: A History of the Mystics, Mediums, and Misfits Who Brought Spiritualism to America.* New York: Schocken Books, 1995. (First published by Martin Secker & Warburg, Limited, London, 1993.)

Waugh, Norah. *Corsets and Crinolines.* New York: Theatre Arts Books/Methuen, 1987. (First published, 1954.)

Waugh, Norah. *The Cut of Women's Clothes 1600–1930.* New York: Theatre Arts Books, 1985. (First published, 1968.)

Wiley, Bell Irvin. *Confederate Women.* New York: Barnes & Noble Books, 1994. (First published by Greenwood Press, 1975.)

Wilson, A.N. *Eminent Victorians.* London: BBC Books, 1989.

Wilson, Colin. *The Misfits, a Study of Sexual Outsiders.* New York: Carroll & Graf Publishers, Inc., 1989.

Woman's Institute of Domestic Arts & Sciences Department of Millinery. *Ribbon Trimmings: A Course in Six Parts.* Martinez, California: Sloane Publications, 1992. (First published, 1922.)

Supply Sources

✦

THE companies listed here supplied materials for the projects in this book. While I am not in a position to vouch comprehensively for anyone's products or services, I admit to being something of a fussbudget, and I have listed only those firms whose goods and services I have used personally and found satisfactory.

For readers outside the U.S., I have marked with an "★" those firms which invite foreign credit card orders. This is by far the easiest way to make purchases from an overseas vendor, principally because it eliminates the need to deal with currency exchange. On the order form, give your credit card number. The shop charges your account in its own domestic currency. The credit card company makes the currency exchange. The currency exchange rate employed is the one prevailing on the day the trans-

action reaches the credit card company, not the day of the purchase; this is usually an issue only when you are spending a large amount of money. When you get the bill, you see the purchase and shipping and handling charges in your own domestic currency, plus a small service charge, typically 1% or less. And, of course, interest, if you're inclined to carry a balance. Shipping charges are, naturally, higher outside of the U.S. than within it. Toll-free "800" numbers are good only for people calling from within the United States.

The following list contains names, addresses, phone numbers, the price of the catalogue, if any, and a very brief description of what is offered for sale. This list was as accurate as I could make it when this book went to press.

Notions, Tools, and Miscellaneous Supplies

THE following companies are resources for tools that your local sewing supplier may not carry, as well as small-scale findings and the many types of threads required for these projects.

Ayottes' Designery ★
43 Maple Street
Center Sandwich, NH 03227
603/284-6915
Weaving supplies and home-study instructions. (Cotton carpet warp.)
CATALOGUE: Call to inquire.

Singer Industrial Sewing ★
Cutters Exchange Division
P.O. Box 7001
Murfreesboro, TN 37133
800/251-2142
Tools. (Scalloping shears, pattern scribers.)
CATALOGUE: $5.95

Clothilde
Two Sew Smart Way, B8031
Stevens Point, WI 54481-8031
800/772-2891 or 715/341-2824
Notions and tools. (Silk thread, wool roving.)
CATALOGUE: $2.00

Greenberg & Hammer, Inc. ★
24 West 57th Street
New York, NY 10019
800/955-5135 or 212/246-2835
Dressmaking supplies. (Threads, fasteners.)
CATALOGUE: Free

Hammer Brothers, Inc. ★
407 Grand Avenue
Kansas City, MO 64106-1175
800/321-2351 or 816/842-7290
Dressmaking supplies. (Threads, fasteners.)
CATALOGUE: $2.00

Lacis ★
3163 Adeline Street
Berkeley, CA 94703
510/843-7178
Specialist handwork materials.
CATALOGUE: $5.00 (non-refundable)

Nancy's Notions ★
P.O. Box 683
Beaver Dam, WI 53916-0683
800/833-0690
Supplies, tools, notions.
CATALOGUE: Free

YLI Corporation
P.O. Box 109
Provo, Utah 84603-0109
800/854-1932 or 801/377-3900
Japanese silk ribbon and thread.
CATALOGUE: $2.50

Books

Y OU cannot have too many reference books. If a good book comes out in your area of interest, buy it when you can; books go out of print and can be impossible to find later. The classics of the design and costume history field tend to come back from time to time, but it is frustrating not be able to get the book you need. The following list includes people who sell reproduction patterns, instructional texts, and reprints. I have also listed several out-of-print search services in case you really want to find something. Most search services request that their customers deal with one service at a time so they are not competing with each other for the same hard-to-locate volume.

Avonlea Books
Box 74T
White Plains, NY 10602
800/423-0622 (New York callers: 914/946-5923)
Out-of-print books
NO CATALOGUE

Amazon Dry Goods ★
2218 East 11th Street
Davenport, Iowa 52803-3760
800/798-7979 or 319/322-6800
Reproduction clothing patterns (Folkwear, Past Patterns, Ladies Only, Amanda)
CATALOGUE: Several; please inquire.

Barner Books ★
69 Main Street
New Paltz, NY 12561
914/255-2635
Out-of-print search service
NO CATALOGUE

Dover Publications, Inc.
31 East Second Street
Mineola, NY 11501
516/294-7000
Reprints and classic texts
CATALOGUE: Free

Drama Bookshop, Inc. ★
723 7th Avenue
New York, NY 10019
800/322-0595 or 212/944-0595
Costume books
CATALOGUE: Free

Fred Struthers
P.O. Box 2706
Ft. Bragg, CA 95437
707/964-8662
Books on cloth and related subjects
CATALOGUE: $2.50

Hobby House Press, Inc. ★
One Corporate Drive
Grantsville, MD 21536
800/554-1447
Books about dolls; paper dolls; patterns
CATALOGUE: FREE

Lacis Publishers ★
3163 Adeline Street
Berkeley, CA 94703
510/843-7178
Reprint 19th c. tailor instructions
CATALOGUE: $5.00 (non-refundable)

R.L. Shep Publications
P.O. Box 2706
Ft. Bragg, CA 95437
707/964-8662
Reprint 19th c. and early 20th c. tailor instructions and deportment manuals
CATALOGUE: Free

Dollcraft Supplies

Dollspart Supply Company, Inc. ★
8000 Cooper Avenue, Building 28
Glendale, NY 11385
800/336-3655 or 718/326-4500
Stands, wigs, cases
CATALOGUE: $3.00

Dollmasters ★
P.O. Box 2319
Annapolis, MD 21404
800/966-3655 or 410/224-3644
Reproductions, books
CATALOGUE: $5.00

Standard Doll Company ★
23-83 31st Street
Long Island City, NY 11105
800/543-6557 or 718/721-7787
General supplier (Stands, wigs, shoes)
CATALOGUE: $3.00 (refundable)

Judith Howe, Inc. ★
1240-D North Jefferson Street
Anaheim, CA 92807
714/63-4677
Doll stands (custom sizes available) and porcelain eyes
CATALOGUE: Free

Kate Webster Company ★
83 Granite Street
Rockport, MA 01966
508/546-6462
Doll costuming supplies, including jewelry and findings
CATALOGUE: $3.00

Mini-Magic ★
3910 Patricia Drive
Columbus, OH 43220
614/457-3687 (1-5 p.m. EST only, Mon.-Fri.)
Small-scale fabrics, notions, ribbons, etc., natural fiber fabrics for dolls' dressmakers
CATALOGUE: $3.00

Fabrics

THE sources below range from companies who specialize in an area of interest (like sellers of natural fiber or reproduction fabrics) to those whose offerings contain only one or two hard-to-find items.

B&J Fabrics ★
263 West 40th Street
New York, NY 10018
212/354-8150
Custom swatch service
NO CATALOGUE

Britex-by-Mail ★
153 Maiden Lane
San Francisco, CA 94108
415/392-2910
Personalized swatch service
NO CATALOGUE.
$5.00 per order (7–10 swatches)

Calico House ★
Route 4, Box 16
Scottsville, VA 24590
804/286-2979
Calicoes and cotton handsewing materials
CATALOGUE: Call to inquire

Classic Cloth ★
34930 U.S. 19 North
Palm Harbour, Florida 34684
800/237-7739 or 813/785-6593
Retail store with custom mail-order swatch service
NO CATALOGUE

Creative Trims ★
218 Woodland Drive
Lincroft, NJ 07738
908/747-1532
Lace and embroideries ("Irish lace"-type edgings)
CATALOGUE: Free

Di Carlo's Fabrics ★
15 Temple Place
Boston, MA 02111
617/426-5749
Custom swatch service, natural fiber fabrics
NO CATALOGUE

Martha Pullen Co., Inc. ★
518 Madison Street
Huntsville, AL 35801-4286
800/547-4176 or 205/533-9586
Heirloom sewing by machine; fine cotton fabrics and laces
CATALOGUE: Free

Patchworks ★
6676 Amsterdam Road
Amsterdam, MT 59741
406/282-7218
Reproduction cotton fabrics
CATALOGUE: $1.00

Philips-Boyne Corp. ★
1646 New Highway
Farmingdale, NY 11735
516/755-1230 or 800/292-2830
Fine-quality cotton shirtings
CATALOGUE: $3.00

Kathleen B. Smith ★
Textile Reproductions
Box 48
West Chesterfield, MA 01084
413/296-4437
Vegetable-dyed threads and reproduction fabrics
CATALOGUE AND SAMPLES: $14.00.

Index

Anthony, Susan B., 42
artificial hair, 26

back stitch, 200
Bakst, 71
beeswax, 198
bicycling, influence on 19th-century dress, 69
black suffrage, 42
blind stitch, 199
Bloomer, Amelia, 69
bodice, half high style, 74
bonnet, 25, 26, 28, 66; poke, 26
bridge dress, 72, 168-207
bustle, 44, 65, 68, 130; true (tournure), 119
bustle pads, 130
butterfly blue, 70
buttonholes, 206
buttonhole stitch, 201
buttons, 66, 143, 206

calicos, 103
catch stitch, 199
Chanel, Coco, 72
chemical dyes, 43
chemisette, 86-88
china dolls, 28, 29, 30, 31, 66, 91, 102, 112
Clark, Edward, 47
cleaning old fabric, 196-97
clothing, 19th-century women's, vii, 25, 29, 31, 42, 43, 44, 46, 47, 65, 67, 68, 69, 70, 71, 72, 74, 75-76, 86, 89, 90, 91, 93, 97, 102, 103, 104, 111, 112, 119, 120, 121, 130, 131, 132, 142, 156, 162, 168, 169, 170, 195
closures, 206-7
colors, 74, 90, 103
commercial paper pattern, 43
cord armhole, 83-84, 93, 107
cord facings, 205
cording, 75, 91, 93-94, 103, 112, 131, 143, 154, 204
corsets, 44
costume, 120
crinolette, 44
crinoline, artificial (or cage), 31, 89
crinoline period, 142

day dresses, 25-26, 26-27, 89-101, 102-110, 74-110
Demorest, Madame, 47
dollmaking, 29
dolls, modeled as children, 102
drawers, 25

Edwardian period, 68, 69, 70, 72
Edwardian skirt and waist, 121, 156-67
eyelets, 207

fabric, 43, 46, 74, 90, 91, 103, 112, 120, 131, 143, 156, 157, 162, 169, 195-97
false hems, 29
feather stitch, 200
felled seam, 202
French fashion doll (Parisienne), 31, 32, 41, 43, 45, 46, 47, 48, 68, 195, 209
French papier mâché, 25
french seam, 108, 202

Gaches-Sarraute, Madame, 60
garrison cap, 41
gathering, 203
Gibson, Charles Dana, 68
Gibson girl, 68
gored skirt, 156
goring, 44
Grenier dolls, 29, 65
Grey, Sir Edward, 72

hand sewing, 195-207
health corset, 70-71
hem stitch, 199
hooks, 206
hoops, 31
Horton, Elizabeth Richards, vii, 17, 30
Horton, Thayer, 17

industrialization, 29
infant bodice, 102
International Doll Collection (IDC), 17

Jumeau, 48

Ketsner, 68

lace, 65, 165, 171, 173, 197; cotton, 195
linens, using old, 162

measuring dolls, 208-12
Mere et Tante, 68, 69, 70, 71, 72

needles, 198

overcasting, 201
overskirt, 169, 170, 172

pagoda; sleeve, 31; day dress, 30-31, 89-101
papier mâché dolls, 25, 26, 27, 30
Parian dolls, 31, 32, 41, 42, 209
Parisienne. See French fashion doll.
pattern scriber, 198
Pierotti, 68
pin stitch, 200
Poiret, Paul, 71
polonaise, 47, 65, 142, 142-55; princess, 48, 65, 142-55
pouter pigeon, 69, 70
promenade dress, 46, 130-41

Rohmer, 41
rolled seam, 204
rolling, 203
running stitch, 199

seams, 202, 204
sewing, style, 75
sewing machine, vii, 43, 47, 121
shoulderplate dolls, vii, 31, 75
silk, weighting of, 43
Singer, Isaac, 47
skirts, changing shape of, 44
steam iron, 198
stitches, 199-201

thimble, 198
Thomas, Eloise and Ron, vii
tightlacing controversy, 44
Train, Elizabeth, 68
trimming, 104, 108, 112, 120, 127-28, 131, 135, 162, 169, 173, 195
tools, 198

undergarments, trends in, 28
undersleeve (engageante), 31, 101

Victorian period, 8, 29, 42, 44, 67, 68, 72, 73, 97, 103, 195-96

walking costume, 42-43, 119-29
weighted cushion, 198
Weld, Hanna, 68
Wenham Museum, vi, vii, 30, 68
whipping, 203
whip stitch, 201
women; rights of, 28, 42, 67; social issues of, 8, 67, 102; wearing men's clothes, 69
worked bars and loops, 207
wrapper, 32, 111-18

Yesteryears Historical Association, vi, vii
yoke bodice day dress, 30-31, 102-10